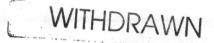
WITHDRAWN

Preparing Adolescents for
Life After Foster Care

Preparing Adolescents for Life After Foster Care

The CENTRAL ROLE of FOSTER PARENTS

EDITED BY

Anthony N. Maluccio

Robin Krieger

Barbara A. Pine

Child Welfare League of America

Washington, DC

CHILD WELFARE LEAGUE OF AMERICA, INC.
440 First Street, NW, Suite 310, Washington, DC 20001-2085

CURRENT PRINTING (last digit)
10 9 8 7 6 5 4 3 2 1

Cover design by Anita Crouch
Text design by Rose Jacobowitz

Printed in the United States of America

Library of Congress Cataloging-in-Publication Data

Preparing adolescents for life after foster care : the central role of
    foster parents / edited by Anthony N. Maluccio, Robin Krieger, and
    Barbara A. Pine.
            p.   cm.
    Includes bibliographical references.
    ISBN 0-87868-433-6 : $24.95
        1. Foster home care—United States   2. Foster parents—United
    States   3. Adolescence.   4. Social work with teenagers—United
    States.   I. Maluccio, Anthony N.   II. Krieger, Robin.   III. Pine,
    Barbara A.
    HV881.P74   1990
    362.7'33'0835—dc20   90-35033
                                                                    CIP

To the foster parents,
who by their endurance serve as an inspiration
to young people in their care

Contents

Acknowledgments

From 1986 to 1988, the Center for the Study of Child Welfare at The University of Connecticut, School of Social Work, received funding from the United States Department of Health and Human Services[1] and from The Annie E. Casey Foundation to conduct a national project on foster parenting adolescents. Its purpose was to improve the ability of foster parents and workers to help teenagers in their care get ready for emancipation. This book is one of several outcomes of that project and is intended for use by child welfare personnel and others as a practical guide to their work with foster parents as they prepare the adolescents in their care for adulthood.

We gratefully acknowledge the generous support of the United States Department of Health and Human Services and our Project Officer, Cecelia Sudia; The Annie E. Casey Foundation and its Director, Martin Schwartz; and Lucille Tomanio, Executive Director of Casey Family Services. We also wish to thank Dean Nancy Humphreys for her continued interest in our work. We owe a debt of gratitude to our editor at the Child Welfare League of America, Carl Schoenberg, for his extensive knowledge of child welfare and dedication to excellence, both of which served to guide us well toward our goals. Respect and appreciation go also to Pamela Harrison for her outstanding secretarial skills and professionalism, and to Elisa Taylor and Virginia Starkie, for their expert help with manuscript typing.

Deep appreciation is extended also to our colleague Migdalia Reyes for her illuminating contributions to the meaning of ethnic competence for those working with emancipating adolescents. And to the

[1]Grant No. 90-CW-0787, U.S. Department of Health and Human Services, Office of Human Development Services, Administration for Children, Youth and Families

contributors of this book, we extend our sincere gratitude for their hard work, flexibility, insights, and patience throughout the lengthy editing phase of the book.

Finally, we are indebted to the many foster and adoptive parents and social workers throughout New England whose experiences and insights formed the basis for many of the case examples cited in the book. Their commitment to the young people in their care offers us all a ray of hope for the future.

West Hartford, Connecticut

ANTHONY N. MALUCCIO
ROBIN KRIEGER
BARBARA A. PINE

Contributors

ROSEMARIE CARBINO, M.S.W.
Clinical Associate Professor
School of Social Work
University of Wisconsin—Madison
Madison, Wisconsin

Alma J. Carten, D.S.W.
Director and Chair of Social Work
  Department
Westchester Social Work
  Education Consortium
New Rochelle, New York
  formerly
Director
Office of Adolescent Services
New York City/Human Resources
  Administration

Susan Whitelaw Downs, Ph.D.
Associate Professor
School of Social Work
Wayne State University
Detroit, Michigan

Robin Krieger, M.S.W.
Curriculum Specialist
Center for the Study of Child Welfare
School of Social Work
The University of Connecticut
West Hartford, Connecticut

Helen Land, Ph.D.
Associate Professor
School of Social Work
University of Southern California
Los Angeles, California

Katherine Gordy Levine, M.S.W.
Child Therapist
SCAN—NY (Supportive Children's
  Advocacy Network)
New York, New York

Anthony N. Maluccio, D.S.W.
Professor
School of Social Work
The University of Connecticut
West Hartford, Connecticut

Hildegarde A. Mauzerall, M.S.W.
Division Director
The Casey Family Program—Idaho
  Division
Boise, Idaho

Emily Jean McFadden, M.S.W.
Associate Professor of Social Work
Associate Director, Independent Living
  Project
Eastern Michigan University
Ypsilanti, Michigan

Barbara A. Pine, M.S.W.
Associate Professor
School of Social Work
The University of Connecticut
West Hartford, Connecticut

Patricia Ryan, Ph.D.
Professor of Sociology
Administrative Director
Institute for the Study of Children and
  Families
Eastern Michigan University
Ypsilanti, Michigan

Bennie M. Stovall, Ph.D.
Executive Director
Children's Aid Society
Detroit, Michigan

Tom Wedeven, M.S.W.
Social Worker
The Casey Family Program—Idaho
  Division
Boise, Idaho

Preface

Much attention has been focused in recent years on adolescents in foster family care, who constitute most of the more than 250,000 youngsters in out-of-home placement in the United States at any given time—with concern, in particular, about their readiness for living on their own following "emancipation" from foster care. This concern has led to the development of a range of programs and services to prepare young people in foster care for independent living, or what we prefer to call *interdependent* living.

As various programs emerge and as public and voluntary child welfare agencies search for better solutions, it is increasingly recognized that foster parents play a central role in helping adolescents to prepare for life after foster care. Foster parents have the most uninterrupted contact with, and knowledge of, the young persons in their care; are expected to guide youths and to teach them independent-living skills; observe and assess progress toward service goals; advocate for services for their children and often manage the provision of these services; and, perhaps most important, deal daily with behaviors that commonly occur in adolescence as well as those that result from adolescents' experiences in having been separated from their biological parents and in living in foster care.

For these reasons, this book deals with the central role of foster parents in helping adolescents to master the tasks required to prepare successfully for interdependent living following discharge from foster family care. It is practice-oriented and draws from the direct experiences of the editors and contributors in research, training, consultation, or practice with adolescents in foster care and their biological and foster parents. Its aim is to contribute to the growing efforts to understand and meet the challenge of helping to prepare adolescents for life after foster care.

Its three major parts comprise twelve chapters. Each chapter provides comprehensive information needed by foster parents and others on a particular aspect of fostering adolescents and suggests practice principles and strategies to guide their work. Where appropriate, case examples are included.

Part I examines the various dimensions of the challenge. In Chapter 1, the editors present an overview of the needs and tasks of young people in foster care, and also define the concept of interdependence as the overarching goal of services for this population. Downs, in Chapter 2, presents a profile of foster parents for adolescents and suggests strategies for recruitment. Chapters 3 and 4 examine adolescent development in the context of the foster care experience: Land discusses the major developmental milestones that are an extra challenge for teenagers in foster care; Levine focuses on the need for these young people to mourn past losses and disappointments before they are able to move onward.

Part II considers meeting the challenges of preparing adolescents for life after foster care from the perspective of policy and program. Following an overview in Chapter 5 of principles and guidelines by the editors, the contributors focus on policy and programmatic responses to the needs of youths in care. In Chapter 6, Wedeven and Mauzerall present the key components of a supervised independent-living program. Carbino, in Chapter 7, emphasizes the importance of involving biological parents as resources for adolescents, while Carten, in Chapter 8, delineates strategies for capitalizing on the important resources that black foster parents offer to teenagers in their care.

In Part III, the contributors focus on practice methods and strategies in work with adolescents and their foster parents. In Chapter 9, Stovall and Krieger discuss the needs of minority teenagers in care and strategies for the development of ethnic competence. McFadden, in Chapter 10, outlines the problems caused by maltreatment that may characterize a foster youth's earlier experience and suggests ways to overcome the resulting obstacles to healthy development. Ryan, in Chapter 11, addresses the special challenge of disciplining adolescents in foster care and examines the issues foster parents ought to consider as they help them to develop self-control. Finally, in Chapter 12, Pine and Krieger discuss the importance of assessing the independent-living skills of adolescents in foster care and review a number of assessment tools and approaches.

The book is intended primarily for child welfare personnel working with foster parents, including social workers, supervisors, administrators, and staff development persons in public and private child welfare agencies, as well as practitioners in such fields as law, psychology, psychiatry, and education. It could also be used as a text for students in child welfare courses in schools of social work and for participants in in-service training programs. The reader, it is hoped, will feel encouraged to create and nurture program efforts to prepare adolescents for life after foster care in ways that are consonant with the principles expressed here. These include the following:

The central roles of foster parents in achieving the goals of foster care services should be more explicitly recognized and valued, and foster parents should receive from the agency and the community the support and services needed to do the job.

Foster parents are an integral part of the service team and should be encouraged to work as partners with agencies and social workers in preparing adolescents for interdependent living.

Preparation for leaving foster care and interdependent living should begin on the first day in care. Moreover, preparation for successful and satisfying adulthood is a lifelong process, best begun in a nurturing family setting.

As a central feature of the philosophy of permanency planning, it is a major goal of the foster care system to prepare young people to develop, sustain, and enrich nurturing relationships with others; to select relationships that are mutually rewarding and growth-producing; and to become adults who are able to participate in caring for others through giving to, and interacting with, individuals and groups in the community.

PART I

Understanding the Challenge

*A*dolescence is a poignant time in life, as young people attempt to sort out and make peace with their own identities. The foster care experience creates unique obstacles for youths in their efforts to carve out distinct selves. Traumatic separations; abuse and neglect; poverty, with its attendant inadequate diet and medical care; feelings of loss, guilt, and shame; and fragmented histories all impede a youth's progress toward competent adulthood. Part I illustrates the multifaceted challenges facing those responsible for the care of older youths leaving the foster care system.

In Chapter 1, Maluccio, Krieger, and Pine review the needs and issues presented by adolescents preparing for life after foster care. Consideration is given to the confluence of factors that jeopardize foster adolescents' ability to develop needed skills, including the negative experiences that initially brought them into care. The importance of preparing for interdependent living is addressed, and the key components of this approach are described. The authors also focus on the central role of foster parents in the lives of youths preparing to leave care and stress the importance of the biological family members to youths at this important juncture.

In Chapter 2, Downs emphasizes the importance of foster parents, both to the youths in their care and to the agencies they serve. The supply of foster parents, however, is inadequate to meet the growing need for foster home placement of adolescents. The author presents data that provide direction to agencies as they work to recruit and retain foster parents of adolescents. Findings include the need for more sharing of information about each adolescent with foster parents; increased involvement with foster parents in planning for and monitoring youths' progress; more realistic reimbursement rates; and recognition of foster parents as vital members of the treatment team.

In Chapter 3, Land discusses the developmental tasks of adolescence, describes how the foster care experience can result in delays, and delineates ways for foster parents and social workers to cooperate as partners in order to reduce psychological risks for adolescents. The three phases of emancipation are presented, as are typical behaviors and strategies for each.

In Chapter 4, Levine describes how the adolescent's emerging ability to think abstractly forces recognition that biological parents *could, in fact, have behaved differently. This realization sparks a need to remourn earlier losses and often includes a period of angry acting out. Commonly troubling behaviors are cast as part of a necessary grieving process, and guidelines are presented to enable the social worker to educate, support, and sustain foster parents and adolescents through this process toward resolution.*

Adolescents and Their Preparation for Life After Foster Family Care: An Overview

ANTHONY N. MALUCCIO, ROBIN KRIEGER, AND BARBARA A. PINE

In response to their growing numbers, adolescents in foster family care in recent years have been attracting increasing attention from policymakers, researchers, administrators, and practitioners in child welfare as well as other agencies. This chapter sets the scene for the rest of the book by offering an overview of these adolescents and their needs and tasks, especially in relation to their preparation for life after foster care. Within this context, the concept of interdependent living is presented as the ultimate goal of services for this population of adolescents, and the roles of foster parents and biological families are highlighted.

Adolescents in Foster Family Care

The proportion of adolescents in foster family care in the United States has been increasing, as the permanency planning movement has been successful in keeping younger children out of care, reuniting them with their biological families following placement, or placing them in adoption or other permanent plans. Representative studies reveal the following:

> Approximately 40 percent of the 275,000 children and youths in foster care (that is, both residential and foster family settings) in 1984 were between thirteen and twenty years of age [American Public Welfare Association 1985].
> Thirty-nine percent of all children and youths in long-term foster family care in 1986 in Connecticut were over age sixteen [Fein et al. 1990].
> The proportion of teenagers in foster care in Maine increased from 46 percent in 1960 to 56 percent in 1980 [Hornby and Collins 1981].
> Adolescents constituted over one-quarter of the children and youths awaiting adoption in 1984, but few of them were placed in adoptive homes [Tatara and Pettiford 1985].

In short, there is no question that "whereas the number of younger children is decreasing, the number of adolescents is on the rise" [Kadushin and Martin 1988: 356]. Furthermore, adolescents in care constitute several different groups:

> Firstly, there are those who were placed at an early age and have had a stable career in foster care, typically growing up in the same foster home; secondly, there are those who were placed at an early age and have been moving from one placement to another, often because they have been described as "difficult to deal with"; and thirdly, there are those who were placed for the first time as teenagers, usually because of their behavioral or relationship problems [Aldgate et al. 1989].

Although policies and programs have tended to lump all of these young people into one category, it is important to understand more clearly and plan more deliberately for their different needs and challenges.

Recent studies have led to increased visibility of the problems and needs of adolescents in foster family care. First, it has been shown that a high number of homeless persons have been in foster care. For example, 38 percent of the homeless in Minneapolis [Piliavin et al. 1987] and 23 percent of those in New York [Susser et al. 1987] reported a history of childhood placement. Second, foster parents and social workers have consistently reported that adolescents approaching emancipation are unprepared for independent living. In a comprehensive study of children and youths in long-term foster care in Connecticut, foster parents and social workers described two-thirds and one-half, respectively, of the adolescents as unprepared for independent living [Fein et al. 1990]. Foster parents and social workers in the same study agreed that adolescents in care have needs in a range of areas, including job skill training, planning a budget and handling money, finding housing, parenting skills, obtaining income assistance, finding a job, maintaining a household, learning how to shop, developing social skills, finding mental health services, sex education, finding recreation services, and using public transportation. Third, follow-up studies of young persons who grew up in out-of-home placement have also pointed to their lack of preparation for life after foster care, especially in interpersonal and social skills, money management, job preparation, and career planning [Festinger 1983; Harari 1980; and Stein and Carey 1986].

Clearly, adolescents in care need to develop or enhance a range of life skills if they are to move toward competent adulthood. Life skills have been defined as those competencies needed to act effectively in social roles and environments [Whittaker et al. 1986]. For adolescents, these include skills in two major categories: tangible or "hard" skills and intangible or "soft" skills. The former refer to those skills that are known or done, such as finding and maintaining employment and housing; obtaining food, clothing, health care, and other services; and managing money. In contrast, the intangible skills are those that are felt, and are related to communication, decision making, and problem solving, as well as the personal attributes of self-esteem, and the ability to confront anger, manage past losses, and develop relationships [Westat 1986: 3–1]. Recent focus on the complex needs of young people leaving foster family care has led to an understanding that both categories of skills are necessary for a satisfying life, and that each relies on the other for full development.

These skills are not unique to young people in foster care. Indeed, as suggested elsewhere in this book (for example, in Chapters 3 and 4, by Land and Levine, respectively), the needs, problems, and tasks faced by these adolescents are typical of those encountered by young people in general. In addition, however, foster adolescents face a variety of unique challenges. These include coping with the effect of separation from their biological families, especially their feelings of loss and grief; making peace with their biological families; coming to terms with a personal history different from the norms that society defines; relating to diverse families (biological parents, foster parents, and, in some cases, adoptive parents); and establishing connections with other significant figures in their social environment without the usual family supports [Fein et al. 1990].

In sum, adolescents in foster care are apt to be triply jeopardized in their struggle to prepare for competent adulthood.

They are typically brought into care by reason of abuse or neglect; their family situations are characterized by poverty, disorganization, and major needs in basic life areas such as health, education, and housing; and their parents often experience serious difficulties such as substance abuse and mental illness.

The foster care experience, which often involves multiple placements and lack of stability, is likely to complicate rather than promote their growth and development; its resources are insufficient, as is attention to their individual needs; and its abrupt and often premature discharge at age eighteen leaves no provision for the continuing support that all young adults need.

The foster care population includes a disproportionate number of young persons of color who have limited economic opportunities and who suffer the consequences of racism and other oppressive social conditions hostile to their achievement of competence.

The increased recognition of the needs and risks faced by adolescents in foster family care has led to important developments in policy, programs, and practice. These will not be detailed here, as they have been reviewed elsewhere [Aldgate et al. 1989; Barth 1986; Stone 1987; and Mech 1988]. Two pertinent federal laws should be mentioned, however: Public Law 96-272, "Adoption Assistance and Child Welfare Act" of 1980, and Public Law 99-272, the "Independent Living Initiative" of 1986.

The Adoption Assistance and Child Welfare Act establishes the legal and policy framework for children and youths coming to the attention of the public child welfare system. In particular, it sets forth several procedural reforms aimed at providing permanent families for young people, preferably with their biological parents but also, if appropriate, with adoptive or foster families. In relation to adolescents, one of the most prominent provisions of this law is its emphasis on the responsibility of public agencies to provide a permanent family for every young person [Maluccio et al. 1986].

The Independent Living Initiative of 1986 focuses on preparation of young people in care for "emancipation" or "independent living," that is, the status of adulthood and self-sufficiency [Hardin 1987]. The law provided a sum of forty-five million dollars per annum, available to the states to support independent-living programs, but required that the effectiveness of these programs be documented, for funding to be continued or expanded beyond 1988. Agency administrators, policymakers, and practitioners have therefore had to go beyond showing that there are foster children who appear to need preparatory and remedial emancipation programs; they must assess program activities and outcomes.

It should also be noted that there is a growing trend toward providing specialized, therapeutic foster family care for certain adolescents entering the foster care system, in recognition of their special needs (cf. Hawkins and Breiling 1989; Hudson and Galaway 1989; and Shaw and Hipgrave 1983).

Preparation for Interdependent Living[1]

As a central feature of the philosophy of permanency planning, a major goal of the child welfare system is preparing young people in foster care to develop, sustain, and enrich nurturing relationships with others; select relationships that are mutually rewarding and growth-producing; and become adults who are able to care for others through giving to, and interacting with, individuals and groups in the community. This goal requires shifting from our current emphasis on *independent* living to a mindset of *interdependence* or *interdependent living* in our work with young people in foster care.

Independent Living

The concept of independent living, while having societal currency and embodying positive ideas such as self-direction and self-sufficiency, also involves negative connotations or consequences. In particular, emphasis on independence for adolescents in foster care increases the following probabilities:

There will be unrealistic/unfair/inappropriate expectations of adolescents, foster parents, social workers, and the service delivery system in general.

[1]This section has been adapted in part from Maluccio et al. 1987.

The American ideal of rugged individualism will be maintained, an ideal that is used to the detriment of people with needs, problems, or disabilities.

The social isolation that is frequently a problem for the families of foster adolescents, and may have been one of the reasons for their coming into care, is reinforced.

The adolescent's need to form attachments or to desire connectedness with other human beings may be regarded as a sign of weakness.

Adolescents whose dependency needs have gone unmet may be denied the services and continuing dependence they may require by pushing for premature independence [Ainsworth 1987].

The burden of preparation for adulthood is placed largely on the adolescent, rather than being perceived as the shared responsibility of policymakers, practitioners, biological and foster parents, and others to help youths who have been in community care become participating adults in that community.

Programs and services may be misdirected. For example, some adolescents may be forced to use programs focusing on learning skills in tangible areas such as budgeting or housekeeping (skills commonly identified with independence), when, first and foremost, they need help in intangible areas such as self-image or interpersonal communication.

Finally, a goal of *independence* may perpetuate a variety of myths and convey unhelpful messages to these adolescents:

"You can't go home again," thereby foreclosing on legitimate efforts to reestablish ties to biological families.

If you come back (to the biological home, foster home, or independent-living program), you (we) have failed.

"If you need any kind of help (from family, friends, mental health services, and the like), there is something wrong with you." This myth of autonomy has been perpetuated in our society and is one reason that our service system lags well behind universal needs for such services.

Interdependent Living

The concept of interdependent living, however, is based on the assumption that human beings are interdependent; that is, able to relate to—and function with—others, using community influence and resources, and being accessible to individuals and groups. Being interdependent means being able to carry out management tasks of daily life and having a productive quality of life through positive or appropriate interactions with individuals, groups, organizations, and social systems. It means recognizing the values of mutuality as well as self-determination and being able to assume responsibility for individual choice and its consequences.

Use of the concept of interdependent living in work with adolescents in foster care has various advantages. It is much more realistic than independent living; it is fair; and it is more consonant with real life and with the ideal concept of a community in which all people are mutually and constructively dependent. It also helps to dispel the myth of total autonomy of individuals, families, and nations. It is consistent with the growth of the self-help movement, which stresses the value of learning to rely on one another, to serve as resources for each other.

In addition, this concept helps to emphasize that a major goal of child welfare practice is helping adolescents in foster care to develop and maintain the essential connections required to meet their common human needs. As Polowy et al. [1986] indicate, interdependent living involves a range of "essential connections" between specific human needs and the ways people seek to fulfill these needs; that is, reciprocal connections between the youth in foster care and diverse components such as family, community, history, and values. "When people have positive connections, they tend to live more stable, satisfying lives. When people are disconnected, even from one essential connection, their well-being may be negatively affected."

The shift to emphasis on interdependent living also highlights a number of guidelines that are especially relevant for services to adolescents in foster care:

Viewing preparation for interdependent living as a process rather than a product or event—as an individualized, lifelong process, "not as movement from one geographical place to another but as a multidimensional process designed to enhance the young person's autonomy and growth toward mastery of life experiences" [Pasztor et al. 1986: 35]

Focusing on opportunities for mastery of both essential tangible and intangible skills

Delineating the different phases in the movement of youths toward interdependent living, from initial placement to leaving care, with differential practice implications in each phase on such aspects as their needs and roles, the roles of foster parents and biological parents, and the roles of social workers and other service providers

Clarifying similarities and differences between foster care and non-foster care youths in relation to preparation for interdependence. For example, the need for lifelong connections to a family cannot be minimized. For young people in foster care, however, the challenge of maintaining connections to foster and biological families is often problematic.

Regarding preparation for interdependent living as a shared responsibility involving the young person, foster parents, biological parents, the agency, and the community, and broadening the focus of intervention from the youth in foster care to the community, assessing the extent to which there is support for interdependence

Supporting foster parents in their efforts to prepare youths for life after foster care, while also recognizing and affirming their continuing meaning for, and relationship with, the youths following "emancipation"

Paying special attention to the roles of biological parents or extended biological family in the process of preparation for independent living, as well as in the post-discharge period

Locating and linking young people leaving care with meaningful community resources, such as those that reflect ethnic heritage, religion, or special interests

Roles of Biological and Foster Families

At the center of preparation of foster adolescents for interdependent living are the roles of biological and foster families.

Biological Families

The role of the biological family in foster care of adolescents in general—and in preparation for interdependent living in particular—needs to be reexamined and strengthened. As underscored by Carbino (Chapter 7 in this volume), the biological family continues to have crucial significance for the adolescent in care. For example, it has been found that many adolescents return to their biological families after leaving care or at least resume their relationship with their parents or other family members [Fein et al. 1990; Jones 1983]. Moreover, families can end by feeling better about themselves for having become involved at least in the end phase of their child's growing up.

For these reasons, biological families should be more extensively considered as potential resources for adolescents during the placement, as well as following discharge. The practice of separating young people from their families must be questioned. As Loppnow [1983: 531] has indicated, "Current knowledge suggests rather that young people need help differentiating from the troubling aspects of their heritage, [while] remaining connected in whatever ways possible to those biological figures central to their identity and experience."

Social workers, foster parents, and others working with adolescents should consider more explicitly whether biological parents can become at least partial resources for their children. This process, however, is one that should begin long before the young person leaves care. In addition, parents as well as adolescents require help to develop the skills that may be useful in learning or relearning to relate to one another. Although the parents may not have been competent in bringing up their children in the earlier phases of development, perhaps they can be helped to learn the skills required to relate to them as young adults.

In this respect, both the youths and the parents may need assistance, since so many of the parents have serious difficulties such as substance abuse and mental illness, and many of the youths have special needs [Fein et al. 1990; Kluger et al. 1989].

Foster Families

As noted in the preface, foster parents play a central role in helping adolescents to prepare for life after foster care. It is they who have the most contact with, and knowledge of, the young persons in their care. For these reasons as well as those related to federal cutbacks in services to children, society has charged foster parents with a full range of professional caregiving responsibilities. Foster parents are expected to guide youths and teach them skills for interdependent living; observe and assess progress toward service goals; advocate for services for their foster children and often manage the provision of these services; and, perhaps most important, deal daily with difficult behaviors that commonly occur in adolescence, as well as those that result from adolescents' experiences in foster care. Clearly, foster parents are an integral part of the service team and should be encouraged to work as partners with agencies and social workers in preparing adolescents for interdependent living. Their roles should be strengthened, supported, and made more visible.

The perspective of interdependent living also calls for maintaining linkages between adolescents and foster families. Often it is the foster family to which a youth remains connected [Jones and Moses 1984]. Yet, at present, youths' relationships with their foster families are officially terminated when they are discharged from care, and payments to foster families are ended. These actions imply that the foster parents' involvement is no longer needed or valued, since the youths are now expected to be self-reliant.

It is true that young people in care struggle to become emancipated from parent figures, including their foster parents, but this fact does not mean that they do not have a need for linkages with a family just as adolescents in general do. On the contrary, in at least some situations the foster family can be a source of ongoing support and connectedness. The continuing importance of a foster family for each youth should therefore be explored and reinforced to maximize connections whenever possible [Kluger et al. 1989].

In short, an interdependent approach would encourage continued involvement between adolescents and foster parents. But this approach also means that the foster parents' continued involvement should be recognized and rewarded through various means, such as educational benefits, retirement plans, and tax incentives. Moreover, as additional expectations of foster parents are established, some form of financial support should continue, especially in light of the low incomes of many foster families of adolescents [Fein et al. 1990]. In accordance with the concept of interdependence, foster parents should also be encouraged to make use of sources of connection, such as support groups and foster parent associations. Foster parents, like the young people for whom they care, should not be expected to go it alone and can receive valuable assistance and validation from their ties with other foster parents.

Conclusion

Successful achievement of interdependence leads to what we really mean when we say "becoming independent"—namely, becoming a self-sufficient person who is comfortable with self and happily connected to significant others in family, community, and society. This situation is what we want for all youths who will constitute the next generation. Why would we want less for the very children for whom society has assumed the greatest responsibility?

To enable adolescents in foster family care to achieve the goal of interdependent living, we must provide them with services that help them to develop the following key components of competent adulthood:

Competence and mastery of a range of tangible and intangible skills
Satisfying and mutually gratifying relationships with friends and kin
Ability to nurture their own children
Responsibility for their sexuality
Contribution to, and participation in, the community
Making essential connections
Positive sense of self

In the following chapters, the contributors delineate a range of principles, guidelines, strategies, and skills useful in providing the required services and programs in behalf of adolescents in foster family care, with emphasis on the central role of foster parents. As various contributors suggest, services for children, youths, and their families are most effective when there is teamwork or partnership among service providers, especially between foster parents and social workers. Yet foster parents have too often had to care for children and youths *independent* of agency supports. Too often, social workers have made case planning decisions *independent* of foster care youths, their biological parents, and their foster parents. Too often, agency administrators and even the courts have made decisions *independent* of clients and direct service providers. The most effective way to prepare youths for *interdependent* living may be for the child welfare field to practice *interdependent* service delivery more directly and systematically.

REFERENCES

Ainsworth, F. "The rush to independence . . . A new tyranny?" Australian Social Work 40 (March 1987): 5–6.

Aldgate, J., Maluccio, A. N., and Reeves, C. (editors). Adolescents in Foster Families. London: B. T. Batsford and Chicago: Lyceum Books, 1989.

American Public Welfare Association. Voluntary Cooperation Information Systems. Washington, DC: American Public Welfare Association, 1985.

Barth, R. P. "Emancipation services for adolescents in foster care." Social Work 31 (May–June 1986): 165–171.

Fein, E., Maluccio, A. N., and Kluger, M. No More Partings: An Examination of Long-Term Foster Family Care. Washington, DC: Child Welfare League of America, 1990.

Festinger, T. No One Ever Asked Us . . . A Postscript to Foster Care. New York: Columbia University Press, 1983.

Harari, T. "Teenagers exiting from foster family care." Unpublished doctoral dissertation. Berkeley, CA: University of California at Berkeley, 1980.

Hardin, M. Legal Issues Related to the Federal Independent Living Initiative. Washington, DC: American Bar Association, National Legal Resource Center for Child Advocacy and Protection, 1987.

Hawkins, Robert P., and Breiling, James (editors). Therapeutic Foster Care—Critical Issues. Washington, DC: Child Welfare League of America, 1989.

Hudson, Joe, and Galaway, Burt (editors). Specialist Foster Care: A Normalizing Experience. New York: Haworth Press, 1989.

Hornby, H. C., and Collins, M. I. "Teenagers in foster care: The forgotten majority." Children and Youth Services Review 3 (1981): 7–20.

Jones, M. A. A Second Chance for Families—Five Years Later: Follow-Up of a Program to Prevent Foster Care. New York: Child Welfare League of America, 1983.

Jones, M. A., and Moses, B. West Virginia's Former Foster Children: Their Experiences in Care and Their Lives as Young Adults. New York: Child Welfare League of America, 1984.

Kadushin, A., and Martin, J. K. Child Welfare Services—Fourth Edition. New York: Macmillan Publishing Co., 1988.

Kluger, M., Maluccio, A. N., and Fein, E. "Preparation of adolescents for life after foster care," in Aldgate, J., Maluccio, A. N., and Reeves, C. (editors), Adolescents in Foster Families. London: B. T. Batsford and Chicago: Lyceum Books, 1989, 77–87.

Loppnow, Donald M. "Adolescents on their own," in Laird, J., and Hartman, A. (editors), A Handbook of Child Welfare—Context, Knowledge, and Practice. New York: The Free Press, 1983, 514–531.

Maluccio, A. N., and Fein, E. "Growing up in foster care." Children and Youth Services Review 7 (1985): 123–134.

Maluccio, Anthony N., Fein, Edith, and Olmstead, Kathleen A. Permanency Planning for Children—Concepts and Methods. London and New York: Routledge, Chapman and Hall, Inc., 1986.

Maluccio, A. N., Krieger, R., Pasztor, E. M., and Pine, B. A. "Life after foster care: Independent or interdependent living?" Unpublished manuscript, 1987.

Mech, E. V. (editor). "Independent-living services for at-risk adolescents." Child Welfare 67 (special issue, November/December 1988): 483–634.

Pasztor, E. M., Clarren, J., Timberlake, E., and Bayless, K. "Stepping out of foster care into independent living." Children Today 15 (March-April 1986): 32–35.

Piliavin, I., Sosin, M., and Westerfelt, H. "Conditions contributing to long-term homelessness: An exploratory study," IRP Discussion Paper No. 853-887. Madison, WI: Institute for Research on Poverty, University of Wisconsin, 1987.

Polowy, M., Wasson, D., and Wolf, M. Fosterparentscope. Buffalo, NY: New York State Child Welfare Training Institute, 1986.

Shaw, Martin, and Hipgrave, Tony. Specialist Fostering. London: B.T. Batsford, 1983.

Stein, M., and Carey, K. Leaving Care. Oxford, England: Basil Blackwell, 1986.

Stone, Helen D. Ready, Set, Go—An Agency Guide to Independent Living. Washington, DC: Child Welfare League of America, 1987.

Susser, E., Struening, E. L., and Conover, S. "Childhood experiences of homeless men." American Journal of Psychiatry 144 (December 1987): 1599–1601.

Tatara, T., and Pettiford, E. K. Characteristics of Children in Substitutive and Adoptive Care: A Statistical Summary of the VICS National Child Welfare Data Base. Washington, DC: The American Public Welfare Association, 1985.

Westat, Inc. Independent Living Services for Youth in Substitute Care. Rockville, MD: Westat, Inc., 1986.

Whittaker, J. K., Schinke, S. P., and Gilchrist, L. D. "The ecological paradigm in child, youth, and family services: Implications for policy and practice." Social Service Review 60 (4) (December 1986): 483–503.

2

Recruiting and Retaining Foster Families of Adolescents

SUSAN WHITELAW DOWNS

I n the United States and Canada, the major resource for children unable to live with their families is the large, publicly supported, child welfare system that administers foster family care programs in every state and province. This system has helped countless youngsters to receive the nurture and support they need to become productive adults. Without the protection of these programs, many vulnerable children would continue to be exposed to family experiences inimical to healthy growth and development. Because of the significance of substitute care for the most vulnerable children, it is important for policymakers and administrators to assess continually the effectiveness of the foster care system. In regard to foster family care for adolescents, one should ask: Who are the foster parents? How adequate are the services that foster families receive from the child welfare agency? How extensive are the potential fostering resources?

These are important and timely questions, especially since about half of the youngsters in foster family care are adolescents; moreover, this proportion is increasing, and more youngsters are entering foster care in adolescence and spending their remaining youth in foster families. As a result, the role of foster parents is being reconceptualized from that of substitute parents to that of professional providers of special treatment services [Galaway 1978; Hawkins and Breiling 1989; Hudson and Galaway 1989; Meyer 1985; Tinney 1985].

In light of these trends, there is a need for further information about foster parents of adolescents that will guide agencies as they adapt foster family care programs to meet the needs of adolescents and their foster families. This chapter addresses that need, through analysis of data from two surveys of foster parents in the public child welfare system. The focus is on these questions:

What are the characteristics of foster parents caring for adolescents, and do they differ from those of other foster parents?

Among licensed foster parents of public agency programs, how many foster parents are willing to take adolescents, and what are their concerns in doing so?

What is the foster parents' perception of the adequacy of services to them provided by the agency, and is this perception related to their willingness to continue to foster adolescents?

What are the reimbursement rates provided to foster parents of adolescents?

Data Sources

The main source of data is the Westat 1980 survey of foster parents in eight states, which involved state child welfare agencies in Alabama, Arkansas, North Dakota, Rhode Island, Texas, Utah, Virginia, and Wisconsin. It covered responses of foster parents to questions concerning their demographic characteristics, experiences as foster parents, and relationships with their agencies. From the random sample of foster families selected in each state, 79 percent returned usable questionnaires ($n = 1,371$). Nearly all (98 percent) of these were affiliated with a public child welfare agency, and all were licensed or approved by the state [Westat 1981].[1]

The second source of data is a 1986 survey of foster parents in

---

[1]Data presented in this chapter were analyzed by the author from data collected by Westat for this survey. Information on receiving copies of the survey data and documentation may be obtained from Soledad Sambrano, Administration for Children, Youth, and Families, U.S. Department of Health and Human Services, Washington, DC 20201.

two child welfare agencies of metropolitan Detroit that provide foster care services under purchase-of-care agreements with the Michigan Department of Social Services [Downs 1987]. Foster parents were interviewed in their homes, using a standard survey instrument adapted from the 1980 Westat survey. Of the 250 foster parents affiliated with these two agencies, 211 (84 percent) completed the interviews.

Information from the 1986 Detroit survey is used to supplement the 1980 eight-state survey, particularly in regard to adequacy of payments to foster parents. Unless otherwise noted, all data presented are from the 1980 eight-state survey. The 1986 survey contained higher proportions of black and single foster parents than did the 1980 survey. These differences may mean that results of the 1986 survey are not generalizable to the broad population of foster parents.

Findings

Characteristics of Foster Parents of Adolescents

Of the 1,371 foster families included in the eight-state survey, 757 (55 percent) reported that they had fostered one or more teenagers during their fostering career. The demographic characteristics and fostering experiences of these foster parents are presented in Table 1 and compared with those of foster parents who had not cared for adolescents.

Demographic Characteristics
Most of the families that had cared for adolescents were headed by two parents (84 percent). Nearly half (45 percent) had incomes of under $15,000 in 1980. Nineteen percent were black, 2 percent Hispanic, 76 percent were white, and the rest Native American, Alaska native, or Asian-American. Sixty-six percent of the foster mothers had graduated from high school, and 61 percent were not working outside the home (full-time homemakers). The majority (54 percent) of the foster mothers were over age forty.

In general, foster parents with experience caring for adolescent foster children were similar demographically to other foster parents. The one exception was that women fostering teenagers tended to be somewhat older than other foster mothers.

TABLE 1. CHARACTERISTICS OF FOSTER
PARENTS BY WHETHER OR NOT THEY
HAVE CARED FOR ADOLESCENT
FOSTER CHILDREN[1]

Characteristic	Cared for Teen (n = 757) (%)*	Not Cared for Teen (n = 614) (%)*	χ^2
Marital status (n = 1,367)			0.81
Married	84	82	
Single	16	18	
Annual income (n = 1,348)			4.39
Less than $7,000	13	17	
$7,000 to less than $15,000	32	31	
$15,000 to less than $25,000	37	34	
$25,000 or more	18	19	
Ethnicity (n = 1,347)			6.43
Black	19	24	
Hispanic	2	3	
White	76	70	
Other	3	3	
Foster mother education (n = 1,344)			3.6
Eighth grade or less	12	11	
Some high school	22	20	
High school graduate	53	58	
College graduate	13	11	
Foster mother employment (n = 1,339)			3.75
Employed full time	24	20	
Employed part time	14	15	
Full-time homemaker	61	66	
Foster mother age (n = 1,347)			8.73**
18–25 years	3	4	
26–40 years	42	49	
41–60 years	44	36	
61 years or older	10	11	
Main reason for becoming a foster parent (n = 1,364)			27.79**
Help a foster child because I was a foster child	3	1	
Provide a home for a child I knew	22	16	

TABLE 1 *(continued)*

Characteristic	Cared for Teen (n = 757) (%)*	Not Cared for Teen (n = 614) (%)*	χ^2
Have more children in the family	21	23	
Increase household income	2	2	
Care for a child but did not want long-term responsibility	6	6	
Adopt a child and thought foster care was a good starting point	3	9	
Fulfill my religious beliefs in doing good deeds	16	16	
Other	10	11	
Inappropriate answer	17	17	
Length of time a foster parent (n = 1,370)			23.91**
Less than 3 years	32	44	
3 to less than 10 years	41	35	
10 years or more	28	20	
Total number of foster children cared for (n = 1,360)			104.44**
0 to 5	41	66	
6 to 10	21	18	
11 or more	39	16	
Number of foster children in home (n = 1,365)			37.28**
0	29	28	
1	31	40	
2	16	20	
3	19	12	
4	5	1	

[1]Source: Westat, 1981
*Total percentages do not equal 100 due to rounding
**Significant at the .05 level

Reason for Fostering

As to the main reasons for becoming foster parents, the largest categories of responses among foster parents of adolescents were to "provide a home for a child I knew" (22 percent); "have more children in the family" (21 percent); and fulfill my religious beliefs in doing good deeds" (16 percent).

Foster parents who had fostered teenagers were more likely than the others to say that they became foster parents to care for a child they already knew, and less likely to say that they wanted to adopt a child and they thought foster care was a good place to start.

Experience

About two-thirds of those fostering adolescents had three or more years of experience as foster parents. Thirty-nine percent had cared for eleven or more children during the course of their fostering career. About 40 percent had two or more foster children in the home at the time of the 1980 survey. Foster parents of adolescents differed significantly from other foster parents in regard to experience; they tended to have fostered longer, to have more children in the home, and to have cared for more children than had other foster parents.

In summary, as a group, foster parents of adolescents were mainly two-parent families with low to middle incomes. Their primary motivation for fostering was to provide a home for a child they already knew, to have more children in the family, or to fulfill religious or altruistic beliefs. Foster parents of adolescents differed from other foster parents mainly in that they tended to be more experienced in fostering, more likely to have become foster parents to care for a child previously known to them, and less likely to be interested in adoption.

Willingness to Take Adolescents and Concerns in So Doing

Given the increasing proportion of adolescents in the foster care population, it was of interest to determine the extent to which currently licensed foster parents were willing to accept children in this age group. Table 2 therefore presents the responses of foster parents in the 1980 survey to the question, "If you were now requested to care for a teenage foster child, would you: probably accept the child; possibly accept the child, depending on age; probably not accept the

TABLE 2. FOSTER PARENTS' WILLINGNESS
TO ACCEPT AN ADOLESCENT FOSTER
CHILD BY WHETHER OR NOT THEY
HAD PREVIOUSLY CARED FOR AN
ADOLESCENT FOSTER CHILD[1]

Willingness to Accept an Adolescent Foster Child	Cared for Teen		Not Cared for Teen		Total	
	n	%	n	%	n	%
Probably would accept	285	38	92	15	377	28
Possibly would accept depending on age	132	18	94	15	226	17
Probably would not accept	158	21	307	50	465	34
Planning to quit fostering	180	24	118	19	298	22
Totals	755	101*	611	99*	1,366	101*

[1]Source: Downs, 1987
*Total percentages do not equal 100 due to rounding
$\chi^2 = 152.35$, $df = 3$, $p = .00$

child; inapplicable, no longer foster parent or intend to stop foster parenting?"

Of the total group of foster parents, nearly half (45 percent) would probably or possibly accept a teenager. Over half would not do so, either because they did not wish to foster a child in this age group (34 percent) or because they intended to stop fostering altogether (22 percent). Of those foster parents experienced in caring for teenage foster children, only a little more than half were interested in continuing to care for a teenager (38 percent probably would accept; 18 percent possibly would accept). Less than a third (30 percent) of those with no experience in caring for teenage foster children were interested in caring for a child in this age group.

These findings suggest that, among currently licensed foster parents, resources for foster home placement of teenage children are limited. Attrition is high, as nearly half of those experienced in fostering teenagers did not plan to continue to do so. Furthermore, interest in fostering teenagers among those who had not cared for a child in this age group is limited and does not compensate for the attrition of experienced foster parents.

All foster parents, whether or not they had cared for an adolescent foster child in the past, were also asked an open-ended question about their major concerns in caring for a teenage foster child. The responses suggest that the overwhelming concern of foster parents is their ability to cope with the adolescent's problems in areas such as behavior, discipline, drugs, or pregnancy. Foster parents also expressed fear of physical harm and concern about the disruptive effect of the teenager on family life as well as on their biological children. Lack of transportation or physical space in the home and acceptance of the foster child in the community were less frequently mentioned as barriers to fostering an adolescent.

Adequacy of Agency Services to Foster Parents

Table 3 presents information on the foster parents' perception of the adequacy of agency services to them during the time that they cared for a teenage foster child. For this analysis, only foster parents of teenagers are included, but results are presented from both the 1980 survey [Westat 1981] and the 1986 survey [Downs 1987]. The 1980 survey provides data on the adequacy of information that the foster parents were given regarding the teenager's background or special needs and on the help or support they received in dealing with the teenager's special needs or problems. The 1986 survey provides data on foster parents' perception of the adequacy of reimbursement rates to cover the costs of caring for an adolescent. The latter question was not asked in the 1980 survey.

The results show that 73 percent of the foster parents in the 1980 survey found adequate the information they received on the child's background or special needs, and 80 percent found adequate the help or support they received from the agency in dealing with the child's special needs or problems. Sixty-four percent of the Detroit foster parents in the 1986 survey found the reimbursements given to cover the costs of care to be adequate.

It is an interesting question whether or not a relationship exists between the foster parents' assessment of the adequacy of agency services to them while caring for a teenager and their willingness to care for another foster child in this age group. To explore this question, a bivariate analysis of data was done. As shown in Table

TABLE 3. FOSTER PARENTS' ASSESSMENT
OF ADEQUACY OF AGENCY SERVICES AND
WILLINGNESS TO CARE FOR ANOTHER
TEENAGE FOSTER CHILD

Agency Service for Previous Teenage Foster Child	Willing to Care for Another Teenage Foster Child?		Total (%)	χ^2 (%)
	Yes* (%)	No* (%)		
Information on child's background or special needs (n = 40)				6.39**
Adequate	77	69	73	
Not adequate	23	31	27	
Help or support in dealing with the child's special needs or problems (n = 741)				1.89
Adequate	82	78	80	
Not adequate	18	22	20	
Data Source: Westat 1981				
Reimbursement to cover the costs of care (n = 72)				2.68
Adequate	73	52	64	
Not adequate	27	48	36	
Data Source: Downs 1987				

*Yes: probably would accept or possibly would accept, depending on age of foster child; No: probably would not accept, or planning to quit fostering
**Significant at the .05 level

3, over three-fourths (77 percent) of the foster parents who were willing to care for another teenage foster child had found adequate the information they had received concerning the background and special needs of earlier teenage foster children; a smaller proportion (69 percent), however, of those unwilling to foster another teenager had found this area of agency service to be adequate. The relationship between adequacy of information received and willingness to foster another teenager was statistically significant ($p = .05$).

Eighty-two percent of those willing to care for another teenager had found the help or support from the agency to be adequate during earlier experiences in caring for a teenager, while 78 percent of those unwilling to care for another teenager were satisfied with the help or support they had received. No significant relationship was found between perception of adequacy of help or support received from the agency and willingness to continue fostering teenagers.

Regarding level of payment, 73 percent of the foster parents in the 1986 survey who were willing to continue fostering teenagers found the reimbursement level adequate to cover the costs of care, while 52 percent of those unwilling to continue believed that they were adequately reimbursed. The relationship between perceived adequacy of reimbursement and willingness to continue was not statistically significant $(p = .10)$, but the direction of the relationship supports the possibility that perceived adequacy of payments may affect the decision to continue fostering this age group.

To supplement the quantitative data presented above, foster parents were also asked an open-ended question as to what additional help or support they had needed from the agency. Answers to this question revealed that, in addition to the areas listed in Table 3, foster parents wanted more help from the agency in relation to discipline and structuring and reinforcing behavioral expectations for adolescents in their care.

Reimbursement Rates to Foster Parents of Adolescents

Table 4 shows the reimbursement rates for fostering various age groups for each study state during the year that the surveys were conducted (1986 for Michigan and 1980 for the eight Westat survey states). Information on reimbursement rates came from agency material and telephone conversations with state-level foster care administrators.

The monthly rates for adolescents ranged from $135 (in Alabama) to $285 (in Utah) in 1980. The rate for Michigan in 1986 was $380. There was also a range among states in the difference between rates for younger children and adolescents. Alabama paid the same rate for all children, regardless of age, while Utah had the largest difference in rates between children of grade school age ($183) and adolescents ($285). There was also variation in the age at which the "adolescent reimbursement rate" started, varying from age ten, in Texas, to age 13, in North Dakota and Virginia.

TABLE 4. MONTHLY REIMBURSEMENT RATES
FOR DIFFERENT AGE GROUPS OF FOSTER
CHILDREN BY STATE

State	Age Group	Rate*	Difference Between Grade Schooler and Teenager
Alabama	0–18	$135.00	$00.00
Arkansas	0–5	$111.00	
	6–11	122.00	
	12–14	140.00	$18.00
	15+	150.00	$28.00
North Dakota	0–4	$161.00	
	5–12	197.00	
	13+	212.00	$15.00
Rhode Island	0–11	$160.00	
	12+	196.00	$36.00
Texas	0–9	$180.00	
	10+	210.00	$30.00
Utah	0–10	$183.00	
	11+	285.00	$102.00
Virginia	0–4	$118.00	
	5–12	149.00	
	13+	187.00	$38.00
Wisconsin	0–4	$129.00	
	5–11	167.00	
	12–14	188.00	$21.00
	15–18	215.00	$48.00
Michigan	0–12	$307.00**	
	13–18	380.00	$73.00

*Rates for Michigan are for 1986 [Downs 1987]; rates for other states are for 1980 [Westat 1981].

**Michigan calculates rates on a daily rather than a monthly basis. The rates given here are estimates per month, figuring 365 days in a year.

Implications for Practice, Policy, and Research

The findings from surveys of foster parents that have been reported in this chapter suggest that a lag exists between the changing foster child population and the responses of child welfare agencies. As discussed below, efforts to respond more appropriately to the needs of foster parents caring for adolescents should include changes in recruitment, agency-foster parent relationships, and reimbursement rates.

Recruitment

As others have noted [Kluger et al. 1989], the pool of foster families currently available for adolescents needing out-of-home placement seems to be increasingly inadequate. Moreover, the changing nature of the foster child population has probably not been sufficiently considered in current recruitment strategies. For example, recruitment campaigns that emphasize care and nurture of vulnerable children attract foster parents who are motivated to help children, but who may not have the requisite skills for, or interest in, caring for adolescents [Coyne 1986; Pasztor and Burgess 1982].

The high attrition rate of those fostering adolescents and the limited interest of other foster parents in caring for children in this age group mean that recruitment for foster parents of adolescents must not only be continued but must also employ different strategies. For instance, the finding that foster parents of adolescents were more likely than others to enter the foster program to care for a child previously known to them suggests that families may be available in the general population who are interested in caring for this age group but who have not been reached by generic recruitment campaigns. For these families, the relatively greater independence and capacity for self-care of adolescents may make them desirable as foster children. Moreover, recent emphasis on the role of foster parents in preparing adolescents for independence suggests that it may be particularly important to recruit foster parents with interest in helping children to live on their own [Pasztor et al. 1986; Barth 1986].

Little is known about recruitment strategies effective in targeting families primarily interested in caring for adolescents. Research directed at this issue would help focus agency recruitment efforts and also, perhaps, expand the supply of foster families available for this age group.

Agency-Foster Parent Relationship

The findings on the foster parents' assessment of agency services to them also indicate a need for change. Foster parents say that they need more information on the background of the teenagers coming into their home and also more help from the agency in regard to discipline, an area discussed in depth by Ryan in Chapter 11 of this volume.

In regard to the need for additional information, it is necessary to take into account that teenagers in foster care have usually suffered deprivations and disruptions that affect their current functioning. Foster parents have a legitimate interest in receiving information about adolescents in their care, particularly as they are viewed as professional foster parents and members of the treatment team (see Chapter 1 and Aldgate et al. 1989). Considerations of confidentiality cannot override the legitimate need of foster parents to know the past experiences and likely feelings and behaviors of teenagers coming into their homes.

Regarding discipline, it seems important to consider that the youngster's legal status vis-à-vis the foster parent is ambiguous. Courts, the child welfare agency, the biological parents, and the foster parents all share responsibility and authority over the child. An adolescent's natural tendency to question authority may become particularly problematic in foster care, where there are so many authority figures and the nature of the foster parents' legal responsibility is unclear. Since agencies and foster parents work together as members of a team, agency involvement in developing and enforcing behavioral expectations for the teenager can be facilitated. Because authority is shared, it is reasonable for both foster parents and agencies to share the responsibility for setting limits. This shared responsibility can not only bolster the foster parents' efforts but also prove less confusing for the teenager.

Reimbursement Rates

In public child welfare, reimbursement rates for regular foster care are generally intended to cover only the direct cost of care of a foster child [Settles et al. 1976]. The differences in rates among states reported here indicate, however, that there is little agreement about the costs of caring for adolescents. Indeed, the variation in rates for teenagers suggests that the amounts are determined less upon empirically based information as to actual costs than from political, historical, or budgetary factors.

Studies of reimbursement rates have generally shown them to

be inadequate to cover direct costs, suggesting that foster parents subsidize the costs of care. This situation is inexcusable, especially in light of research showing that over one-fifth of foster families have incomes below the poverty line [Fein et al. 1990]. Furthermore, rates do not cover indirect costs such as wear and tear on the family home and the value of the foster parents' time in caring for the child [DeJong 1975; Settles et al. 1976]. Foster parents must therefore subsidize these costs as well. Past research indicates that this foster parent subsidy negatively affects the amount of foster care they are willing to provide [Simon 1975; Campbell and Downs 1987; Downs in press].

The findings reported here lend some support to the view that if those fostering adolescents perceive the rates to be inadequate, they may discontinue fostering children in this age group. That interpretation is presented cautiously, since the relationship between perceived adequacy of board rates and willingness to foster adolescents is not conclusive, and information on perceived adequacy of board rates was not available from the 1980 survey, with its large, multi-state sample.

Common sense suggests, however, that given the low incomes of most foster families, it is unreasonable to expect that they can subsidize the financial costs of caring for teenagers in addition to offering love, emotional support, and guidance to the troubled teenagers in their homes [Kadushin 1980]. In general, it seems reasonable to assume that increasing reimbursement rates would enable more foster parents to care for adolescents.

At the same time, it should be noted that further information is required on the direct and indirect costs that foster parents incur in caring for adolescents, to advance consideration of a rational basis for setting reimbursement rates. It would also be important to understand the relationship, if any, between reimbursement rates and quality of care and to know more about the characteristics of those who consider providing foster family care to teenagers but decide that reimbursement rates are insufficient. Finally, it would be helpful to consider extending stipends for foster children beyond age 18, in order to ensure more gradual transition from foster care to a return home or to interdependent living.

Conclusion

The number of foster parents is inadequate to meet the growing need for foster home placement of adolescents. The findings considered in this chapter suggest that this number can be expanded through such means as recruitment efforts focused on the need for families to care for teenage foster children, increased sharing of information about the adolescents with foster parents, more active involvement with the foster parents in planning and monitoring behavioral expectations of adolescents in their care, and higher (as well as more realistic) reimbursement rates. Above all, the findings suggest that recent efforts to reconceptualize the foster parents' role from caregiver-parent to member of a treatment team would be particularly relevant to adolescent foster care [Aldgate et al. 1989; Galaway 1978; Hudson and Galaway 1989; Tinney 1985].

REFERENCES

Aldgate, J., Maluccio, A. N., and Reeves, C. (editors). Adolescents in Foster Families. London: B. T. Batsford and Chicago: Lyceum Books, 1989.

Barth, R. P. "Emancipation services for adolescents in foster care." Social Work 31 (May–June 1986): 165–171.

Campbell, Claudia, and Downs, Susan W. "The impact of economic incentives on foster parents." Social Service Review 61 (December 1987): 599–609.

Coyne, Ann. "Recruiting foster and adoptive families: A marketing strategy." Children Today 15 (September–October 1986): 30–33.

DeJong, Gerben. "Setting foster care rates: I. Basic considerations." Public Welfare 33 (Fall 1975): 37–41.

Downs, Susan W. Foster Parents and Children's Aid Society: Preliminary Report. Detroit, MI: Wayne State University, School of Social Work, 1987.

———. "Foster parents of mentally retarded and physically handicapped children." Children and Youth Services Review, in press.

Fein, E., Maluccio, A. N., and Kluger, M. No More Partings: An Examination of Long-Term Foster Family Care. Washington, DC: Child Welfare League of America, 1990.

Galaway, Burt. "PATH: An agency operated by foster parents." Child Welfare 57 (December 1978): 667–674.

Hawkins, Robert P., and Breiling, James (editors). Therapeutic Foster Care—Critical Issues. Washington, DC: Child Welfare League of America, 1989.

Hudson, Joe, and Galaway, Burt (Editors). Specialist Foster Care: A Normalizing Experience. New York: The Haworth Press, 1989.

Kadushin, Alfred. Child Welfare Services, 3rd edition. New York: Macmillan, 1980.

Kluger, M., Maluccio, A. N., and Fein, E. "Preparation of adolescents for life after foster care," in Aldgate, J., Maluccio, A. N., and Reeves, C. Adolescents in Foster Families: London: B. T. Batsford and Chicago: Lyceum Books, 1989: 77–87.

Meyer, Carol H. "A feminist perspective on foster family care: A redefinition of categories." Child Welfare 64 (May–June 1985): 249–257.

Pasztor, Eileen Mayers, and Burgess, Elyse M. "Finding and keeping more foster parents." Children Today 11 (March–April 1982): 2–5.

Pasztor, Eileen Mayers, Clarren, Jean, Timberlake, Elizabeth M., and Bayless, Linda. "Stepping out of foster care into independent living." Children Today 15 (March–April 1986): 32–35.

Settles, B. H., Van Name, J. B., and Culley, J. D. "Estimating costs in foster family care." Children Today 5 (November–December 1976): 19–21.

Simon, Julian L. "The effect of foster care payment levels on the number of foster children given homes." Social Science Review 49 (September 1975): 405–411.

Tinney, Mary Anne. "Role perceptions in foster parent associations in British Columbia." Child Welfare 64 (January–February 1985): 73–79.

Westat, Inc. Final Report: 1980 State Surveys of Foster Parents. National Study of Social Services to Children and Their Families. Prepared for Division of Program Development and Innovation, U.S. Children's Bureau, Administration for Children, Youth and Families, U.S. Department of Health and Human Services, Washington, DC 20013, Contract No. HEW 105-76-1127. Rockville, MD: Westat, 1981.

3

The Coming-of-Age in Foster Care

HELEN LAND

W hen asked about the meaning of the term "emancipation,"
most people might think of setting a slave free from bondage
rather than accomplishing the developmental process that results in
an identity distinct from parental figures, the achieving of greater
independence, and leaving home. To adolescents who are psychologically ready to leave home, negotiating a more separate life from parents
and family appears as an eagerly anticipated event filled with fantasies
of freedom and jubilation, albeit one coupled with some anxiety. For
a sizable group of adolescents who are not psychologically ready, however, the process of leaving home is quite a different experience. For
some, it is a time of fear; for others, it is a time filled with feelings
of abandonment; for still others, it may be the start of a long career
as an identified client [Haley 1980].

Emancipation is both an act and a process. Historically, for the
adolescent in foster care, emancipation has received attention primarily as an act not involving a process. Yet coming of age in foster
care embodies a unique set of developmental tasks that require adequate time to fulfill. The fact that foster adolescents face artificial
and often inflexible discharge deadlines, as well as possible developmental delays, places them at particularly high risk for failure. This
chapter discusses the process of emancipation for adolescents in foster

family care, identifies the developmental tasks necessary for its successful completion, and alerts foster parents and social workers to methods of intervention aimed at reducing psychological risk within this vulnerable population and thus increasing chances for healthy interdependent living after foster care.

Developmental Tasks of Adolescence

To clarify the unique issues of the process in foster care, it is useful to review the developmental tasks that face all adolescents as they confront leaving home. Success is characterized by the achievement of these developmental milestones within adolescence [Specht and Craig 1982; Leveton 1984; Oldham 1980]. Expectations of when it is appropriate for certain developmental tasks to be accomplished may vary, however, according to ethnicity, class, or gender. For example, in many Latino cultures, adolescents are not considered deviant or delayed should they continue to reside at the parental home through young adulthood or until marriage [Falicov 1982]. In other cultures, because of economic necessity and cultural values, many generations may reside within the same household, with no expectation of leaving the parental home. Moreover, in wealthier societies, the process of emancipation may be extended and the act of emancipation delayed by advanced educational opportunities. But regardless of cultural differences in developmental expectations, adolescents in foster care are expected to become emancipated during late adolescence.

Identity Formation

Despite cultural and social differences and some disagreement as to the degree of normative turmoil within adolescence, most would agree that the primary agenda of adolescence is a renegotiation of the separation and individuation process to gain greater independence from parental figures and solidify an identity of one's own [Oldham 1980; MacIntyre 1970; Specht and Craig 1982]. Identity formation is a progressive process, involving several dimensions. The process begins early in life, but it is primarily during adolescence that individuals judge themselves in light of how others judge them. Simultaneously, they assess the worthiness of others' judgments in light of how they perceive themselves in comparison to the judgers and to significant others [Erikson 1968]. Adolescence is also a time of solidifying gender identification and negotiating sex roles.

Identity formation involves a process of repeatedly looking back on one's life history and looking forward to the ideals and opportunities ahead. It is a time of judging one's capacities to achieve those ideals. In addition, it is a time of relating significant events in one's life, and significant actors in one's life history, to personal qualities and to the social ideals and opportunities ahead. It is also a time of identifying with those who are significant in one's life and of assuming ethical stances [MacIntyre 1970]. What the adolescent is to become is influenced by what the environment has allowed and will now allow. Erikson [1965: 23] states that these processes give meaning to an individual's identity "by relating it to a living community and to ongoing history, and by counterpointing the newly won individual identity with some communal solidarity." The importance of stable family and community life cannot be overemphasized, as discussed by Pine and Krieger in Chapter 12 of this book.

The emancipation process during adolescence also strongly recalls Mahler's concept of refueling during toddlerhood [Mahler et al. 1975]. Completion of object constancy and of the separation/individuation process depends upon the young child's internalization and awareness of a parental presence when the parent is out of sight. The child engages in a series of autonomous actions, venturing away from the parent and returning to the parent for emotional refueling. The adolescent's final steps to autonomy are similar. The emancipation process often involves a series of episodes of venturing out from the family, rejecting the status quo of family life, testing the waters outside the family home, and returning to it for emotional refueling to regain stability and security. Hence, just as for the toddler, a necessary component in the adolescent's developing autonomy is an internalized awareness of a stable parental presence.

Transaction with the Environment

Achievement of developmental milestones such as emancipation results from interactional processes. The transactional nature of life span development, however, is often inadequately recognized. Bloom [1980: v] eloquently reminds us that much of the literature on human growth and development is "presented as if one person moves through the life span in splendid isolation, like a spotlight following the star of the show across a stage, while the supporting cast dash in and fade out, as if fully subordinate to the star."

It follows that the adolescent attempting to prepare for adult roles affects and is affected by the relative health and stability of the near ecological environment—the family, peer group, and the neighborhood—as well as by the relative health of the far ecological environment—the community, the state, and the society. For example, in many families with adolescents, the parents are approaching midlife and experience a similar period of self-reflection and evaluation of their life history. These parents and their adolescents must negotiate individual but tandem life-stage issues, with each affecting and being affected by the others. Other families may be facing an adolescent's emancipation process at the same time that aging grandparents are growing increasingly dependent. For these and other reasons, for parent and adolescent alike, the road to a successful emancipation may not be a smooth passage. The youth's accelerating physiological development, coupled with pseudoemotional maturity, may tempt parents to expect more maturity and autonomy at a dangerously early age, resulting in what Elkind [1979] describes as the "hurried child." Conversely, a delay in clarifying roles and in developing congruent self-perceptions in the family may result in an adolescent out of synchrony with family or peer expectations.

Going beyond the parent-adolescent relationship, the lack of job opportunities resulting in extraordinarily high unemployment rates for black and Hispanic adolescents also illustrates the negative effect of the environment on achievement of developmental task and successful emancipation [Edelman 1987]. Finding and keeping a job is an important life skill, necessary for survival as well as contributing to a youth's sense of self, which is denied many minority youths.

In light of the above, it is clear that emancipation is truly a multidimensional and transactional process. Because of the manifold family developmental issues occurring at the time of emancipation, even under the best conditions, the emancipation process can be a difficult time for parent and child alike. Yet every adolescent must confront the developmental steps leading to a distinct identity formation and emancipation. These steps involve judging self and others, reflecting back on one's life ahead to one's future, identifying with significant others, obtaining emotional refueling, assessing oneself within society's domain, and, extremely important, being received by a stable community.

The Coming-of-Age in Foster Care

"My parents didn't want me anymore." "Mother ran out on me . . . I think she went to jail." "Being foster is like being a piece of garbage. You're just something somebody tossed out." "Because I was bad." "I don't know."

These are the responses of some adolescents to the question: "Why are you in foster care?" [Gil and Bogart 1982: 8; Lee and Park 1978: 523]. With answers like these, there remains little mystery as to why foster children may be at risk for problems associated with identity formation and emancipation. The developmental steps that may be difficult to achieve under normal circumstances are even more so for adolescents in foster care. Their judgment of self in light of how others judge them often renders a verdict of guilty. In addition, as several studies indicate, many adolescents in foster care are confused and frustrated in their efforts to put together their life story—who they are, and why they are where they are [Lee and Park 1978; McDermott 1987; Pasztor et al. 1986; Mauzerall 1983].

It follows that the life review process, a cornerstone of identity formation, can be painful or, at best, greatly encumbered for adolescents in foster care. Judging one's capacity to meet future ideals may result in significant depression and developmental delay at the time of a forced emancipation [Lee and Park 1978]. Furthermore, adolescents in foster care may internalize negative parental identities or attributes as they relate significant events in their lives and significant actors in their life histories to their own personal qualities. Conversely, adolescents may develop an idealized view of their parents and label their out-of-home placements a result of their own unworthiness as children [Tiddy 1986].

In addition, the realities of foster care placement may inhibit adolescents' attainment of the two requisites for identity formation mentioned earlier: permanence in ongoing life history and communal solidarity [Erikson 1968], even while their importance has been noted repeatedly [Maluccio et al. 1986]. There is often little sense of a stable parental presence in the lives of adolescents in foster care. Finally, the progressive series of episodes described above as emotional refueling are simply not available to adolescents who do not have the opportunity to leave and later return to the parental home. Leaving the foster home is most often accomplished in a single act, even when programs such as halfway houses are used before a move to full independence [Simonitch and Anderson 1979; Furrh 1983].

Given these dilemmas, it should come as no surprise to helping professionals that studies examining adolescents and adults who had been in foster care frequently reveal distressing life statuses. Compared to their cohorts raised in their own families, those who have lived in foster care have higher rates of marital dissolution, higher rates of problem pregnancies and births [Meier 1965]; lower intellectual performance; higher rates of alcohol abuse and criminality [Jones and Moses 1984; Bohman and Sigvardsson 1980]; higher rates of reactive depression [Anderson and Simonitch 1981]; lower rates of educational attainment and employment [Festinger 1983]; and higher rates of poverty [Zimmerman 1982]. In addition, those with a greater number of foster placements have fared more poorly than those with fewer placements [Fein et al. 1983].

Although study results are by no means decisive, and we cannot conclude that all foster children will experience difficulty as a result of their out-of-home placement [Maluccio and Fein 1985], the statistics often confirm that former foster children are at greater risk for a more difficult life. This fact is not surprising, because frequently their histories include abridged educational experiences; physical abuse, neglect, or abandonment in childhood; multiple caregivers and foster family placements resulting in changes in neighborhood, school, and community settings; and scanty guidance at the time of emancipation [Barth 1986; Fein et al. 1983].

Service approaches must take into account each foster adolescent's own history and life experience, as he or she is helped to achieve the developmental milestones in negotiating passage through the stages leading to emancipation and interdependent living.

Aiding in the Emancipation Process

As a result of growing attention to the needs of adolescents in foster care for help in preparing for interdependent life, a number of support programs have been instituted [Barth 1986]. Some programs include semisupervised apartments for emancipating adolescents [Furrh 1983; Mauzerall 1983; Simonitch and Anderson 1979]. Others emphasize group intervention approaches to assist in the emancipation process [Lee and Park 1978]. But few have capitalized on the strengths of the ecological environment in which the adolescent resides—in particular the foster family—and the natural partnership that exists between the social worker and the foster family.

Role of the Foster Family

When adolescents who are in their own homes display dysfunctional behavior and are referred for social services, intervention may involve individual and group treatment, with service frequently centering on some type of family intervention, and, ultimately, work with the parents, who act as architects of family life. Service providers often view dysfunctional adolescent behavior in light of issues pertaining to autonomy and impending emancipation and in light of the adolescent's transactions with other family members and with his or her ecological environment. Similarly, teenagers in foster care may display a variety of dysfunctional behaviors. Many may struggle with unresolved life issues, as well as with the impending emancipation. They may attempt an eleventh-hour effort to sabotage the foster placement, an obvious signal for help (see Chapter 4 by Levine). Yet in many cases, unlike their practice with other troubled adolescents, service workers underutilize family intervention in their work with foster adolescents, even when the foster family may be a valuable resource in smoothing the transition toward greater independence.

In a very real sense, foster parents are the bridge between the emancipating adolescent and society, and, in this role, they may provide a crucial linking function. Their status is an ambiguous one, however. Although they function *in loco parentis*, the state typically holds final legal responsibility for the adolescent. As foster parents, their power is attenuated. In addition, because of the many ambivalent and distrustful feelings the adolescent may hold toward parenting figures—both foster and biological—foster parents may find themselves in a seemingly untenable situation, living with an acting-out adolescent and trying to cope with unresolvable issues. Hence, foster parents meet resistance and major struggles in their effort to assist adolescents in the processes of separation/individuation, identity synthesis, and emancipation.

One or more of the following situations is not uncommon. An adolescent may feel little sense of loyalty to the foster parents as parents; hence, their influence in his or her life may be diminished. An adolescent may perceive little possibility of a future relationship with them and may therefore not invest emotional attachment in the relationship. Other adolescents have a tendency to glorify emancipation and negate the value of family life and the foster home, especially when stable family relationships have been absent. In other cases, adolescents may engage in an offensive rejection of the foster parents before their perceived rejection by foster parents results in the inevitable disruption of the foster placement. They may feel jealousy toward other children who will remain in the home. Finally, foster parents in some families may be struggling with developmental life issues of their own, which, in combination with those of the foster adolescent, may produce a highly conflicted living environment. Although this potential for conflict may seem to suggest a diminished role for foster parents, in fact the reverse is true. The identity-centered conflict illustrated above will not resolve itself and must be attended to; avoiding or suppressing the conflict impedes the adolescent's resolution of feelings about placement history and past life events and their subsequent effect on identity issues and emancipation.

Foster Parent-Worker Partnership

The chances for a successful emancipation are increased when social service providers and foster parents work in partnership and *use* naturally occurring conflict and resistance in family life to solve problems. Foster parents should be alerted to potential conflict, to typical parental responses to emancipation, to issues inherent within their own life stage, and, most important, to those parental responses that facilitate a healthy emancipation. Hence, by negotiating the areas of conflict described above and others that may be manifested among foster adolescent, foster family, and the child welfare agency, the adolescent may be helped to untangle pertinent life issues and synthesize an autonomous identity as well as prepare for the realities of adult relationships.

The roles of the participants may vary from case to case. For example, how the foster parents' role is realized depends on the history of agency involvement and the degree of permanence in the relationship between the particular adolescent and the foster family. Even in intact families, parents often look to helping professionals for consultation and support as their adolescent negotiates emancipation. Because families often require extra support during this time, therefore, chances for a smoother emancipation increase when foster parents and worker act as a team in providing support for the adolescent.

Again, the adolescent who has been living in a foster family since childhood may allow a different type of role to be enacted by the foster parents than will the adolescent who has experienced a number of moves and a lack of permanence. In the first case, the role of the foster parents more closely parallels that of parents in an intact family. In the second case, the foster parents may perform a quite different role, that of consultant or advisor, or a social worker may more easily provide direct emotional support for the adolescent. In either case, it is helpful to examine each of the phases of emancipation and the manner in which roles of foster parents change in concert with the adolescent's evolving self-identity.

Pre-Emancipation Phase

Negotiating the pre-emancipation phase is perhaps the most difficult task for foster parents and foster adolescents as well. It is a preparatory phase. Success in this phase may prevent many identity-related problems and post-emancipation issues for the adolescents. Hence, the foster parents play a sensitive role in guiding adolescents through it.

It is a major challenge to foster parents to recognize the varying responses of adolescents to the pre-emancipation phase, because the responses signal conscious and subconscious preoccupation with emancipation issues in many different ways. Some regress developmentally; others deny the upcoming emancipation; still others dramatize their awareness of upcoming emancipation by assuming stereotyped roles that change often and reflect an unevenness in maturity level. Eugenia is an example of the latter:

> Eugenia appeared ready for school on Monday looking like a character out of a Mickey Spillane novel. In spike heels, trench coat, and a pound of makeup on her face, she routinely asked if anyone had seen her favorite stuffed animal. The following day, it was back to blue jeans and tennis shoes.

Regardless of how an adolescent responds to impending life changes, either the foster parents or the worker must broach the issue of emancipation no later than the beginning of the last full year in placement. In doing so, it is important to frame the issue positively to prevent the adolescent's feeling rejected, of being cast out of the family once more. The message, "You look so grown up today; we will certainly miss you when you have a place of your own," is an example of a supportive way to approach the topic.

Judging Self and Others; Reflecting Back and Ahead

Once the topic of emancipation has been approached, foster parents should expect erratic behavior and conflict as the adolescent wrestles with ambivalent feelings about assuming greater independence in living. To the degree that the adolescent will allow, the foster parents may support him or her in a life review process, by using more formal tools such as a life history chart and/or informally by discussing and revealing some of their own ambivalent feelings about the process of gaining greater independence and leaving home. The life history chart, or time line, provides an opportunity to document and probe earlier experiences regarding the adolescent's remembrance of and feelings about the biological family, reasons for entering and remaining in foster care, and experiences in out-of-home placements [Pasztor et al. 1986]. These remembrances help to construct self-definitions and build self-identity. Where the adolescent is not emotionally close to the foster parents, mutual aid groups, and other individuals, such as social service providers, may carry out this activity.

Identification with Significant Others

Where permanence in foster care has been achieved, adolescents most often will identify with current caregiving figures. In many cases, however, in assessing their identity—who they are, where they have come from, and where they are going—adolescents in foster care evidence an interest in reconnecting with biological parents or others historically significant in their lives. Should the adolescent voice a wish to reconnect with the biological parents at this time, foster parents should validate this interest, review the options available to the adolescent, and discuss the possible scenarios. Throughout this process, foster parents should be alerted not to respond defensively to the adolescent's multiple and perhaps conflicting messages, but rather to use areas of distress as potential discussion topics concerning emancipation. By emphasizing their confidence and pointing out the adolescent's positive attributes and strengths, foster parents can help to solidify his or her autonomous identity.

Competence, Gender Identification, and Sex Roles

Over the course of the following months, a number of issues involved in gaining greater independence in living must be negotiated. Foster parents should encourage the adolescent gradually to assume greater responsibility for daily living skills such as planning a week's menu, grocery shopping, cooking, doing laundry, and budgeting money and time. Allowing the youth to make mistakes and assuming the role of "senior partner" in achieving life skills is the preferable stance for foster parents. The adolescent should be encouraged to show off newly acquired skills by inviting friends to a self-prepared dinner or teaching other children in the home the mysteries of doing laundry or completing other independent-living skills. In addition, the adolescent should be helped to obtain items such as cooking utensils, bedding, and linens for the new residence.

In light of increasing concern for adolescent pregnancy, parenting, and contracting sexually transmitted diseases such as AIDS, the adolescent in foster care should be well educated about human sexuality, contraception, and health care. Foster parents should not assume that the school system provides adequate sex education. Hence, foster parents may need to discuss issues involved in human sexuality or refer the adolescent to appropriate community resources, such as planned parenthood clinics.

Planning for a New Living Environment

By the time of emancipation, every adolescent in foster care should have a plan for obtaining an apartment or transitional living arrangements, and a plan for further education, training, or a job. Helping the adolescent to explore these avenues and secure a plan is an essential role for foster parents during the pre-emancipation phase.

The foster parents may well need to apartment hunt with the adolescent, help with rehearsing for job interviews, visit training programs, or encourage a more sheltered, supervised living environment, if necessary, and assure the adolescent of the foster family's continued availability and support. To prevent or limit feelings of social isolation once separate living arrangements have been made, foster parents should encourage adolescents to acclimate themselves to the new community by getting acquainted with neighbors, shopping, attending recreational opportunities, and participating in mutual aid groups of emancipated foster adolescents, if such groups exist.

Obtaining Emotional Refueling

Above all, adolescents should be given the message that their relationship with their foster family does not end when they leave the home. Child welfare agencies must press policymakers to grant foster parents a post-emancipation stipend so that adolescents can be allowed to meet their developmental needs for emotional refueling. Guiding the youth to plan and carry out the many decisions involved in more independent living is not an easy task for biological parents; the role of foster parents in serving this function is far more difficult because of the adolescent's expectable feelings of rejection, abandonment, insecurity, and denial, which derive from a lack of permanence in life as a foster child. Perhaps these difficulties explain why foster parents often do not fulfill this transitional function, and why so many foster adolescents leave foster care unprepared to meet the demands of living on their own.

Emancipation Phase

Preparation for the actual day of emancipation should be set far in advance of its arrival. On or close to the date, the adolescent in foster care might benefit from a celebratory ritual such as a party. A festive occasion serves to cement the gains the youth has made. As with the cotillion in Latino cultures or the coming-out party in Anglo culture, the foster family might invite relatives, friends, or other significant people in the youth's life and ask them to bring a small gift as a token of the occasion. Foster parents and other family members should actively help with the move into new housing, making sure there are sufficient necessities and food. This process may occur over a weekend or a period of days and may include several visits to the new living environment before the adolescent spends the first night away from home.

On Friday evening, the Greens hosted a party for Josephina and invited her friends from school as well as some friends of the family. After the gifts had been opened and the barbecue finished, Josephina took the group to her new neighborhood for a tour of her apartment. Over the weekend, the Greens gradually helped her move, buy groceries, and settle in. It was not until midweek that Josephina spent her first few nights away from the foster home. She returned for a weekend visit.

Post-Emancipation Phase

The tolerance and capacity of foster parents adequately to handle the post-emancipation phase may dramatically affect an adolescent's ability to succeed.

Assessing Oneself within Society's Domain

Following the feelings of anxiety during pre-emancipation, the adolescent living independently predictably experiences subsequent phases of elation, loneliness, and fear, and, it is hoped, finally confidence [Simonitch and Anderson 1979]. Feelings of elation typically last about a month and are characterized by the adolescent's tendency to ignore or overlook potential problems. It is the foster parents' role to anticipate these problems and to be consistently available for support and guidance.

Feelings of loneliness and fear follow, as the adolescent encounters the daily problems of living on one's own. Maintenance of a routine becomes boring, money is scarce, and there is little time for entertainment. Loneliness may predominate. Friends may drop away, and other peers may be living at home while the foster adolescent is assuming a more adult role by working and maintaining an apartment. As these more negative aspects of independence become reality, the adolescent is at some risk of a failed effort.

During this time, foster parents continue to play a crucial role in helping the adolescent to become autonomous by providing a link between the adolescent and the receiving community, and between the present situation, past events, and the future. Because of the youth's heightened insecurity, respite visits to the foster home are a necessity and are predictable. They should be routinely scheduled in the first months following leaving home. The adolescent should be welcomed back, nurtured, and should return to the apartment knowing that the foster family has confidence in his or her ability to succeed. Inviting the foster family to the new residence and serving as host may also reinforce the adolescent's autonomy. The relationship between adolescent and foster parents gradually evolves into one characterized by greater degrees of reciprocity.

Furthermore, if not accomplished earlier, the post-emancipation phase may be an excellent time for the adolescent to initiate or repair the relationship with biological parents or other relatives, however tenuous these connections may be. By quietly advocating and normalizing these reconnections, and by reassuring the adolescent of their continuing support, foster parents help alleviate feelings of divided loyalties to parenting figures. Foster parents may convey the message that, at different points in the life cycle, each of us relates to our parents in a different way. Emancipation may be one opportunity among many to reconnect. The Chins, Tom's foster parents, provide a good example of how foster parents can assist in the post-emancipation phase:

> Although over the last six months Tom had talked about little else than having a place of his own, a few weeks after the move his euphoria dissipated. Despite his enrollment in a job training program, he frequently expressed self-doubt and admitted to being lonely, even fearful during the evening hours. He found it difficult to concentrate on his homework and said that his friends had it easy—someone to cook and clean up after them.
>
> Over dinner at the Chins' home, he seemed to say over and over, "Who am I and where am I going with my life? My family never amounted to anything and neither will I." The Chins reviewed with Tom some of the circumstances that had led to his placement and emphasized that he was his own person and that they had confidence in his abilities. In their discussion, Mr. Chin was able to normalize Tom's anxiety by disclosing that he had felt confused and lonely after moving out of his parents' home, but that after several months his relationship with his parents eventually evolved into a more mutually interdependent one. By the end of the evening, Tom was exploring the possibility of reconnecting with some relatives across town, and Mr. Chin invited Tom to join his bowling league. In his delight at the invitation, Tom hosted the Chins to a potluck at his apartment and later invited them to a family night at his job training site.

Because of the Chins' supportive nature, Tom had allowed himself to share his sense of being directionless and lonely. In turn, the Chins were able to express their confidence in him and in who he was. Through this process, they had helped him take another step toward developing an autonomous identity and a more interdependent relationship with them and others.

Conclusion

Because it provokes painful memories and anxiety, the emancipation process is one of the most difficult times in the life of an adolescent in foster care. The potential for growth or regression may emerge at each phase of the process, as the dynamics involved in forming an autonomous identity are played out. Foster parents play a crucial role in the life of an emancipating adolescent, yet the presence of a supportive social worker also underlies a successful process. The foster parents act as a bridge for the adolescent to society, but without the strong support of a social worker, the bridging function may not be possible.

Working with emancipating adolescents in foster care may provoke the social worker to ask, "Why me?" The job appears to be an impossible one, filled with conflict and unresolvable developmental knots. But we might also wonder at the resiliency of the adolescent spirit, which emerges strong in spite of repeated trauma. And we may wonder how there can be people such as foster parents who are willing to guide a young person in foster care through the process of becoming an autonomous person. We are an interdependent people. Without the navigating role that foster parents play, the adolescent, who is trying to negotiate the process of identity formation and emancipation, travels uncharted waters. Without the social worker's support and training, foster parents' chances of carrying out their crucial guiding function are diminished.

REFERENCES

Anderson, J. L., and Simonitch, B. "Reactive depression in youths experiencing emancipation." Child Welfare 60 (June 1981): 383–390.

Barth, R. "Emancipation services for adolescents in foster care." Social Work 31 (May–June 1986): 165–171.

Bloom, M. (editor). Life Span Development. New York: Macmillan, 1980.

Bohman, M., and Sigvardsson, S. "Negative social heritage." Adoption and Fostering 3 (1980): 25–34.

Edelman, M. W. Families in Peril: An Agenda for Social Change. Cambridge: Harvard University Press, 1987.

Elkind, D. "Growing up faster." Psychology Today 12 (9) (1979): 38–45.

Erikson, E. "Youth: Fidelity and diversity." In E. Erikson (editor), The Challenge of Youth. New York: Anchor Books, 1965, 1–28.

———. Identity, Youth and Crisis. New York: W. W. Norton, 1968.

Falicov, C. "Mexican families." In McGoldrick, M. (editor), Ethnicity and Family Therapy. New York: Guilford Press, 1982, 134–163.

Fein, E., Maluccio, A. N., Hamilton, V. J., and Ward, D. "After foster care: Outcomes of permanency planning for children." Child Welfare 62 (November–December 1983): 485–560.

Festinger, T. No One Ever Asked Us . . . A Postscript to Foster Care. New York: Columbia University Press, 1983.

Furrh, P. "Emancipation: The supervised apartment living approach." Child Welfare 62 (1983): 55–61.

Gil, E., and Bogart, K. "Foster children speak out: A study of children's perceptions of foster care." Children Today 11 (1982): 7–9.

Haley, J. Leaving Home: The Therapy of Disturbed Young People. New York: McGraw-Hill, 1980.

Jones, M. A., and Moses, B. West Virginia's Former Foster Children: Their Experience in Care and Their Lives as Young Adults. New York: Child Welfare League of America, 1984.

Lee, J., and Park, D. "A group approach to the depressed adolescent girl in foster care." American Journal of Orthopsychiatry 43 (1978): 516–527.

Leveton, E. Adolescent Crisis: Family Counseling Approaches. New York: Springer, 1984.

MacIntyre, J. M. "Adolescence, identity, and foster care." Children 17 (1970): 213–217.

Mahler, M., Pine, F., and Bergman, A. The Psychological Birth of the Human Infant: Symbiosis & Individuation. New York: Basic Books, 1975.

Maluccio, A., Fein, E., and Olmstead, K. A. Permanency Planning for Children: Concepts and Methods. London and New York: Routledge, Chapman and Hall, Inc., 1986.

Maluccio, A., and Fein, E. "Growing up in foster care." Children and Youth Services Review 7 (1985): 123–134.

Mauzerall, H. "Emancipation from foster care: The independent living project." Child Welfare 62 (January–February 1983): 46–53.

McDermott, V. A. "Life planning services: Helping older placed children with their identity." Child and Adolescent Social Work Journal 4 (1987): 245–263.

Meier, E. "Current circumstances of former foster children." Child Welfare 44 (1965): 196–206.

Oldham, D. "Adolescent turmoil." In Bloom, M. (editor), Life Span Development: Bases for Preventive and Interventive Helping. New York: Macmillan, 1980, 270–285.

Pasztor, E. M., Clarren, J., Timberlake, E. M., and Bayless, K. "Stepping out of foster care into independent living." Children Today 15 (March–April 1986): 32–35.

Simonitch, B., and Anderson, J. "On their own: An Oregon experiment." Children Today 8 (1979): 28–31.

Specht, R., and Craig, G. Human Development: A Social Work Perspective. Englewood Cliffs, NJ: Prentice-Hall, 1982.

Tiddy, S. "Creative cooperation: Involving biological parents in long-term foster care." Child Welfare 65 (1986): 53–62.

Zimmerman, R. B. Foster Care in Retrospect. New Orleans, LA: Tulane University School of Social Work, 1982.

4

Time to Mourn Again

KATHERINE GORDY LEVINE

A ll foster children struggle with the need to make sense of placement in the least hurtful way possible. The loss of home and family is a deeply wounding experience, and it must be explained and fully mourned before the foster child can begin to plan for the future. If the past makes no sense or the hurts of the past remain open wounds infecting the present, the path to the future is full of dangers.

A primary question posed by placement is: "How come you can't stay with your own family?" How this question and others raised by placement are answered will have an effect on the placed child's future well-being [Brown et al. 1986]. Moreover, the questions must be answered twice, for the cognitive limitations of childhood dictate one set of answers, and the expanded cognitive abilities of adolescence raise doubts about the explanations that earlier mollified and comforted the placed child.

The youth who learns to think abstractly understands perhaps for the first time that his or her parents could have behaved differently. The pain created by this cognitively forced examination of old explanations brings about a need to mourn once again the losses associated with being a foster child. Some adolescents manage this remourning adaptively. Others find the pain nearly overwhelming and, in an effort to deal with that pain, act out against themselves or against others—or perhaps both. That reaction can threaten their ability to prepare for adulthood as well as jeopardize the stability of the foster placement. This chapter places acting-out behavior within the context of a necessary grieving process brought on by changed cognitive abilities and suggests ways in which the social worker can educate, support, and sustain foster parents and adolescents through this crucial time. One such case illustrates the process.

Consider John. He was originally placed in foster care when nine years old. His three- and five-year-old sisters were placed in another foster home at the same time. John's parents were alcoholics, and all three children had been neglected and abused. At the time of placement, John was a quiet child, slightly withdrawn, compliant and ready to please. He was also eager to be reunited with his sisters and parents. He denied that his parents had a drinking problem. John used the fact that his father had an ulcer and his mother suffered from chronic lower back pain, caused by a drinking-related accident, to explain why he and his sisters could not live with their own parents. "They were sick and we didn't help them enough," he explained to his social worker.

Efforts to reunite the family failed. The parents separated, the father left town, and the mother's alcoholism worsened. Eventually, all parental rights were terminated, and the girls were adopted by their foster parents. John, then twelve, did not want his foster parents, the Browns, to adopt him and instead maintained that his mother would be hurt by the adoption. He periodically contacted his mother and accepted her vague plans to have him live with her again.

Six months after his sisters were adopted, John began to complain about his foster parents. His complaints were generally vague; he felt they were too restrictive and not understanding enough. Moreover, he was argumentative and angry most of the time. Soon after he began complaining about the Browns, his behavior deteriorated even more: his school performance declined; he began to cut classes; he often stayed out past curfew. Fortunately, the Browns had had considerable experience with adolescents and were tolerant of his behavior.

Three days after John's thirteenth birthday, however, he showed up at his social worker's office and demanded that he be placed in another foster home. His request was at first denied, but when he ran away and threatened to keep running away if not re-placed, he was finally moved to a second foster home. He did well in this home for three months, but then began to abuse drugs and engage in other self-destructive behavior. When he refused to go for treatment for his drug problem, his foster parents requested his removal. John was then placed in a residential treatment center from which he often ran away. He was frequently found at his mother's home. During this time he visited the Browns twice.

During one of his runaways, he was arrested for robbery and was placed in a locked detention facility. His mother promised she would get him released to her custody, but when the time came for the court hearing, she failed to appear. Much to John's surprise, however, the Browns did come. Moreover, they agreed to have John live with them after he had received treatment for his drug problems. John entered a drug treatment program; during individual sessions with the social worker, it became clear that his denial of his parents' drinking and other problems had broken down. He used the sessions to review the hurts his parents had inflicted on him, and was finally able to see that drinking was the primary reason his parents had not been able to care for him. After six months in the treatment program, and with help to mourn what might have been, John returned to live with the Browns.

John was luckier than most adolescent foster children: he worked through his losses, he had foster parents willing to maintain a long-term bond with him, and he had a social worker who helped reunite him with his foster parents. A great many foster children are not as fortunate as John. They either remain stuck in the mourning process or, during the course of remourning and working out their rage, destroy all possibility of remaining with their foster families. Whether the placement survives the remourning process is often determined by the foster parents' willingness to understand and endure the acting-out behavior.

More than endurance, however, foster parents offer a pivotal and sustaining force in helping assure that the adolescent moves through the remourning process adaptively. Their help can promote growth and healthy interdependence. Lack of help and understanding on the part of foster parents, as well as lack of agency support to foster parents, can lead to placement disruption and solidification of maladaptive behavioral patterns. To be helpful, foster parents must recognize that adolescence is a time of renewed mourning brought about by changes in the way the adolescent thinks.

Foster parents attempting to care for a remourning adolescent need to understand a number of dynamics, including the losses connected with being a foster child; how the preadolescent child mourns losses; how the emerging cognitive processes of adolescence lead to mourning; the course of the remourning process; and, finally, the effect of remourning on the adolescent, the foster parents, and the biological parents.

The Foster Child's Experience of Loss

Foster children experience a number of losses. Viewed from a cognitive standpoint, their suffering involves the four major sources of uncertainty: the new, the unpredictable, the contradictory, and the conflicting. Foster children confront these sources of uncertainty in relation to inner self and connections with significant others, both of which intensify the psychological burden [Kagan 1978]. They must deal with the new, such as family, home, values, and status. They must live with the unpredictability and impermanence associated with placement. Perhaps foremost, they must deal daily with the contradictions and conflicting beliefs about self, worth to others, control over decisions, and the meaning of separation from parents.

From an analytic perspective, these uncertainties and losses constitute the four calamities of childhood: loss of object, loss of love, loss of power, and punishment or loss of self-esteem. Uncertainty results from fear of the possibility that these calamities might occur; depression exists when the feared loss has occurred [Brenner 1982].

Foster children experience both uncertainty and loss in relation to each of these calamities. They experience object loss, for they are no longer in their parents' physical presence, and they have lost the familiarity of their homes, their neighborhoods, their schools, and their friends. Even if they hold steadfastly to the idea that their parents do love them, they no longer have a daily experience of that love and therefore view foster care as a diminishment or loss of parental love. Moreover, placement forces children to confront their own and their parents' weaknesses. They believe that loving parents do not willingly place a child in foster care. No child really wants to be moved from his or her home; placement clearly constitutes a loss of power. Finally, placement is experienced as punishment, and the child suffers a diminished sense of self-worth.

The question, "How come you can't stay with your own family?" epitomizes all of the potential hurts facing placed children as they try to explain to themselves why they are not able to live in their own homes and with their own parents. Most clearly, however, the question raises the very real possibility in the child's mind that placement means a lack of parental love. Loss of love is a key component in the remourning process.

Adolescents not living with their parents have been found to be significantly more depressed than their counterparts [Teri 1982]. The loss is particularly threatening when it entails the loss of mother's love. As Kagan [1984: 265–266] notes:

> A mother's love for the child is treated as a mysterious force which, if sprinkled plentifully over young children, guarantees salvation. But for the child who is not fortunate enough to have had a loving mother, the future is poisoned. This faith in the power of love does not operate across all cultures, nor has it been consistently held to throughout the history of our society. Nevertheless, it is a potent assumption today, and one that greatly increases the pain of the foster child.

In their examination of the effect on foster children of parental failure to visit or maintain contact, Fanshel and Shinn underscored this basic need of children to believe they are loved. As the authors note:

> Our data suggest that total abandonment by parents is associated with evidence of emotional turmoil in the children. We can think of no more profound insult to a child's personality than evidence that the parent thinks so little of the relationship with him that there is no motivation to visit and see how he is faring. Good care in the hands of loving foster parents or institutional child care staff can mitigate the insult but cannot fully compensate for it. [Fanshel and Shinn 1978: 487–488]

All adolescents suffer when faced with a loss of parental love. Adolescent foster children confront the potential loss of parental love daily; it is a testament to human adaptability that so many accomplish as much as they do. Suffering is better endured if it makes sense, and suffering children seek to understand their pain. Their efforts to understand depend upon the level of their cognitive abilities.

Changing Thought Processes

Pre-Adolescent Thinking: What Is, Ought To Be

When children are placed in foster homes, explanations and reasons are sought by all involved parties. Consequently, children are often presented with a number of conflicting views about why they are in placement. Often the explanations will involve blaming someone or something, since one of the principal ways people resolve uncertainty is by finding someone or something to blame [Kagan 1978]. Many parents will blame outside forces; practitioners will often blame psychodynamics or societal forces; foster parents might blame the child's own parents; and most pre-adolescent children will look inward for an explanation and will blame themselves.

Consider how abused and neglected children often explain their parents' hurtful treatment of them: "All parents beat children." "Of course, my mother beats me; she has to teach me right from wrong." No matter how parents treat them, most pre-adolescents believe that this is how loving parents treat children. Pre-adolescent children have difficulty in imagining that children are treated differently from the way they are treated. They cannot deal with the abstract; they can think only about what they know and live with. They believe that "what is, ought to be." When the "what is" turns out to be something painful, they will think the pain is deserved punishment. They will seek the cause of the pain and punishment in their own being and behavior.

To a certain extent, such self-blaming thought processes serve a useful purpose, for they permit foster children to maintain some control and some belief that they will be able to return home someday. The alternative is too bleak to be considered: if the cause is not in the children, but in parental limitations, the children are forced to consider the possibility that their parents either do not love them or are weak and powerless. Both of these beliefs are untenable and are defended against by the placed child, whose emotional and physical survival depend on alliance with a greater and more powerful force. No matter how weak or abusive are the parents, the child needs to believe that they are the best of all possible parents. Childhood is, therefore, a time when parental limitations are for the most part denied by blaming the self.

Adolescent Thinking: An Interest in the Possible

Unlike the pre-adolescent child, however, adolescents can think abstractly; they can deal with ideas and possibilities. This ability allows adolescents to imagine a better world, a better self, and better parents. Moreover, unlike pre-adolescents, they can compare their parents to other parents, and in doing so become aware of their parents' limitations. Their faith in parental infallibility erodes. Eventually, the belief system regarding parents shifts, and the perfect parents of childhood are lost. Viewed from the perspective of mourning theory, childhood represents the first stage of mourning—denial of loss. The changing thought processes of adolescence break down this denial, and the adolescent enters the next stage of mourning—anger.

The realization that parents are not perfect creates anger in all children. The sense of having been betrayed by the people they loved and trusted most is strong. The greater the discrepancy between the child's view of the parents and the adolescent's more objective views, the greater the sense of betrayal and the greater the anger. Much of the moodiness, the anger, and the despair of adolescence begins in the uncertainties created by the loss of childhood's beliefs, particularly beliefs relating to self and parents.

Fortunately, for most adolescents the readjustment of thoughts and feelings about parental limitation occurs slowly. Strong feelings do not run dangerously high. This permits a manageable resolution to occur. Gradually, the bad-good parent seesaw stabilizes, and parents are viewed more realistically. Anger, grief, and blame subside. Resolution of the conflicting beliefs is achieved. The loss of the perfect parents of childhood is accepted, and the third stage of mourning, the period of resolution, occurs.

Placed adolescents are not so fortunate, however, for placement greatly complicates the adolescent's ability to objectify parents. Placed adolescents do not compare abstract parents. They live trapped between two sets of parenting figures: their own parents, either as experienced or imagined, and foster parents. Moreover, the discrepancy between the idealized parent of childhood and the objectified parent of adolescence is usually greater for foster children than for children who are raised by their own parents. When combined with changes in the belief system inherent in an adolescent's cognitive development, being in placement frequently forces a premature and too rapid awareness of parental limitations upon the adolescent.

This effect is similar to the process called "treatment shock," which refers to the shock of a therapeutic and nurturing environment on a deprived child. The child's denial of parental limitations is suddenly overturned, and the child's former view of the world no longer exists. Treatment shock is characterized by mass evacuation of anger, a fear of closeness or love, and unrealistic longings for more than can be [Redl and Wineman 1957].

In the case cited earlier, John's behavior involved venting of hostility, fear of closeness to his foster parents, and unrealistic expectations or longings for love from his mother as well as his foster parents: he expected love and approval from all of his parenting figures no matter what his behavior. Both treatment shock and remourning involve the same dynamics. Treatment shock, however, is caused by a shift in environments; remourning is caused by a shift in cognitive abilities. Both, however, involve uncertainties about the quality of parental love.

The concept of love is abstract and cannot be thought about by the pre-adolescent child. For example, a pre-adolescent child does not really understand the golden rule. When a pre-adolescent child who has been hit by another child is asked what action the golden rule suggests, the response will likely be to hit the person back. Thinking of an alternative is too abstract a task for the pre-adolescent.

An adolescent can, however, think about the true meaning of loving behavior and can interpret the golden rule accurately. The adolescent can think about love as not wanting to hurt the beloved even in the face of hurt from the beloved [Kohlberg and Gilligan 1972]. This change in the ability to think about love imposes new hurts on adolescents as they struggle to explain why they do not live with their own parents. Adolescents can see that their parents have hurt them, and this recognition leads them to question whether or not they were loved. Remourning has begun.

The Remourning Process

Remourning follows the same process as mourning proper: a period of denial, a period of strong feelings, and a period of acceptance. The major loss of love being experienced during the remourning process, however, is a loss occurring in the child's mind as a result of increased cognitive abilities. It may or may not reflect an actual change in life events.

Denial

The pain created by realizing for the first time that placement might mean being unloved is immense and cannot be immediately tolerated. Regression frequently accompanies pain. The regression that results from a foster child's recognition of parental limitations most frequently leads to a rebound denial: biological parents, particularly if they are absent, are idealized.

Despite the remourning adolescent's efforts to deny parental limitations, the pain remains: the foster child cannot completely discount the parents' absence and a growing awareness of their limitations. The denial is incomplete. The adolescent is forced to explain feelings of hurt and uncertainty in a way that does not add to growing doubts about parental love. As adolescents look about for a cause or an explanation of their current uncertainty and pain, often their eyes first light on the foster parents, who are, after all, there. Moreover, there is a strong human tendency to view two simultaneously occurring events as sharing a cause-and-effect relationship.

The adolescent is aware that being in foster care hurts. The pains of being a foster child justify, in the adolescent's mind, making the foster parents targets for retaliation. The combined idealization of parents and concurrent denigration of foster parents is a clear indication that remourning has begun. It is important to remember that the adolescent's changing thoughts are not sufficiently developed to permit an understanding that the felt rage is displaced anger created by past parental wounds, the uncertainty of shifting beliefs, and the breakdown of denial surrounding the biological parents' limitations.

Similar dynamics operate in some of the adoption breakdowns that occur during adolescence. As one adolescent, placed in foster care because her adoptive parents were unable to tolerate her acting out, explained to her social worker: "When I was a kid, I thought my adoptive parents were the most wonderful people in the world. Now I wonder how I could have been so blind. All the things I've done, I've done because I can't stand my adoptive parents any more. Just looking at them makes me angry." A number of months later, when this girl was able to consider her anger toward her biological mother, her anger toward her adoptive parents began to ease, and eventually she was able to return to her adoptive home.

The adolescent's initial tendency to blame foster parents is exacerbated by the fact that, as suggested earlier, the nurturing from the foster parents often becomes salt in old unhealed wounds. One youth placed in a short-term foster home asked his foster parents repeatedly to treat him more harshly. "You're nicer to me than my parents," he said. "That hurts. Get meaner. You'll see that I'll calm down." It is a little-understood and perverse fact of any foster parent's life that normal nurturing can become a constant reminder for some placed children and adolescents of their own parents' failures. The very acts the foster parents believe will comfort and aid a foster child may only increase pain.

Moreover, living with nurturing parents forces adolescents, particularly if they have previously experienced abuse and neglect, to endure a component of treatment shock called "Starvation Hunger in The Promised Land" [Redl and Wineman 1957]. Even as adolescents are undergoing a major belief system change—coping with feeling betrayed by their parents and learning to deal with their limitations—they also yearn to take advantage of the gifts of love and affection being offered by foster parents. As adolescents realize their needs have not been met, they feel like the starving man who suddenly finds himself in a four-star restaurant with unlimited funds but a seriously shrunken stomach: he tries to satisfy his hunger; he asks for more and more. Adolescents who try to glut themselves on foster parents' offerings eventually fall victim to the realization that strangers are offering more love and nurturing than their biological parents. This realization traps the adolescents between betraying either their own parents or their own wants and needs.

The loss of the placed adolescent's idealized view of biological parents as well as the loss of their physical presence is deeply traumatizing. Moreover, the adolescent's identity rests on identification with biological parents, and the loss of them as caring persons strikes a painful blow to the adolescent's feelings of self-worth. The hurt and rage the adolescent feels can reach monumental proportions; strong feelings can run dangerously high.

Strong Feelings

Remourning's second stage, the stage of strong feelings, is marked by acting out. The adolescent, with increased cognitive abilities, is better able to assess whether the punishment experienced fits the crime. Since placement is felt to be extreme punishment, the youth believes he or she must have been very bad to deserve such a fate. Such thoughts can lead to extensive acting out as the adolescent tries to document the badness in order to justify parental rejection. Frequently, the acting out not only documents the youth's badness but, particularly when taking risks or substance abuse are involved, simultaneously helps numb the pain.

Moreover, the angry behavior can be used to force foster parents to become cold and rejecting. If all parents are bad, then the adolescent's parents are not unusual. "All parents are alike, they all care more about themselves than their kids," observed twelve-year-old Mary to her social worker, as she was being moved from yet another foster home. Mary's mother placed her when conflict developed between Mary and her stepfather. Within six months of placement, Mary had lived in three different foster homes. With uncanny psychological discernment, she discovered the one piece of behavior that each family found impossible to tolerate. In her first home, Mary had repeatedly stolen from the foster mother and a number of the foster mother's friends. This behavior was upsetting to the foster mother, but she was able to tolerate Mary's stealing until it spread to some local stores. When Mary was arrested for shoplifting, her foster mother asked that Mary be re-placed. Mary was then moved to a Jewish foster home, where she proceeded to spray-paint swastikas on both the inside and outside walls of her foster family's home. She was placed with another family noted for being able to work with difficult teenagers. Mary managed her move from this home by sexually assaulting the foster parents' three-year-old niece. By forcing her various foster parents to reject her, Mary proved to herself that rejection was the norm. Her familiar view of the world was maintained, and any uncertainties created by the differences between her various foster parents' and her own parent's treatment of her were thereby resolved.

These interlocking issues of intensified self-blame, displacement of feelings, and rationalization underlie the acting out of many placed adolescents experiencing the remourning process. The acting out creates even further difficulties, since it usually generates guilt and the concomitant need for punishment. Unless a punishment acceptable to the adolescent is forthcoming, both the existential and guilt-related anxieties and uncertainties increase.

The remourning-induced acting out can become circular and self-feeding. Adolescents act out to prove their badness, to numb their pain, and to force their foster parents to reject them. As guilt over the acting out and displaced anger increases, the acting out also comes to serve punishment needs. Severe enough punishment will ease the adolescent's conflicts temporarily. If, however, punishment is not forthcoming, the youth's uncertainty and guilt intensify, leading to increased acting out and increased guilt, anguish, and uncertainty.

Adolescents can become frantic in this circular repetition of efforts to explain the losses and hurts of their lives.

Acceptance

Adolescents can make peace with their status only when they ultimately say: "Yes, my parents, no matter how much they may love me, hurt me." Resolution means accepting things as they are [Jewett 1982]. It has occurred when the past can be recalled without undue anger or grief. Achieving this is not easy. Just as mourning is not accomplished in finite stages, remourning involves moving back and forth among the three stages. Denial slowly turns into recognition of the loss and hurt. Strong feelings emerge, but the pain cannot be endured, and denial is thus resurrected. Eventually, as the pain can be tolerated, the strong feelings predominate, and moments of acceptance begin to occur. Gradually, acceptance begins to predominate, and eventually it is reached.

"My anger and hurt just wore out," was the way one articulate foster child described her movement into acceptance. "I figured my social worker was right when she pointed out my parents had done the best they could and I should try to think about that and go on from there. With her help, I stopped raging. I tried to think about the few good times we had and that helped me get on with my life."

Another described it this way: "The hurt and anger slowly dried up, and one day I realized they were gone. I kept going to see my social worker, but I didn't want to talk about the past anymore. I had more important things to do with my life than to keep looking back. I have scars, but the big hurts have healed. I survived my parents' limitations, and maybe I'm even stronger because of their problems."

Not all youngsters can articulate such feelings. For less verbal youngsters, acceptance has occurred when behavior becomes less controlled by strong emotions. The angry acting out subsides, the grief lessens, and the calm periods become longer, until it is eventually clear that the youngster is moving forward with his or her life: the past has been accepted both intellectually and emotionally.

Helping the Adolescent Remourn Childhood Losses

There are a number of ways the adolescent can be helped to remourn childhood losses. Traditional supportive approaches are useful. Some adolescents are helped by verbally reviewing their past or by the use of devices such as time lines [Court 1980] or life books [Backhaus 1984], both of which highlight important personal events. Others need to ventilate and talk about their painful feelings. The picture becomes more complicated when remourning takes the form of acting out.

As long as discharge of feelings can be accomplished by way of acting out, the youth will not face underlying conflicts. Mourning requires that the pain be experienced if acceptance is to be achieved. Because the acting out serves to prevent pain, containing it is not always immediately possible. Unfortunately, the acting out of an angry adolescent is difficult to tolerate; once remourning begins, the current foster care placement may be threatened.

Preserving the Placement

The first task facing the practitioner is preserving adequate placements. Foster parents frequently become targets of the remourning adolescent's anger and hurt, and it is imperative that they be helped not only to understand the remourning process, but that they be supported and sustained while the acting out is running its course. This approach will not be easy; the remourning adolescent's acting out creates feelings of uncertainty and powerlessness in the foster parents.

Limiting Blame

If the youth needs to force rejection, the foster parents are essentially out of control as parents, leading to feelings of failure, uncertainty, and a need to find someone to blame. Foster parents can often blame the adolescent, any and all former caregivers, including biological parents, the social workers, and each other. But blaming only provides a temporary release from the uncertainty created by living with an angry, blaming adolescent. Moreover, if too much blame is assigned to the adolescent, not only is the placement endangered, but so too is the child's ongoing relationship with the foster parents.

Once a remourning adolescent begins to act out, maintaining an existing placement demands the existence of a strong alliance between foster parents and social workers. Social workers need to understand their role regarding foster parents and acting-out adolescents; the latter will want the social worker to join in blaming foster parents. Simultaneously, foster parents may want the social worker to join them in blaming the adolescent, which merely perpetuates problems.

Instead, families can often be helped by the social worker's use of an educational approach, which includes encouraging foster parents to see the youth's behavior as part of a grieving and, ultimately, healing process. This knowledge allows them to see the acting out as a positive and necessary step to resolution of grief. And while it is in the best interest of youths to help them to contain their hostility, foster parents will also be helped to understand the value of the anger.

Social workers can also help angry adolescents and foster parents to cease blaming each other by clarifying the difference between "good enough" and failed parenting. Most parents are "good enough" parents [Bettelheim 1987]. A failed parent often feels love but does not translate that love into minimally appropriate behavior. Failed parents are parents who assault, sexually abuse, abandon, or severely neglect their child. The fact that most abused and neglected children do not know what normal family life is can lead them to expect too much of foster parents and to assign blame whenever foster parents fall short of expectations.

Practitioners can also overstate the foster parents' role in creating the remourning adolescent's acting-out difficulties, thereby implying their failure. To determine that the foster parents are "good enough" parents, it is useful to recall the foster family's level of functioning before the acting out began. When the foster child and the foster family have shared a positive relationship before the onset of adolescence, the most helpful stance for the practitioner is to view the problem as related to the remourning process. The cause of the acting out lies in the adolescent's handling of painful feelings; when the youth has worked through the feelings, discord within the foster home usually fades.

Relieving Guilt

When it has been determined that the foster parents are "good enough" parents, direct efforts to relieve their guilt are often useful. Sometimes just knowing that acting out has a name and a purpose relieves the foster parents' guilt and stabilizes a deteriorating placement. Such relief permits the foster parents to stop personalizing the hostility. If the foster parents are going to be able to avoid becoming enmeshed in the adolescent's acting out, they must learn to see the youth's anger as separate from them, as illustrated by the following example.

Mr. and Mrs. Green had reached the point of despair regarding their ability to maintain thirteen-year-old Delphine in their home. She had been in their care for three years, and was being freed for adoption: the Greens had hoped they could become her adoptive parents. But after two years of a positive adjustment in the Greens' home, Delphine had begun to pick fights with them. The fights always ended with Delphine's running to a friend or a neighbor's house, or, on occasion, to the local police. During these episodes, Delphine had the friend's parents, the neighbor, or the police intervene in her behalf with the Greens. The Greens were threatened and embarrassed by continually being forced to explain their behavior.

Moreover, in response to Delphine's provocations, the Greens had violated their personal standards of good parenting: one or another had yelled. Both Mr. and Mrs. Green believed raised voices were a sign of failed parenting. Despite the efforts of their social worker to be supportive, the Greens were enmeshed in Delphine's acting out. They felt guilty; Delphine sensed their guilt and this awareness exacerbated her uncertainty.

Fortunately, the Greens and their social worker both attended a foster parents' training session in which remourning was discussed. During the discussion period that followed the presentation, Mrs. Green broke into tears of relief. She later told her worker, "Just knowing we weren't to blame gave me the strength to go on." Following the training session, the Greens connected with a Tough-Love group. The support of that group helped them cope with Delphine's acting out. Eventually, Delphine was adopted by the Greens.

Overcoming Anger

In a recent study of cognitive-behavioral interventions for reducing parental anger in the face of perceived provocation by children, helping the parents maintain empathy with the child's feelings was deemed important. Another finding of this study suggests that problem solving directed toward the control of parental anger is also useful; the use of cognitive restructuring and problem-solving skills appeared to be of definite value in alleviating parental anger [Whiteman et al. 1987].

The case of Delphine and the Greens offers a good example of the importance of a cognitive restructuring approach:

As long as the Greens believed Delphine's behavior was proof that she did not care for them, their frustration grew. As they understood that her behavior was a displacement of anger created by earlier hurts and had more to do with her growing awareness of her own parents' limitations than with feelings about them, the Greens were able to defuse their hurt and understand Delphine's pain. A cognitive reframing of their beliefs led to their willingness to learn how to deal more appropriately with Delphine's provocations.

Anger can also be managed through the use of time-outs, thought-stopping, and barb-training. The time-out is a frequently used behavioral device that can prevent reinforcement of angry or aggressive behavior; it usually involves removing the aggressor from the scene of the aggressive behavior. A simplified version of a time-out involves an agreement between two angry persons to take a break from discussing a problem because tempers are mounting and a cooling-off period is indicated. More complicated time-outs involve contracting with a youth that certain aggressive behaviors will signal a time-out, during which he or she will be expected to go to a quiet and unrewarding place for a specified period of time. If the youngster's behavior continues to be unacceptable, the time-out period can be extended [Barth 1986]. Both Delphine and the Greens were taught to call a time-out when either felt they were reaching a boiling point in their efforts to deal with her difficulties.

Thought-stopping involves identifying dysfunctional thoughts, encouraging the individual to think those thoughts and then signaling the individual to stop, usually by yelling "Stop!" Eventually, the client is able to stop the dysfunctional thoughts without outside help [Martin and Pear 1988]. Mr. and Mrs. Green were taught to say a loud "Stop!" to Delphine whenever she began castigating them or saying they did not love her. They were also told to follow their command to stop with a strong statement about their love for her. Eventually, Delphine connected her anger to feelings of being unloved and was told to remind herself when upset: "The Greens care about me."

Barb-training involves desensitizing individuals to anger-creating situations and, most particularly, to dysfunctional reactions to criticism. Youths are advised to maintain eye contact with the barb deliverer, to keep a neutral or pleasant facial expression, to respond in a calm tone of voice, and to develop and carry out a plan of action that will eliminate the problem. Role-playing is used to rehearse the individual in handling barbs. The next step is helping the individual to handle barbs from an increasing number of individuals [Barth 1986]. These techniques can best be taught through a small-group, problem-solving approach that allows time for skill building and then supports the maintenance of new skills once they have developed.

Placement Disruption

Sometimes disruption cannot be avoided. In John's case, his displaced anger at his parents resulted in his demanding that he be replaced. Fortunately, he had a social worker who was prepared to use the disruption as a way for John to mourn his losses, while deepening his relationship with his foster parents. They were helped to sustain their interest and concern in John because Mr. Smith, the social worker, understood the Browns' need for guilt relief. Mr. Smith made it clear to the Browns that John's request for re-placement indicated his difficulties in handling his mother's limitations and was not an indictment of the Browns' ability to provide good care.

Moreover, he ultimately made the decision that John needed to be placed in another home, since it is usually not possible to maintain an adolescent in a foster home when he has decided that he wants to live somewhere else and is willing to act out in order to achieve re-placement. In those situations, planned intermittence is generally preferable to acted-out disruption.

The decision to re-place a foster child is never easy. Too often the entire burden rests on the foster parents. As long as foster parents are willing to tolerate the acting out, the general pattern seems to be not to disrupt placement. Failure purposely to intermit or disrupt placement, however, may allow the acting out to reach the point where the relationship between the adolescent and the foster parents is breached.

Disruption Criteria

As reluctant as most professionals are to re-place an acting-out adolescent, re-placement or temporary intermittence of a placement should be considered when the following events occur simultaneously: *(1)* the youth is requesting a re-placement; *(2)* the youth's acting out is continuing to escalate in the face of reasonable countermeasures; and *(3)* the youth is using drugs or alcohol abusively, is endangering his or her physical life by taking risks, or has committed violence against property and now threatens violence against individuals.

Although re-placement should not occur precipitously, some youths caught in the agonies of remourning might well be helped through a cooling-off period in a treatment facility or in a temporary foster home. And surely, planned intermittence is more appropriate than waiting until the foster parents and adolescent reach the point of irreconcilable differences.

Re-Placement in Foster Homes

It is also important to note that a youth who has been removed from a foster home for acting out can be re-placed in another foster home, rather than in an institution. Distance from the foster parents can clarify for youths the source of their anger, thus helping to facilitate the grief process. Indeed, some children need to be in a number of homes before resolving the uncertainty about the limitations of their parents and coping with the remourning process. Recent research indicates that even after a number of disrupted foster care placements, some children seemed to adjust well to a subsequent placement [Fanshel et al. 1987; Fein et al. 1983]. In fact, in contrast to prevailing practice wisdom, there seems to be no correlation between the number of placements and ultimate success in the final placement [Fanshel et al. 1987]. A child who has objectified biological parents and reached an acceptance of their limitations is often finally able to live with another family.

Maintaining Ties

If the way has been kept open, some adolescents can be reunited with former foster parents, as in John's situation. Only after he had begun to accept his mother's limitations was he able to live with his former foster family. Mr. Smith's efforts to help the Browns to remain emotionally connected to John maintained the possibility of return when the time was right. Throughout his work with them, Mr. Smith recognized that the Browns were clearly "good enough" foster parents. He believed their rules were reasonable and reasonably enforced. He believed their responses to John's acting out were also reasonable. He did not view the Browns as creating or contributing to John's difficulties. He was therefore able to alleviate their guilt and help them to stop personalizing John's attacks, while supporting their continuing interest in being of help. Of equal importance was Mr. Smith's having taken responsibility for deciding to re-place John, alleviating the need for the Browns to assume the burden of deciding when enough was enough. Consequently, it was not difficult for the Browns' doors to remain open since it was not they who had closed them.

Once re-placement occurred, Mr. Smith maintained contact with the Browns and kept them abreast of John's status. He encouraged them to write John and let them know that, even though John did not respond, the letters were important to him. Once it was clear that John was beginning to accept his mother's limitations and to control his acting out, Mr. Smith actively worked with the Browns to accept John once again back into their home.

Conclusion

Mourning and remourning are processes that require time. Maintaining a longitudinal approach is essential. Inability to offer immediate comfort is painful for both foster parents and social workers. Whether the adolescent is mired in depression or desperately resisting it by angry behavior, caring people want to help. When the adolescent's hurt cannot be quickly eradicated, feelings of failure on the part of caregivers ensue.

These feelings may lead to a "dance of blame" in which all parties lose. It is the job of the social worker to keep the blaming process from becoming circular. By maintaining a longitudinal approach, providing needed support and information, and focusing on the process, social workers can help to soften feelings of failure and the circle of blame can be avoided. Given enough time, old wounds may heal, and the adolescent in foster care can then move forward toward adulthood and interdependent living.

REFERENCES

Backhaus, Kristina A. "Life books: Tools for working with children in placements." Social Work 29 (November–December 1984): 551–554.

Barth, Richard P. Social and Cognitive Treatment of Children and Adolescents. San Francisco: Jossey Bass Publishers, 1986.

Bettelheim, Bruno. A Good Enough Parent. New York: Alfred A. Knopf, 1987.

Brenner, Charles. The Mind in Conflict. New York: International Universities Press, Inc., 1982.

Brown, G. W., Harris, T. O., and Bifulco, A. "Long-term effects of early loss of parent." In Rutter, M., Izard, C. E., and Read, P. B. (editors), Depression in Young People. New York: Guilford Press, 1986, 251–296.

Court, Nancy J. "The 'Time Line': A treatment tool for children." Social Work 25 (May–June 1980): 235–236.

Fanshel, D., Finch, S., and Grundy, J. "Collection of data relating to adoption and foster care." Unpublished paper. Washington, DC: U.S. Department of Health and Human Services, Office of Human Development Services, Administration for Children, Youth and Families, September 1987.

Fanshel, D., and Shinn, E. Children in Foster Care: A Longitudinal Investigation. New York: Columbia University Press, 1978.

Fein, E., Maluccio, A. N., Hamilton, V. J., and Ward, D. "After foster care: Outcomes of permanency planning for children." Child Welfare 62 (November–December 1983): 485–560.

Jewett, Claudia. Helping Children Cope with Separation and Loss. Harvard, MA: The Harvard Common Press, 1982.

Kagan, J. The Growth of the Child. New York: W. W. Norton, Inc., 1978.

———. The Nature of the Child. New York: Basic Books, 1984.

Kohlberg, L., and Gilligan, C. "The adolescent as a philosopher." In Kagan, J., and Coles, R. (editors), Twelve to Sixteen: Early Adolescence. New York: W. W. Norton and Company, 1972, 144–179.

Martin, Garry, and Pear, Joseph. Behavior Modification: What It Is and How to Do It. Englewood Cliffs, NJ: Prentice Hall, 1988.

Redl, F., and Wineman, D. The Aggressive Child. Glencoe, IL: The Free Press of Glencoe, 1957.

Teri, L. "The use of the Beck Inventory with adolescents." Journal of Abnormal Child Psychology 10 (1982): 227–284.

Whiteman, M., Fanshel, D., and Grundy, J. "Cognitive behavioral interventions aimed at anger of parents at risk of child abuse." Social Work 32 (November-December 1987): 469–476

Meeting the Challenge: Policies and Programs

*T*he sudden popular interest in older youths leaving foster care has created a temptation to believe that these young people, through participation in a single training program or similar effort, can progress through a complex set of adolescent life tasks at accelerated speed. Efforts to "fast-forward" youths through a process that takes less vulnerable adolescents years to complete creates expectations that few foster youths can meet. Effective independent-living policies and programs create springboards, formed at the point of entry to the foster care system, from which youths can gain experiences that promote readiness for adulthood. Part II covers the key policy and programmatic considerations by which agencies can be guided in the development of services for youths in foster care.

In Chapter 5, Pine, Krieger, and Maluccio present a range of principles and guidelines to meet this challenge. Basic premises include the concept that foster care services ought to be youth-driven, not government-driven or agency-driven; recognition of a young person's developmental rather than chronological age; and the conviction that foster parents are essentially extended agency staff members who need to be accorded rights and responsibilities consistent with the work they are charged with performing.

In Chapter 6, Wedeven and Mauzerall draw on their practice experiences with a supervised independent-living program to offer principles for planning and implementation. The focus is on creating an environment that promotes achievement of tangible skills, as well as developmental milestones. Through a team effort among the agency, foster parents, social workers, and youths, learning opportunities can be found that promote individuation, integrate past trauma, establish unique histories, and clarify sexual identity.

In Chapter 7, Carbino takes an expanded view of the roles the biological families can play in preparing youths in foster care for interdependent living. The process of reconnecting to the family is presented as an important step toward achieving satisfying adult functioning. The variety of roles that biological families can play are explained, as are the complementary ways in which foster parents, social workers, and the agency can provide support.

We see a disproportionate number of black youths who have grown up in foster care and who have a discharge plan of independent living. In Chapter 8, Carten outlines key principles to guide agency *practice and foster parent training to enhance the contribution of black foster parents in preparing foster adolescents to leave care. The black family, with its tradition of valuing children, emphasis on mutual help, and capacity to cope with adversity, is seen as the most appropriate setting for ensuring a young person's successful transition to adulthood.*

5

Preparing Adolescents to Leave Foster Family Care: Guidelines for Policy and Program

BARBARA A. PINE, ROBIN KRIEGER, AND
ANTHONY N. MALUCCIO

I ncreased attention to the number of adolescents in foster care and their need to prepare for adulthood has resulted in a burgeoning of independent-living programs. Currently, several hundred agencies report the provision of services to help adolescents exit from out-of-home placement [Mech 1988]. As noted in Chapter 1, this development has been spurred, in part, by the availability to the states of forty-five million dollars per year in federal money since 1985 under the "Independent Living Initiative."

Unfortunately, to date, few efforts have been made to evaluate systematically the effectiveness of these services in preparing foster adolescents for competent adulthood. Evaluation studies should constitute a significant portion of the research agenda in child welfare. What has emerged from a number of studies of youths currently and formerly in out-of-home care is a fairly clear picture of their various service needs [Barth 1986; Westat 1986; Barth 1988; Festinger 1983]. These findings, building on the existing knowledge in child welfare and the experiences of administrators and practitioners in the field, suggest some policy and program responses to meeting these needs. This chapter develops and illustrates a set of principles and guidelines that draw on current knowledge to suggest ways of framing these responses.

Understanding the Foster Care Experience

The dominant principle guiding the development of policies and programs for youths in out-of-home care is their foundation on a thorough understanding of the factors associated with the experience of foster care placement, which includes the range of possible events leading to the removal from family and placement in foster care, as well as the placement experience itself and its potential effects on preparation for interdependent living. As considered in Chapter 1, the factors associated with the foster care experience for the most part constitute risks for adolescents and threaten their potential to achieve competent adulthood. In particular, adolescents in foster care face the triple jeopardy resulting from the risks of abuse, neglect, poverty and its correlates, and family breakdown leading to placement; the lack of permanence and stability and other experiences that may characterize foster care placement; and the hostility of the social environment to emancipating adolescents, particularly the disproportionate number who are persons of color and with handicapping conditions.

In general, policies and programs based on the principle of understanding the foster care experience would seek, first, to diminish whenever possible the risks described above; second, to mediate their effect; and finally, when necessary, to provide remedial help to adolescents affected by them. Prevention and remediation can be realized when programs to prepare adolescents for interdependence are also guided by two other important principles to be discussed below: use of a youth-driven approach and appreciation of the centrality of the role of foster parents.

Use of a Youth-Driven Approach

The needs of young people in care should be the starting point for developing policies and programs. A youth-driven approach is sensitive to the following aspects of achieving adulthood:

Individual developmental needs and strengths
Attainment of both tangible and intangible skills
Ethnicity and culture
Preparation for adulthood as a process

The implications of each of these aspects of a youth-driven approach are considered below.

Individual Developmental Needs and Strengths

This aspect includes an understanding of, and sensitivity to, the developmental needs of all adolescents, as well as those in foster care; recognition of the potential effect of the foster care experience on adolescents; program strategies to prevent, attend to, or overcome any resulting deficits; and recognition that all adolescents in foster care experience grief and loss that they must be helped to manage.

Assessing the developmental status of each young person in care and basing a comprehensive case plan and services on his or her strengths and needs are of primary importance. As Pine and Krieger consider in Chapter 12, a number of instruments and approaches exist for assessment and case planning with adolescents in foster care. From a programmatic perspective, it is important that developmental assessment, regardless of the particular approach, be institutionalized and systematic, and that case planning and intervention begin as early as possible for all pre-adolescents and adolescents in care, not at the time emancipation is approaching, as is often the case.

Disagreement currently exists about the responsibility of child welfare agencies to prepare all adolescents for adulthood or only those whose discharge plan is independent living. Waiting for the development of such a definitive placement goal, however, may leave little time for intervention and deprive adolescents of vitally needed services. This situation is an example of programmatic responses on the agency's time clock rather than on an adolescent's "developmental clock" [Pine and Jacobs 1989]. Moreover, as Barth [1988] found, a number of adolescents leave care at seventeen years, well before their eligibility for foster care services ends, suggesting the need to start early with effective services that encourage remaining in care.

Assessment of individual developmental needs and strengths should take into account that, of all the possible negative effects of foster care on development, none is more compelling than the grief and loss that seem to characterize the experience of every adolescent in foster care (see Chapter 4 by Levine in this volume). In addition, past abuse, neglect, rejection, or loss may deplete a young person's psychosocial resources and undermine the development of skills needed for interdependence (see Chapter 10 by McFadden in this volume). Barth [1988] found high levels of depression among former foster youths. Even more serious was the finding that 13 percent of the young adults in his study had experienced hospitalization for mental illness after leaving care. Anderson and Simonitch [1981] found reactive depression to be common among adolescents who were preparing for emancipation in one independent-living program. These authors, therefore, characterized those young people as having difficulty in coping with the losses and disappointments of life brought on by too much deprivation and misfortune and not enough adaptive capacity.

The universality of the experience of grief and loss among adolescents in foster care must be recognized and dealt with. Experiences of loss while in care must be minimized by fewer moves, as much regular contact with biological family members as possible (see Chapter 7 by Carbino in this volume), and the involvement of adolescents in making the essential attachments and connections to significant persons and groups needed for a secure future. Opportunities to work at resolving past losses and grief should be provided early in the placement to every adolescent through individual or group therapy.

Attainment of Both Tangible and Intangible Skills

In Chapter 1, Maluccio et al. outlined the range of interrelated skills needed for interdependence. These included "hard" (tangible) skills as well as "soft" (intangible) skills. Achievement of interdependence, the goal of services to adolescents in foster care, was identified as mastery of these skills to the extent that the young persons were self-sufficient, comfortable with themselves, and satisfied with their connectedness to family, community, and society.

The case for helping adolescents to develop this range of needed skills has been made by many researchers. Cook and Ansell [Westat 1986] found that only about one-third of the eighteen-year-olds studied had completed high school. Timberlake and Verdieck [1987] found that a quarter of the adolescents leaving care needed some type of academic remediation, as well as having other problems such as limited self-control. Barth [1988] found a high rate of unwanted pregnancies, suggesting the need these adolescents had for more knowledge and skills in planned parenthood.

Service strategies that promote the attainment of both tangible and intangible skills include comprehensive skill assessment using approaches similar to those described by Pine and Krieger [Chapter 12 in this volume] and the provision of multiple opportunities for adolescents to develop both types of skills. It should be stressed that, among the most important intangible skills, are decision making, problem solving, self-control, and the assumption of responsibility for one's own actions.

Too often adolescents in foster care have been excluded from participation in important life decisions; other persons have been in control, stepping in and, for example, finding a new placement when the old one had broken down. These teenagers have little opportunity for decision making and for predicting the consequences of decision options. For them, "Things just happen." The concept of empowerment provides a useful lens through which to view service strategies that are youth-driven. This concept implies that adolescents play a central role in case planning and the review of their own progress; in decisions about services to use, as well as in evaluating them; and, more broadly, as active participants in agencywide efforts as advisors, training consultants, and even as mentors for younger adolescents in foster care.

Ethnicity and Culture

Cultural heritage is an integral part of self-identity. Learning about cultural values and the ability to convey them to the next generation is an adult responsibility common to all ethnic groups. Moreover, preparation for adulthood is itself determined by ethnicity, as discussed by Stovall and Krieger in Chapter 9 of this volume.

Policies and programs aimed at helping adolescents in foster care to prepare for interdependence must first recognize cultural differences and their importance to these adolescents. Second, the valuing of culture must be expressed systematically. This approach is essential, given the high proportion of children of color in out-of-home care. The following are components of a program that systematically addresses culture and ethnicity:

Placing adolescents in foster families whose ethnicity is the same as that of the young person

Mobilizing resources of the foster families through training and other supports (see Chapter 8 by Carten in this volume)

Hiring and training child welfare workers from among the ethnic groups served

Developing supports for youths in the community; for example, working with a black church congregation on a mentor program

Ensuring that all agency staff members have opportunities to become ethnically competent; that is, aware of their own culture and its effect on viewing others; open to understanding other cultures; and able to use cultural resources effectively (see Chapter 9 by Stovall and Krieger in this volume)

Preparation for Adulthood as a Process

As Cook [1988] has pointed out, tangible and intangible skills are acquired and refined throughout life, beginning in childhood. Thus it is appropriate to view preparation for adulthood as a series of events occurring along a continuum. This view would require a much-expanded notion of what constitutes independent-living services and who is to receive them. For example, younger foster children would be provided with planned opportunities to develop skills in decision making and problem solving. Their caregivers would be encouraged to begin early to teach them basic living skills in the natural environment of the foster home.

For older adolescents, opportunities to live on their own while still in care would be essential. Barth [1988] found that the young people in his study felt they needed a transitional housing program to *practice* independent living while continuing to receive financial support; having to support oneself as well as to master basic skills was a dual and often unmanageable burden.

In addition, since all adolescents in care, even those still in an educational program, would be encouraged to work and save some of their earnings for future needs, policies that limit savings should be examined. For instance, the adolescents in Barth's study were limited to $999, a low figure considering that the initial costs of starting a home were nearly that much [Barth 1988]. Following discharge of youths from foster care, drop-in centers and perhaps a continuing contact in the agency are needed, as well as an emergency loan program and the continuation of health care and dental coverage for at least a year [Barth 1988].

For adolescents who remain in foster homes after age eighteen, or who return regularly to the foster family, ways to legitimize and support the foster families' continued involvement must be found [Aldgate et al. 1989]. A number of examples are presented in Chapter 1. Moreover, expanded care arrangements should be encouraged and maximized. The informal but important arrangements that foster parents often make on their own underscore their central role in helping adolescents to prepare for adulthood.

The Central Role of Foster Parents

The centrality of foster parents' roles should also guide policy and program responses to the needs of adolescents in out-of-home care. Foster parents have enormous, often untapped, potential for preventing, minimizing, or remediating the risks, described earlier, that are associated with foster care placement. They are the logical teachers of the range of skills that adolescents need to master. Since the foster home is most like the family environment in which these skills are naturally developed, teenagers in care can learn and practice informally and over a span of time; learning opportunities can be geared to the adolescent's individual needs and strengths [Ryan et al. 1988]. Finally, as foster parents practice the wide variety of skills in daily life as consumers, members of organizations, community residents, and family members, they serve as role models for adolescents in their care.

Foster parents who share an adolescent's cultural heritage are more likely to engage in culturally relevant emancipation rituals [see Chapter 9 by Stovall and Krieger in this volume] and to value their heritage. They are also better able to link teenagers to a network of community groups that they will need as interdependent adults. Finally, foster parents who are persons of color have generally had experience in preparing their own children to deal with the unfortunate realities of racism and can provide the same support to foster children. Skills in managing and overcoming the effects of oppression are important for adolescents who are preparing for adulthood.

Foster parents can also help adolescents in their care to deal with the task of reconnecting with their biological families as emancipation approaches, a task that is increasingly being recognized as crucial by child welfare practitioners and researchers [Aldgate et al. 1989; Carbino in Chapter 7 of this volume]. It has long been known that the biological family continues to be important for foster children in relation to their sense of identity and connectedness [Laird 1979]. More recently, it has been found that many foster adolescents resume their relationships with their parents or other members of their biological families upon discharge from foster care, in some cases returning to live with them even though there had not been an ongoing relationship while they were in placement [Jones and Moses 1984].

Foster parents can facilitate the process of adolescents' reconnecting with their biological families, or strengthening those connections, through being sensitive to their conflicted relationships with, and attitudes toward, biological parents; encouraging the young people to talk about their feelings and concerns in this area; appreciating their sense of divided loyalty concerning the biological and foster parents; promoting contacts between the foster adolescents and their parents, siblings, and other relatives; and providing opportunities for biological parents to participate in decisions and activities involving their children, particularly with regard to preparation for interdependent living. Above all, foster parents and social workers can work cooperatively to recognize and mobilize biological families as potential resources for young people during placement as well as following discharge.

In sum, foster parents can be an important resource for the teenagers in their care, for child welfare agencies, and for the community. New approaches to foster parenting are essential, however, if foster parents are to provide a stable living arrangement for adolescents, teach skills, advocate for services, serve as role models, help adolescents to develop connections with biological family members, and convey cultural values. Roles and expectations must be more clearly delineated; new relationships between foster parents and the agency must be defined; and extensive supports such as money, training, and community resources must be provided [Aldgate et al. 1989].

New Roles for Foster Parents

Recent reforms in child welfare have resulted in new service outcomes and new roles for foster parents as partners in permanency planning. They have increasingly become active participants in case planning and review and as supporters of biological parents. With current attention to the high numbers of adolescents in care, the foster parents' additional role of preparing youths for emancipation has emerged [Pine and Jacobs 1989].

The intended outcome of foster care service to adolescents in care is their readiness to assume adult roles. As outlined in Chapter 1, the following are the key components of competent adulthood:

Competence and mastery of a range of tangible and intangible skills
Satisfying and mutually gratifying relationships with friends and kin
Ability to nurture one's own children
Responsibility for one's own sexuality
Contribution to, and participation in, the community
Making essential connections
Positive sense of self

This service outcome should guide the delineation of roles and expectations for foster parents, and implies the need for specialized foster parenting that may be provided in family homes, group homes, or supervised apartments [Barth 1989]. Because adolescents need adults in different ways, as friends, mentors, or parent figures, a range of foster parenting options and settings for living should be provided.

Foster Parents as Partners

The rapid development and expansion of foster parenting roles and activities have been paralleled by greater equality and mutuality between foster parents and staff members in child welfare agencies, reflected in recruitment, selection, and training, as well as in the organization and provision of services. Although true partnership is still much more an ideal than a reality, agencies aiming toward this new configuration of relationships should organize their programs to reflect the following:

New models of recruitment and training, such as MAPP and NOVA [Pasztor 1983, 1986], that emphasize self-selection and the identification of family strengths by the families themselves
Joint training of social workers and foster parents, emphasizing their collaborative, complementary, and individual roles
Clearly delineated roles, tasks, and responsibilities of workers and foster parents, as well as a process for negotiating conflicts that may arise [Jacobs and Crowe 1988]
Participation of foster parents in case conferences

Opportunities for foster parents to support and learn from one another
Involvement of experienced foster parents in program advisory commit-
tees, as trainers, and as spokespersons for the agency

Provision of Adequate Supports

It is ironic that, as the system of social services has become
more complex and the needs of children in out-of-home care greater,
the available resources have diminished, and at the same time more
is expected of foster parents who are caring for perhaps the most
challenging of children—adolescents in foster care [Pine and Jacobs
1989]. Much is needed to support these caregivers if they are effectively
to help their young people to prepare for interdependent living. At
the very least, there should be adequate training for their roles and
tasks, adequate compensation for their work, and the development
and enhancement of a range of community resources on which they
can draw.

Training
Foster parent training is only one component of a foster care
program. Training foster parents to assume their ever-expanding roles
as caregivers of adolescents must be considered within the context
of an agency's overall readiness to meet the needs of this foster care
population.

Clearly defined policy goals and program objectives for out-of-
home care are necessary foundations for successful training efforts.
Guidelines for determining agency readiness to implement training
for foster parents are not discussed here because they are available
elsewhere [Pine and Jacobs 1989]. Two recent training resources that
incorporate a number of the principles discussed earlier will, however,
be described here: *PUSH/GOALS* [Ryan et al. 1988] and *Preparing
Youth for Interdependent Living* [Pasztor et al. 1988].

Both of these comprehensive curricula, developed with federal
funds, are for use in training child welfare staff members and foster
parents in preparing adolescents for adulthood. They stress the importance of collaboration and partnership-building between social workers
and foster parents in helping with mastery of the tangible *and* intangible skills needed. Much attention is given to understanding and
helping foster adolescents to overcome the obstacles to achieving
competent adulthood that might be associated with the foster care
experience mentioned earlier.

Well-trained and adequately supported foster parents can be a stable placement resource for adolescents, the system's most demanding children. These parents know what is expected of them, what to expect, and how to be effective in meeting the daily challenges that will inevitably arise.

Compensation

New roles and responsibilities for foster parents, as well as the new substitute care models such as those mentioned earlier, require different approaches to compensation. A higher level of skilled care provided by caregivers who work with a small number of adolescents might result in fewer disruptions and premature emancipations. These foster parents, however, would need increased board rates as well as specialized training [Barth 1988].

Increasingly, as program models become more varied, foster parents are being considered more like staff members and are compensated with salaries and benefits rather than the more traditional board and care payments. Some agencies with supervised living programs hire foster parents to live in homes and apartments, to serve more as landlords than as parental figures, and emphasize self-reliant functioning for the adolescents who live there (see Chapter 5 by Wedeven and Mauzerall in this volume). For younger staff couples working in these programs, the provision of housing may be an attractive benefit, especially considering the present high costs of housing.

Community Resources

To gain competence in the many dimensions of adulthood, adolescents in foster care need a wide range of supports. These are generally provided by organizations that specialize in recreation, education, health and mental health care, employment and job development, housing, religion, and the provision of personal social services.

Foster parents can be effective in helping adolescents to connect with the services and facilities they need in the community only to the extent that those resources exist and are accessible. Moreover, foster parents quite rightfully look to child welfare agencies to provide the necessary linkages for adolescents in foster care to gain access to the resources they need. Foster parents and child welfare agency staff members can work in partnership to advocate for the development of needed services with organizations and policymakers.

Conclusion

This chapter has delineated guidelines for policymakers and administrators seeking to develop programs for adolescents in foster care. To meet the needs of these young people—society's most vulnerable adolescents—as they prepare for the challenges of adulthood, programs must be guided by three key principles: an understanding of and accounting for the factors associated with the experience of foster care placement, the needs of adolescents in care as the starting point for program development, and the centrality of the roles of foster parents in helping these adolescents to achieve competence.

REFERENCES

Aldgate, J., Maluccio, A., and Reeves, C. (editors). Adolescents in Foster Families. London: B. T. Batsford and Chicago: Lyceum Books, 1989.

Anthony, J. L., and Simonitch, B. "Reactive depression in youths experiencing emancipation." Child Welfare 60 (6) (June 1981): 383–390.

Barth, R. P. "Emancipation services for adolescents in foster care." Social Work 31 (May–June 1986): 165–171.

———. On Their Own: The Experiences of Youth After Foster Care. Berkeley, CA: University of California at Berkeley, School of Social Welfare, Family Research Group, 1988.

———. "Programs for interdependent living." In Aldgate, J., Maluccio, A., and Reeves, C. (editors), Adolescents in Foster Families. London: B. T. Batsford and Chicago: Lyceum Books, 1989, 122–138.

Cook, R. "Trends and needs in programming for independent living." In Mech, E. V. (editor), Child Welfare (Special Issue on Independent-Living Services for At-Risk Adolescents) 67 (6) (November–December 1988): 497–514.

Festinger, T. No One Ever Asked Us . . . A Postscript to Foster Care. New York: Columbia University Press, 1983.

Jacobs, M., and Crowe, C. "Developing partnership strategies that work." Unpublished manuscript, 1988.

Jones, M. A., and Moses, B. West Virginia's Former Foster Children: Their Experiences in Care and Their Lives as Young Adults. New York: Child Welfare League of America, 1984.

Laird, J. "An ecological approach to child welfare: Issues of family identity and continuity." In Germain, C. B. (editor), Social Work Practice—People and Environments. New York: Columbia University Press, 1979, 174–209.

Mech, E. V. "Preparing foster adolescents for self support: A new challenge for child welfare services." In Mech, E. V. (editor) Child Welfare (Special Issue on Independent-Living Services for At-Risk Adolescents) 67 (6) (November–December 1988): 487–495.

Pasztor, E. M. Preparation for Fostering: Preservice Education for Families. Ft. Lauderdale, FL: Nova University, 1983.

————. Model Approach to Partnerships in Parenting. Atlanta, GA: Child Welfare Institute, 1986.

Pasztor, E. M., and Associates. Preparing Youth for Interdependent Living. West Hartford, CT: Center for the Study of Child Welfare, University of Connecticut School of Social Work, and Atlanta, GA: Child Welfare Institute, 1988.

Pine, B. A., and Jacobs, M. "The training of foster parents for work with adolescents." In Aldgate, J., Maluccio, A., and Reeves, C. (editors), Adolescents in Foster Families. London: B. T. Batsford and Chicago: Lyceum Books, 1989, 151–165.

Ryan, P., McFadden, E. J., Rice, D., and Warren, B. P.U.S.H. for Youth G.O.A.L.S.: Providing Understanding, Support and Help for Youth Going Out and Living Successfully. Ypsilanti, MI: Institute for the Study of Children and Families, Eastern Michigan University, 1988.

Ryan, P., McFadden, E. J., Rice, D., and Warren, B. "The role of foster parents in helping young people develop emancipation skills." In Mech, E. V. (editor) Child Welfare (Special Issues on Independent-Living Services for At-Risk Adolescents) 67 (6) (November–December 1988): 563–572.

Timberlake, E. M., and Verdieck, M. J. "Psychosocial functioning of adolescents in foster care." Social Casework 68 (April 1987): 214–222.

Westat, Inc. Independent Living Services for Youth in Substitute Care. Rockville, MD: Westat, Inc., 1986.

6

Independent-Living Programs: Avenues to Competence

TOM WEDEVEN and HILDEGARDE A. MAUZERALL

Attention to the needs of foster youths who are preparing for adulthood has resulted in an array of innovative programs and services planned to enhance this transition. Among them are specialized residences designed to help youths assume increasing responsibility for themselves. Time-limited, these independent-living programs typically prepare youths to learn adult living skills, such as those concerned with obtaining employment, finding housing, managing money, and relating to others. Mastering these skills can become very difficult for foster youths, many of whom experience delays due to past trauma. For adolescents truly to make use of the opportunities available in independent-living programs, the services must be developmentally sensitive; that is, designed to help them achieve developmental milestones as essential steps toward satisfying adulthood.

This chapter identifies the components of adolescent development that are necessary for competent adulthood. It then demonstrates how these components provide a theoretical framework on which an independent-living program was designed. The chapter also presents guidelines and principles for planning and implementing developmentally sensitive independent-living programs.

Developmental Components of Emerging Adulthood

Blos [1979] identifies four preconditions of adolescent development, without which healthy adulthood cannot be attained. An examination of these preconditions identifies those arenas in which foster youths are particularly vulnerable and in need of supportive experiences.

Individuation

The first is the emergence of individuation, the awareness of oneself as separate. This awareness evolves from the gradual loosening of childhood ties to parents, which is a struggle for any adolescent. Foster youths frequently have weak ties to their parents and extended family and tumultuous histories of separation and trauma. They have had neither the natural supportive family framework from which to let go, nor a continuous sense of personal history from which to establish an experiential and solid sense of "I am." They characteristically display a diffuse sense of self and a fragile capacity, marked by mistrust, for relationships. Independent-living preparation must include opportunities for youths to develop trust and a positive self-image.

Integration of Past Trauma

A second precondition for adolescent character formation is the opportunity to rework and reintegrate the leftover remnants of past trauma and deprivation. Due to the nature and extent of childhood loss, adolescence can be a prolonged and major struggle for foster youths, extending well into adulthood, occupying much time and attention needed for early adulthood issues of intimacy and productivity. In a support group for former foster youths, in which a range of issues related to adulthood were discussed, Connie, age twenty-seven, told of her feelings about a visit with her mother, who had surrendered her for adoption, and her own subsequent depression and turmoil:

> Connie had anticipated a "nice little mother-daughter chat," and instead found herself "towering over this petite little lady who seemed more like a daughter than a mother." She was glad to have made the visit,

but she was surprised by the lingering feelings of sadness and disappointment that she felt.

Connie has achieved commendable educational and professional success and would accurately be characterized as a warm, empathic mother. Her adult needs for personal intimacy, however, have been haunted by the unanswered questions and concerns about the past. Unable to untangle the web of past losses, she acknowledges her need to "rescue" others and the resultant lack of confidence in her judgments about relationships. The design of independent-living programs should facilitate a youth's resolution of past loss, providing opportunities to recognize the sources of their grief, as discussed in Chapter 4 by Levine in this volume.

Unique History

Establishment and clarification of oneself as having a unique history, or a sense of continuity from child to adult, form the third precondition of adulthood. The legacy of the past for foster youths is complex. Fragmented memories, gaps in one's sense of personal history, and a fragile identity impair self-worth and increase the sorrow of one's losses over time. Isolation, lack of social experience, and loneliness pose formidable problems for many foster youths. Depression is often characteristic of foster youths attempting to live independently [Anderson and Simonitch 1981]. Young people can be helped to overcome feelings of isolation and depression if they are given the chance to connect fragments of their own histories.

Sexual Identity

The fourth precondition that advances adolescent development is the emergence of sexual identity. Many foster youths have experienced sexual and physical abuse and have been exposed to poorly functioning adult role models, leaving them unclear about the appropriate expression of sexual feelings. Moreover, many have not received adequate information about sex to understand their own bodily changes and feelings (see Chapter 10 by McFadden in this volume). A youth's sexual development must be considered when devising independent-living programs.

Solnit [1979] comments that the fit between the individual adolescent's search for competence and the social supports or obstacles for or against it is critical. It is essential that independent-living programs provide ways for youths to achieve the four preconditions of adolescent character formation to attain that competence and identity development. The following is a presentation of a program that bases its preparation of youths for independence on the achievement of these developmental milestones.

An Independent-Living Program

In 1978, a voluntary long-term foster care agency began a series of groups to teach adolescent youths the skills needed to live independently [Mauzerall 1983]. This program evolved into the establishment of a supervised independent-living residence in which a youth could experience the realities of taking responsibility, making decisions, and related consequences, within a protected environment.[1] This facility, a split-level frame home, has six bedrooms, a recreation room, and a separate kitchen for residents. The staff members are licensed foster parents who serve as landlords and a relief worker who is a trained social worker and experienced group worker; they work in close team cooperation with agency staff members and under the supervision of an agency social worker.

Participation in this program provides emancipation experiences and services to youths as part of a long-term foster care placement or a subsequent step for youths who need particular help to function successfully apart from family and agency. Initially developed as a skills-teaching approach, the experience gained from working with emancipating youths over time has underscored the need for a developmental perspective and a strategic team-based framework. The developmental perspective provides guidelines that promote a youth's achievement of developmental tasks. The team approach, composed of agency, social worker, foster family, and youth, recognizes that preparation for adulthood requires mutual effort and has the added benefit of demonstrating interdependent functioning for the youth.

[1]The concepts described are those that guide practice at Lemmon Grove, an independent-living program established by the Idaho Division of The Casey Family Program.

Nearly a decade of experience in conducting this developmentally sensitive independent-living program has pointed to a set of key principles and guidelines, which follow.

Program Principles and Guidelines

Youths need to be accepted into an independent-living program after the development of a contract covering educational and vocational goals as well as the skills needed to live on one's own. Following guidelines discussed elsewhere [Maluccio and Simm 1989], the contract is best developed by the teenager, with the support and consultation of the social worker, who then meets with the entire program staff to present the contract and advocate admission.

A true indication of the commitment of youths to their contract is the amount of energy they are expending on themselves. Foster parents, social workers, and program staff are to *support* the youth's work, not engage in it directly. It is important to convey that a youth's eventual success in meeting the goals of the contract is his or her responsibility.

The ideal independent-living program provides a supportive framework in which young people can work on their contract, make their own decisions, and experience the consequences of those decisions. A room-and-board atmosphere, rather than a parental home, helps increase the emphasis on self-reliant functioning, thus preventing illusions or overdependence on the home. The treatment approach that is promoted calls on youths to be active participants in the planning and processing of their own lives. Critical components of the framework are described below.

Screening

Independent-living programs are appropriate only for those skilled youths who are developmentally ready for intensive training and practice in adult skills. Too often such programs are used as shelters or as a last resort for young people whose needs have not been met through other child welfare services, such as foster home or group residence care. These youths, many of whom have large developmental gaps, are assuredly not suited for the high level of performance expected in independent-living programs. The staff must be prepared to help social workers, foster parents, and youths to evaluate each youth's potential for success.

Participation as a Privilege and an Opportunity

Youths need to choose, rather than be required to enter, an independent-living program. Making the choice is evidence of, and further promotes, autonomy. Choosing to enter, however, mandates the meeting of school, work, and personal goals. Failure to achieve goals as contractually agreed is an indication that the individual is choosing to leave substitute care without help. The youth may be evicted just as a landlord might evict an errant tenant:

> Arthur, nineteen, entered an independent-living program, having had a part-time employment history. Central to his contract was job hunting with a goal of obtaining employment. Two weeks into his stay, Arthur was continuing to resist passively: sleeping well into the day, watching television, and hanging out at local parks. He was quietly and firmly evicted temporarily for failure to participate in his share of the contract. He returned in two days with a job.

Program and Staff Flexibility

The uniqueness of each individual who enters the program must be recognized. In line with the first and third preconditions of adolescence, the staff should help youths explore their sense of identity and their personal histories. Staff members must not impose their own reality but should enable the youths to focus on their unique feelings by helping to answer questions about who one is, what one's dreams consist of, and what special assets and gifts one has.

Just as each youth's assets are different, so are his or her needs. Some youths may come to the program directly from their foster homes. Some may come only for weekly independent-living groups. Still others may spend planned weekends, performing needed learning tasks. And others spend a month or two. A point of diminishing return is reached with a stay beyond twelve months. Needs vary dramatically, and individual planning, assessment, and programming are critical.

"Apartmentalizing"

Residents must develop a budget and agree to pay monthly rent, purchase food, prepare meals, wash clothes, and generally function as tenants in an apartment. It is important that the staff not be seen as family and that the program not be thought of as a group home; in the effort to promote abilities and a positive self-image, staff members should instead be resources, support systems, consultants, and cheerleaders. The program is structured to operate as a supervised boarding home. Residents are given a house key and can come and go as desired. They maintain responsibility for their own hours.

Susan, seventeen, developed a typical monthly budget of $180 for rent; $100 for food; $25 for clothing; $25 for personal needs; and $20 for transportation; $400 is the agency maximum for independent-living payment. The check is received by Susan on the first of the month. The rent is due to the landlords by the third of the month, or the young person must make other shelter arrangements until the rent is paid. When Susan obtained employment, her wages were used to save and prepare for living on her own. Through skills classes, she purchased household items and started a savings account for a rent deposit. As Susan's salary increased, it was also used to pay her expenses at the independent-living program, reducing the financial help provided by the agency and thus promoting a solid sense of self.

Time Framing, Goal Projection, and Monitoring of Progress

Setting a calendar of events and goals becomes an essential part of the work. Each week the residents make a schedule of plans, medical appointments, and priorities. Contract targets are translated into visible short- and long-term time plans. Residents are regularly to be encouraged to denote progress toward their targets and to project new goals for achievement in a step-by-step manner. Job attainment and other achievements should be celebrated. Pre-planning is valuable in reducing the surprises youths experience along the way. It normalizes the inevitable feelings of anxiety that accompany steps to independence.

Coping with Separation

As youths reach mid-adolescence, they begin to deal with the emerging developmental issues and conflicts of independence and dependence. The desire to be separate from parents and caregivers is coupled with clinging and fear. Children who have lived in foster care have experienced traumatic separations. Often these feelings are triggered again as the young persons face emancipation, which creates an ideal opportunity to help them to integrate past trauma and overcome their understandable reluctance to move on. Many wary adolescents are helped by having tasks broken down into very small steps and receiving reassurance and support for each achievement. This process allows them to separate at their own pace, avoid feelings of failure, and remain connected to caregivers.

> Sally, age eighteen and living in foster care, complained frequently about the foster parents' expectations and said she wanted to live on her own. Yet, when the time came to leave the foster home, she kept postponing the date while becoming increasingly belligerent toward her foster parents. She displayed especially provocative behavior by running up a $150 phone bill.
>
> The social worker noted that during several previous leaving experiences she had run away after fights with her former foster parents. She was asked if she needed to run away again or if she would like to try to leave planfully with everyone's support. By acknowledging her anxiety and previous explosive separation history, the worker helped her to develop activities and time frames for moving. After five months of assuming increasing responsibility under the supervision of independent-living staff members, Susan was able to move to her own apartment.

Depersonalization of a Myth

The youth's "myth of emancipation" attributes responsibility to the caregiver for the young person's anxiety or discomfort about leaving home. The youth characteristically focuses on excessive parental rules or expectations as the origin of the problem. To challenge, argue, or engage in a power struggle at this stage affirms the credibility of the myth to the youth. To perceive the youth's reactions as rejection or betrayal is to become part of the youth's projection, thus colluding with him or her in the avoidance.

A helping person's alignment with the child against the foster parents or the foster parents against the child creates a power struggle that perpetuates the myth. Rather, foster parents and social workers are encouraged to help youths associate their uncomfortable feelings with their source: separation anxiety. Reflective and empathic listening, coupled with assurances that the struggle to assume responsibility will eventually benefit the youth, is useful in helping adolescents to identify and work through their feelings during this potentially explosive stage.

Use of Resistance

As a next step to confronting the myth of emancipation, it is productive to frame the youth's challenge of authority as an opportunity for caregivers to rally around the individual and explore plans for independent living, which can be defined as part of a healthy, normal, necessary transition. It is important that all of the parties bond together to acknowledge the roots of the conflict, dealing directly with the anxiety and ambivalence elicited by separation.

Donald, a foster youth who was previously responsive to household rules, began to rebel at age sixteen. Major temper outbursts occurred over chores and curfew. Donald was challenging the foster parent's authority, exploring the parameters of freedom, and asserting his masculinity—a particular issue in this single-parent family. The social worker explained to Mrs. Z, the foster mother, and Donald that Donald's thrust toward independence was normal for a sixteen-year-old, and encouraged him to explore just what living on his own would mean for him and require of him.

Given the choice and researching the possibilities, including taking residence in an independent-living program, Donald was able to recognize clearly the benefits of remaining home despite the rules. Following this decision, the social worker helped Donald and Mrs. Z to formulate an independent-living plan, detailing the skills Donald needed to learn and ways in which he would learn them. This process normalized the struggles for Mrs. Z, alleviating her anxiety and stress, while acknowledging the rights and responsibilities of growth for Donald.

Empowerment and Participation

The staff should avoid doing anything for youths that they can do for themselves. The staff should encourage youths to plan, acting as a consultative sounding board. Youths need to be invited to share experiences and feelings in regular group sessions. This process builds self-esteem and self-confidence and helps them to clarify personal values and goals, affording movement from the external focus of what foster parents, agency, and residential staff members desire to the personal internalizing of "What do I want for myself?" Rigorous staff self-examination as to whose agenda is being addressed (youth or staff) is essential if one is to avoid intrusive and demeaning planning *for* the youth.

Donald, described above, entered the residential-living program before his seventeenth birthday. His independent-living contract included a commitment to attend weekly living-skills groups. Problems with attendance became an issue, with Donald insistently maintaining, "I can do it on my own."

Staff members and Mrs. Z, the foster mother, believed that Donald needed the opportunity to try living on his own. The state caseworker was enlisted in giving the message to Donald that "as you are seventeen and the law recognizes emancipation only at eighteen, know that if you get into trouble you will be returned to care."

Donald left with the support of the staff and Mrs. Z. Despite several crises, Donald did make it and at age eighteen and a half was steadily employed, had returned to school, and maintained frequent contact with the agency and foster family. He is justifiably proud of his accomplishments.

Motivational Strategy

Rather than doing more to develop motivation, staff members are best advised to do less. Many foster parents have done an excellent job of nurturing and meeting the dependency needs of children who have been neglected and abused. With this history often comes a learned helplessness, however, that impedes progress toward adult functioning. When unmotivated youths have been able to have their needs met without corresponding effort on their part, staff members and foster parents are encouraged to inventory what they are doing for them and to let go of that which the youths are developmentally capable of handling. Generally, caregivers can expect an escalation of attack, escape, or avoidance behaviors at the onset, but in time, with consistent support and encouragement, youths can redirect their energy and assume responsibility for their decisions.

Sophie, seventeen and a half, is of Apache ancestry. She was adopted at infancy by a Caucasian family. After a disrupted adoption and a foster home placement, she entered an independent-living program. She was passively angry, unmotivated, and skilled at manipulating former caregivers. She was also completely uninformed about her culture (see Chapter 9 by Stovall and Krieger in this volume). A consultant enabled her to learn about her ancestry initially via Pow Wow attendance, a visit to her reservation, and more recently by a prolonged legal effort to open the adoption records. Sophie was receiving failing grades, refusing to get a job, stealing, and displaying a generally apathetic response to any efforts to motivate her. Her legacy of pain, anger, and mistrust was internalized, becoming manifested in avoidance and nontrusting behaviors.

The staff approached Sophie in frequent conjoint interviews, involving her and residence and agency staff members, in which clear, firm, bottom-line messages were delivered in a caring way. Drawing on two years of experience with Sophie's passivity, manipulation, and avoidance techniques, the staff was concerned that the program had failed her. Indeed, grades and stealing had escalated. It appeared that Sophie would be better served on her own or with another program. The staff members felt that Sophie knew what she needed and affirmed their interest in helping her work more productively with the program or, if she decided, to move into other acceptable living arrangements. She was given two weeks to make a decision and meet with the staff. Within that time, Sophie's grades improved; she obtained a job, negotiated with her probation officer, and entered therapy. The recurring theme of avoidance/manipulation/confrontation continued but with longer episodes of self-reliance. She slowly learned to trust others and gain confidence in herself.

Establishing Boundaries

The staff must be sure to delineate clear physical and emotional boundaries. Nineteen-year-old Tim, who managed to undermine every job and educational opportunity that developed, was reprimanded for vacuuming and dusting the living room at his residence. His attempts to ingratiate himself with the staff, though compelling, were inappropriate in this situation. He was immediately sent from the house to hunt for a job, which was a primary element of his contract.

Disequilibrium

When emancipating youths are comfortable, they have either learned all the skills necessary to live independently or, more often, it is time for exposure to new learning experiences. It may then be appropriate for the staff to create anxiety that stimulates action. Youths are best given direct feedback compatible with what they might receive in the workplace or school setting.

Ken, nineteen, consistently found seemingly plausible reasons not to move out of the residence program and into his own apartment. "This apartment didn't work out; I don't have enough money saved." Finally a projected date of two months hence was given Ken, at which time he was to be living in an apartment. Slowly, tentatively, Ken moved ahead. A year later, a college freshman, he laughingly admitted, "I'd have never left if you hadn't pushed me out the door."

With Freedom Comes Responsibility

Although young people are not required to account for their free time or held to a curfew, they must behave in ways characteristic of competent young adults. This behavior includes assuming sexual responsibility. The staff must be prepared to give youths the information needed to make decisions about their own sexuality: to avoid exploiting and exploitative relationships, to be careful not to contribute to the spread of sexually transmitted diseases or to unwanted births, and to prepare for parenthood. Coming to terms with one's sexual identity requires a sense of separateness, a healing of past trauma, and an awareness of one's uniqueness. Helping youths in this important facet of their development is a critical chance to promote healthy adulthood.

Ken also struggled with his sexual identity and complained in group sessions that girls just saw him as a brother and never as a potential boyfriend. The group showed him that he had become comfortable playing a poor waif, victimized by a traumatic past. This role stimulated sympathy and mothering responses from girls, rather than attraction to him as a boyfriend. He learned, not without discomfort, through information-sharing, self-reflection, and role-playing to behave in ways that more closely and appropriately expressed his sexual feelings.

Normalization of Mistakes

It is important to see mistakes as opportunities to learn. Some of the best learning can take place when an adolescent carrying out a task makes a mistake. Successful staff members take pleasure when a young person can say: "I did it myself." Helping youths learn to laugh at themselves is also important in teaching the determination and resilience that will enable them to cope outside the framework of a supervised program.

Several times over a two-year-period, John, who became emancipated at age seventeen, called the office in a state of crisis. Each time he had either lost a job or was struggling in a difficult relationship. He would return to the program for a one- to three-month stay and then would quickly recoup, again moving toward a more durable vocational effort. This process enabled him, despite a rather rigid personality structure that lent itself to job and relationship disappointments, to continue his development without a return to the program, but he regularly lunches with the staff, checking out his perceptions and thinking.

Reframing the Past

The second and third preconditions of adolescent character formation involve reworking past traumas and searching out and making peace with the past. Affirming the importance of these tasks can be healthy and productive. Helping young people make contact with parents or relatives from whom they have been separated can often open the door to the past. Youths may discover that family members can be a resource in answering identity questions or providing a relationship previously unavailable (see Chapter 7 by Carbino in this volume).

Part of the work with Mrs. Z and the agency included locating information and people from Donald's past. He had clouded and guilty memories regarding the early deaths of his mother and his older sister, events that ultimately led to his placement in foster care. Painstakingly, information was collected that clarified the facts and helped Donald deal with his "naughty mean little boy," guilt-evoking memories. A trip to his hometown with his social worker resulted in a renewed relationship with a brother and the discovery of cousins and other extended family members.

Magical Thinking Versus Reality Testing

Many adolescents move toward adulthood with a naive vision of the world they are seeking to enter. Expectations of what the world will do for them color their planning. They say, "I am going to be an artist" and "I am going to build houses," without genuine motivation or the realization that any planning or preparation effort on their part would be required. Responsibility and initiative are particularly frightening to youths who lack self-esteem.

The task is to help youths assess alternatives and frame positive solutions. It is essential to support their curiosity about "what's out there." The staff can use clear questions to help youths explore ideas and understand the real challenges of adult life, while avoiding judgments in doing so.

"Society owes you nothing; there are no guarantees; life is not fair" are comments that can be used by the staff to reduce the avoidance responses of residents. Conversely, young people should be told they do have choices and they do not have to be victims.

Meeting Staff Needs

The needs of child-care staff members must be met through validation. They should be included in weekly agency staff meetings where their input is considered a vital part of the process. If they feel isolated, burnout will rapidly ensue. The attacks, criticism, and manipulation so frequently displayed by youths in the early phases of moving toward adult functioning are difficult to accept.

It is important to meet regularly as a staff team to share experiences, laugh, and redefine goals. These sessions energize the program and are the key to its success. The staff members must not judge the success of their work by the immediate behaviors of the youths; they must recognize instead that, in the short term, things may have to get worse before they get better.

Letting Go

For child-care staff members, foster parents, and social workers, letting go of a young person after meeting dependency needs for so long can be difficult. It is a time when individual, marital, and family issues can become enmeshed with the behavior and activities of the youth in transition. It is important for adults to avoid taking responsibility for the outcome of a teenager's choice of behaviors. This attitude interferes with the youths' learning and experience of self as a separate and independent individual. Awareness by foster family and staff members of their own experiences with separation and emancipation can help them to sort out issues accurately. Although one's own experience cannot be used to measure another's, remembrance of it can promote empathy and reflection on the enormity of the tasks one faces when entering young adulthood.

Letting go of Donald was particularly hard for Mrs. Z. She had fears for him as a young black male in a predominantly white rural western state. Her reaction was based on her own childhood and adult years in the South during the 1930s and 1940s, when she was a target of flagrant racism. She was also responding to Donald's naivete as to the extent of discrimination against black males in the area.

The social worker dealt with three critical issues. He listened to the foster mother's personal experiences and helped her to sort out what pertained only to her own situation and could not be useful to Donald. Second, by normalizing Donald's struggle for independence, he helped her recognize the support Donald needed. A black male consultant from an urban agency worked with Donald to affirm the importance of letting go and to provide a healthy black role model. Third, the social worker arranged for Donald to spend a month in a large city with a sizeable black population and a wide range of cultural resources. These strategies helped Donald and Mrs. Z to separate from each other with pride and optimism.

Conclusion

Participation in an independent-living program represents an ideal opportunity for many adolescents in foster care to learn the skills required for productive life after foster care. For young people to take full advantage of these innovative programs, they must reflect the primary need of the youths to master specific developmental tasks. Attention to the preconditions of adolescent development, sustained through a team effort among the agency, foster parents, social workers, and the youths, can ensure that young people are adequately prepared to assume adult responsibility.

REFERENCES

Anderson, J. L., and Simonitch, B. "Reactive depression in youths experiencing emancipation." Child Welfare 60 (1981): 383–390.

Blos, Peter. The Adolescent Passage: Developmental Issues. New York: International Universities Press, 1979.

Maluccio, Anthony, and Simm, Mike. "The use of agreements in foster family placements." In Aldgate, J.; Maluccio, A.; and Reeves, C. (editors), Adolescents in Foster Families. London: B. T. Batsford and Chicago: Lyceum Books, 1989, 102–121.

Mauzerall, Hildegarde. "Emancipation from foster care: The independent living project." Child Welfare 62 (January–February 1983): 46–53.

Solnit, Albert. "The adolescent's search for competence." Children Today 8 (1979): 13–16.

7

Participation of Biological Families in Preparation of Adolescents for Interdependent Living

ROSEMARIE CARBINO

The potential contribution of the biological family in the preparation of adolescents in foster care for interdependent living has been largely overlooked. This attitude echoes a pattern of neglect of the family that once pervaded foster care services, but which has been substantially reformulated due to an emphasis on permanency planning.

The strong refocus on work with parents that has taken place in recent years has been largely absent in relation to preparing youths for independent living, in part because of the inappropriate assumption that families who are not a placement resource may not be a resource in other ways. This assumption sometimes limits reunification work only to those steps that can result in the adolescent's becoming reunited with kin. Older youths preparing to leave foster care, however, have a clear need to relate to their families in other ways.

Meeting this need requires that social workers take an expanded view of the roles that families can play in the lives of older youths. The process of reconnecting to the family represents an important step toward interdependent living, one that has the potential to help solidify an adolescent's identity, clarify personal history, and reintegrate past trauma (see Chapter 6 by Wedeven and Mauzerall in this volume). For this potential to be realized, social workers and foster parents must be alert to ways in which families can assist youths in their path toward adulthood.

Following a brief consideration of the importance of the biological family, this chapter focuses on the family's potential contribution to preparation for interdependent living and recommends ways in which foster parents and agency staff members can assist.

Importance of Biological Family

The significance of the family in the growth and development of children and youths in foster care has been extensively considered [Blumenthal and Weinberg 1984; Laird 1979; Maluccio and Whittaker 1988], and emphasis is increasingly placed on maintaining parent-child contact through visiting [Hess and Proch 1988; Millham et al. 1986]. In addition, as various authors have stressed, the family assumes renewed importance for adolescents who are moving toward emancipation from foster care. Anderson and Simonitch [1981] note that even where parent-child relationships are strained, adolescents in foster care gravitate toward family contact, and even limited family support eases reactive depression. Barth [1986] concludes that research consistently has demonstrated improved outcomes for emancipated youths who have had contacts with parents and siblings during foster care. Festinger [1983] reports that sibling contact was recalled as very important to former foster children, and that those who had had contact with other relatives were less likely to show problems at discharge. Zimmerman [1982] finds that foster children considered important even infrequent visits that were not mentioned in case records, and that a large proportion of them would have liked more family contact, particularly with siblings.

Especially if connections with the foster family are ended, biological family members represent the youth's sole ties to a family. For example, Timberlake et al. [1987] note that all youths in an emancipation project identified reconciling with their families as their most pressing need. Furthermore, parents and other relatives may welcome some role and connection in the young person's new life, particularly since they are unable to take him or her back into their homes. In addition, now that the youth has less need for physical care and nurture than a younger child, changed roles with the family may be more workable. In short, the family continues to be important. Moreover, the concept of biological family should be construed broadly, since a variety of kin may be important to the foster adolescent, and because a large number of family connections and supports is desirable. The family thus may include parents, stepparents, siblings and stepsiblings, grandparents, aunts, uncles, cousins, and any other appropriate kin and close friends.

It must also be acknowledged that large numbers of parents are clearly unavailable to their children, particularly in the exit phase of foster care. Fanshel [1982] reports that half of the mothers were completely unavailable for contact, due to death, unknown whereabouts, hospitalization for mental illness, and other factors. This finding makes an even stronger case for helping youths to maintain ties to the broadest network of kin. At the same time, it should be noted that some relationships between parents and their placed children are so inappropriate for the children that they may elect to disassociate themselves from the parents.

In addition, as emphasized in a study by Fein et al. [1983], parents may be living in very difficult circumstances, with limited incomes, inadequate housing, and multiple life stresses. These conditions can pose substantial barriers to the involvement of parents with their children and are areas in which social agencies can help by making resources available.

In most cases, however, young people in foster care want contacts with their parents and other family members. Furthermore, parents and other kin are more available to youths than is commonly assumed. As various studies have shown, many children maintain contact with family members; foster parents generally encourage such contact; and some youths return to their families or otherwise intensify their ties with them following discharge from foster care [Festinger 1983; Furrh 1983; Kluger et al. 1989]. Family members can also be a resource on broader levels. Parents of foster children have demonstrated their ability to help one another in groups, in education/training of foster parents and social workers, and in advocating successfully for change in foster care practice [Carbino 1981; Edinger 1970; Hess and Williams 1982; Murphy 1976].

Since it is clear that contact with family members often takes place, it should be satisfying and productive. It becomes imperative that family members, particularly parents, be involved in a planned way in emancipation services, so that continuing or renewed family relationships are helpful for both youths and families. Moreover, most programs for emancipating adolescents are guided by the principles of permanency planning [Maluccio et al. 1986]. The philosophy of permanency planning should be expanded to include connectedness to kin and community among other outcomes for youths (see Chapter 1 in this volume).

Finally, as youths in foster care are helped to prepare for adult roles, it is vital to draw on all available resources, which include those derived from the family. The concept of family resources encompasses both tangible and intangible assets needed by youths to master the transition. Information on the past, family records, genetic history, and pictures help in the formation of a firm identity. For example, Indian tribal membership about which a child may be unaware would be a critical family resource (see Chapter 8 by Carten and Chapter 3 by Land in this volume). Tangible assets such as actual and potential legacies and veterans' benefits are of obvious benefit. Even if resources from the immediate family are limited, other assets such as sharing skills, job opportunities or apprenticeships, and a place to spend holidays may be available from an extended network of kin (see Chapter 12 by Pine and Krieger in this volume).

Roles of Biological Families

As already noted, family members are an underrecognized and underused resource in emancipation services. Nevertheless, as the following discussion demonstrates, they can play a variety of roles, first with their own family member in care and, second, with other young people in care.

Roles of Biological Families with Their Youths

Developing a Plan for Interdependent Living
Parents can collaborate with foster parents, social workers, and their youths to develop and support the plan for transition to interdependent living. The plan will generally include a proposed living arrangement, a set of tangible and intangible skills a youth needs to acquire, consideration of continued and/or renewed ties with foster and biological family members, and a timetable for achieving the transition. The participation of parents or other significant members of the family to any degree, from active participation in joint planning

meetings to simply acknowledging an already formulated written plan, can be markedly supportive.

Strengthening Linkage Between Families and Youths

Foster parents can invite and encourage family members to strengthen their connections to their teenager and suggest occasions and means. As much as possible, this process should begin long before the youth leaves foster care. For instance, foster parents could use holidays or milestones such as a birthday or completion of schooling as occasions for reinvolving family members. As another example, foster parents can work with youths in their care to gather information about their families and their past, in a life book or other collections of records and memorabilia.

Although not all contacts may work out successfully, even limited family contact can be supportive. Furthermore, since youth and family may be reacquainting themselves after an extended lapse of time, success in contact may best be viewed as gradual and incremental, while all parties get used to one another. Foster parents can help youths to see and appreciate even subtle efforts to connect on the part of their families.

Promoting Interdependent-Living Skills

Family members, such as parents, aunts, and uncles, can work jointly with foster parents, to teach/train youths in such skills for interdependent living as money management and budget planning, job finding and job preparation, finding housing, shopping and running a household, maintaining family ties, interpersonal skills, parenting skills, and sex education [Kluger et al. 1989].

Foster parents can encourage young people to report their progress to their parents and other relatives, thus increasing pride and further cementing relationships. Parents of foster youths are less likely to be helpful on parenting and interpersonal skills and sex education, but they can support the efforts of social workers or foster parents to be helpful.

For example, if parents are informed of the goals toward which foster parents and social workers are striving, they can communicate to their children that these are important matters to learn, that these topics would have been helpful to the learning experiences of the parents in their own youth, and that they hope their children will make good use of these learning experiences.

Supporting Youths After Exit from Foster Care

Family members can encourage their adolescents to continue with the plan and not become discouraged when the initial euphoria of independence has waned and problems in living loom large. Simonitch and Anderson [1979], positing four phases of youths' reactions to independent living in a subsidized apartment program, report success in repairing parent/youth relationships in the third of the four phases of the program: anxiety to get into the apartment; elation, lasting less than a month; loneliness and fear, as money dwindles and friends drop away; and quiet confidence, as solutions are thought out and new friends appear. During the third stage, the social worker tries to help youths establish as many contacts as possible with friends, family, and others. Contact with parents is always encouraged, although there may have been great difficulties with parents in the past. Family support and encouragement are important to youths, especially at this time, whether through personal visits, telephone contact, and/or messages from other family members. Such support can ease the loneliness and fear by underscoring the continuation or resumption of family connections and help to sustain youths in continuing with the independent-living plan. Support also provides a useful role for family members in this important transitional phase. In short, foster parents can encourage young people to view their families as resources during this critical time.

Additional Roles

Family members, particularly parents, can play other roles that go beyond direct involvement with their own youths. Parents of children in foster care have already demonstrated their capacities to assist one another in groups, to participate in training of foster parents and social workers, and to advocate successfully for changes in foster care practice and services [Carbino 1981, 1983; Hess and Williams 1982; Murphy 1976]. It is time to consider ways through which they can contribute to preparation of adolescents for interdependent living, thus enhancing their self-esteem and promoting their own competence [Maluccio et al. 1986].

As Resources to Other Youth in Care

In selected instances, family members may serve as resources to youths other than their own in such areas as planning for emancipation, encouraging contact with family members, teaching basic skills, and supporting youths through transition. Indeed, one fairly common human experience is that it often proves easier to get along with the relatives of others. Parents unable for various reasons to work well with their own adolescents may quite possibly be able to assist other teenagers. From such an experience they may also derive understanding and skills that will improve their relationship to their own offspring. Social workers should be alert to these changes, for, when communicated to foster parents, they can pave the way for renewed or enriched ties between adolescents and their own families.

As Linkages to Other Parents

Members of families may serve as linkages to the parents and relatives of other youths whom the agency would like to see involved in preparation for interdependent living. Family members already involved can be available as credible sources of information and support to families uncertain of involvement with agency programs. This situation may be particularly true for minority families whose cultural systems, including language, are different from those of agency staff members and foster families. Foster parents are often aware of family members willing to reach out to relatives of other youths and can be a valuable resource to the agency in this respect.

As Resource Persons to Foster Parents and Agency

Parents and other relatives might assist as resource persons or panelists in training foster parents as to the roles they can take with biological families. They might be especially helpful, for example, in highlighting the need for sensitivity to cultural differences in family patterns, the feelings of members of the biological family, ways to avoid competition between foster and biological families, and successful strategies for overcoming tensions in reestablishing relationships between adolescents and their families. Perhaps family members might be invited to a foster parent training session in which they can talk about these subjects as part of a panel and then remain available for questions from the audience. These interchanges would provide important and useful information and also model positive collaboration for biological and foster families.

In addition, parents, siblings, and other kin might participate in the agency's development of resources such as videotapes or manuals, to be used to acquaint youths, social workers, foster parents, other parents, or community members with various facets of interdependent living. Among other possibilities, this type of participation can take the form of a direct presentation on videotape; a review of developing materials; and in-person participation to augment use of the materials.

Of course, not all families could contribute extensively or even appropriately. They would vary in availability and in social, emotional, cognitive, and physical abilities, but it is impressive to see the contributions that parents have been able to make when given the chance to assume new and more positive roles, such as teacher or team member, as in the following illustration.

> Five inner-city parents agreed to participate in a workshop to train child welfare workers to deal with resistant, hard-to-reach parents of children in placement. Responding to a request for one hour of their time for a token fee, these parents assisted the trainer to demonstrate the potential helpfulness of groupwork services for inner-city parents of placed children. They did not previously know the trainer or one another, and they were aware that their participation could not be expected to influence agency action in behalf of their own children.
>
> Following a successful demonstration of group process, the parents volunteered to stay for the remainder of the afternoon and respond to questions from the staff. They made excellent suggestions on how to work with parents in their situations—for example, to explain fully the purpose and processes of foster care rather than to assume that the parent knows, to respond to parents' requests for help before the situation requires placement, or to look beyond a parent's behavior to the total person and his or her needs. Feeling certain enough of their roles to leave the safety of the group, the parents then met individually in small groups with agency staff members. Here they continued to respond to questions and to offer opinions. These contributions of modeling group processes, sharing experiences and opinions, and giving their time to the training altered workers' attitudes substantially and demonstrated positive roles for parents.

The expanded roles of family members should be part of the training budget as well. Parents or other family members should be paid for their participation in foster parent training or other agency services. Even a token payment underscores to all that the contributions of family members are valued. Moreover, parents or other family members may be in economically stressed circumstances and should not be expected to donate their time. Foster care trainers are paid for their time; it seems reasonable and feasible to acknowledge and support this new role for family members with some compensation.

In addition, they should receive other supports, such as reimbursement for transportation, child-care fees, or lunch, that are available to foster parents attending training.

Enlisting Participation of Family Members

A valid question at this point is whether all families can be considered potential contributors to interdependent living. We would say yes, even though we recognize as realistic certain obstacles to appropriate participation of family members, such as health problems, lack of money for transportation or telephone, large geographical distances, and refusal of some youths to have contact with their families. If we were to rule out those families that appear to have little or no potential for constructive involvement in independent living, we would be left with few families to consider. We would be considering too narrowly the forms that involvement can take and limiting the benefits that adolescents and families can gain from their association. It is preferable to invite the participation of family members and explore with an open mind how they might be involved.

How can one assess the potential of family members to participate? The best approach is to ask them and the adolescents in care. A foster youth may have an interest in starting with particular family members, can sometimes provide information on them, and can be helped to contact them. Family members, advised of the plan and goals for interdependent living, can decide if and how they will participate and can suggest other family members as well. It is likely that the capacity of family members to participate helpfully will evolve over time, as they, the emancipating youths, and the staff members begin to understand a joint approach to interdependent living.

In addition, as noted earlier, the invitation to play new roles may produce surprisingly positive results. We have therefore recommended expanding the potential roles to include collaborating with foster parents and social agency, providing services for emancipating youths in addition to their own, and assisting with training of foster parents, other biological parents, and agency staff members. To be effective participants, however, family members will need continuing support and training from the agency and from foster parents.

Roles of Foster Parents and Agencies

Foster Parents' Roles

Foster parents can for good reasons be helpful to biological family members. Though agencies may assume that primarily negative feelings exist between foster and biological families, foster parents often do recognize the importance of biological family members for their adolescents and can support positive relationships. Foster parents are also able to use agency training and group support from other foster parents to reassess negative responses to biological families and to develop understanding. Foster parents, from their own experiences with their agencies, can understand how biological families, vis-à-vis the social agency, can feel isolated, uninformed, dependent upon one worker's decisions, and lacking power. Even where there may be tension between foster and biological parents, this constraint does not necessarily extend to other biological family members.

In addition, foster parents who have been active members of foster parent associations or have received foster care education are also likely to view parents as needed participants in foster care. In some instances, foster parents may be more open to family participation than social workers [Carbino 1981]. Foster parents can appreciate some of the challenges families face in getting along with their teenager and can relate to some family members at least. In instances where they are unable to work with the family of their foster adolescent, foster parents may still be quite able to collaborate with families of other foster teenagers, through roles such as those delineated above.

Foster parents can adapt the skills they have used in other phases of foster care to help members of the family become a part of the youth's transition to interdependent living. Some strategies for doing so follow.

Invitation and Engagement
Foster parents can invite and encourage family members to strengthen connections to their teenager and can suggest occasions and means.

Information and Advocacy
Foster parents can inform family members of available resources

and can advocate with various organizations to provide needed resources to the family, especially parents. For example, they are likely to know about low-cost sources of clothing, furniture, and health services; about day camp scholarships and free activities for children; and about available volunteer services. They are often in a position to inform family members and encourage them to make use of resources.

Modeling and Teaching Skills

Foster parents can model successful relationship patterns with foster youths in general and consult with biological parents on dealing with a particular teen whom they know well. As the following example shows, this type of help can be particularly valuable to family members who have not had continuous relationships with their foster youths during adolescence and who are now uncertain about how to relate to this physically and socially changed young person.

> A mother of an adolescent who had run away and then lived in a group home for some time, reflected this uncertainty in a parents' group: "My daughter is seventeen years old and I don't know her any more. I don't even know her dress size if I wanted to buy her something to wear." Foster parents can be helpful by providing both verbal support for the family member's situation and the support that comes from concrete information—such as photos and school and athletic records; mention of the youth's interests and activities; and, yes, clothing sizes—that further recognition and familiarity and give the biological family direction in the relationship.

Foster parents can also show biological parents or other family members the ways in which they teach youths new skills and new ideas, as demonstrated in the next example.

> During visits of family members at the foster home, a foster mother told them what she had learned at foster parent training about getting along with teenagers, particularly in terms of handling discipline, which was an issue in both the foster and biological families. The family members—a mother, her boyfriend, and her mother—heard from the foster mother what new techniques she was using, such as jointly negotiating

rules and consequences where possible; clear and firm holding to rules and consequences without anger; rewarding positive behavior; and suggesting various ways for her foster youth to solve problems.

The foster mother responded to the family's reliance on physical restraint and punishment by saying she was once at that point too, but she has found that these other techniques work better. She told them of her early frustrations in changing her style and waiting for her foster child's new responses, but showed them that the responses do come in time. She said that over time this recognition helped her deal with her initial frustrations with the teen.

The mother and grandmother were quite interested, borrowed some of the training exercise materials from the foster mother, and eventually tried some of the techniques. They needed frequent support from the foster parents, often via phone contacts, and gradually began to use more appropriate responses during the teen's contacts with them. The relationship between the two families also became more collaborative.

Using Family Ties

In addition to helping adolescents to strengthen connections with their families, foster parents can encourage families and emancipating youths to make the best possible use of family ties in preparing for life after foster care. In the following example, the work of an experienced foster mother in initial contacts with the family of her seventeen-year-old foster daughter illustrates how this situation can be aided to happen.

Soon after the teenager moved into the foster home, the foster mother, with the agreement of the girl, got the caseworker's permission to make phone calls and send letters to her mother and stepfather. The foster mother used these early contacts to invite their contact with the girl, offered to keep in touch, and emphasized whatever positives she could find in this estrangement. She told the parents how she could see that they had been helpful to the daughter in some ways in earlier periods of her life, and that she felt they were important to her now. She stressed the notion of partnership between the two families toward assisting the girl into independent living.

In sessions with the social worker, the foster mother acknowledged her initial shock and awe at the anger the family felt because their daughter had made them "look like a failure." With the caseworker's assistance, she overcame her own negative feelings toward the family by viewing all people as having problems and having different ways through which they try to solve them. She realized that parents make mistakes and sought what she called forgiveness of the parents. She was supported by the worker in her efforts to initiate visits and phone contact with the teen and with the parents. She also sent photos from time to time and notes that emphasized something good that the parents had helped instill in their daughter. This practice, she felt, would help the parents realize some of their own good qualities.

When the parents and an older daughter first visited the foster home, the foster mother gave them lunch and talked about their possible involvement in planning the future with the foster daughter. Feeling that it would be important to give them specific roles, she asked if they would wish to join her and their daughter in apartment hunting and/or shopping for sheets and towels. The parents did not indicate interest in these activities, but appeared more willing than previously to have their daughter visit them and to meet with the foster mother again at some time in the future. The older sister did express interest in shopping.

The foster mother plans to support this interest and to continue to invite participation of the family. She will be joined in this effort by the caseworker. She has talked with the teenager and caseworker about telling the family of the overall plan being developed for interdependent living. She has suggested a goodbye party to be given toward the end of the foster placement, to which family members could be invited.

The preceding example gives rise to the following principles that foster parents can consider when trying to involve the family:

Encourage phone calls between youth and family.

Emphasize to the youth positive family attributes.

Consider the particular stresses on the family that prevented them from caring for their children.

Recognize that people find ways to cope to the best of their ability.

Welcome the family to the foster home or other places where they might meet with their children.

Suggest ways in which the family can be involved in a youth's life.

Try not to be discouraged; it may take repeated invitations to involve family members before they become ready to participate.

Agencies' and Social Workers' Roles

Agency support for involving families in preparing adolescents for life after foster care is essential. Without direct agency assistance, individual social workers or foster parents would be able to accomplish only limited goals. It is imperative that agencies come to view emancipation as a final phase of foster care services that requires family involvement to promote continuity and permanency for youths. It is important that agencies emphasize this view in their training of staff members and foster parents, in their practice with biological families, and in the resources that agencies provide.

As implementers of agency services, social workers can help family members to play a larger role and can help foster parents to work with them. Workers may also have to influence their own agencies to think differently about what the family can do. Family members have to be regarded as important to their children, and their involvement must be encouraged whether or not they are a placement resource.

Training

Foster parents and social workers will profit from emancipation-directed training. One useful in-service training method for staff members is a panel of foster and biological parents who share their perspectives, needs, and ideas. In those situations where training has been provided for foster parents from the beginning of their careers, they will have learned ways to understand parents of placed children, deal with negative feelings toward them, realize the importance of family contact with foster children, and work toward reunification. This basic education for foster parents could be adapted to that phase when the foster child is now a young adult, one who will not be returning home to live yet nevertheless needs connections with kin.

When foster parent training has been incomplete or nonexistent, however, the training regarding independent living may need to include the basics of understanding, accepting, and working with family members. Experienced and trained foster parents are invaluable in sharing their insights and in supporting teamwork roles. As suggested earlier, parents can participate as resource persons in the training of social workers and foster parents.

Curriculum content and other approaches for training social workers and foster parents to work with adolescents in foster care are considered in further depth by Pasztor and Associates [1988] and Pine and Jacobs [1989]. It should be stressed that family members also need education for their part in the emancipation process. Participation by biological and foster parents in joint training programs can change their perception of the parental role by adding collaborative roles, such as helping other adolescents, parents, and foster parents.

The content of training should cover agency purpose and services for interdependent living, including the skills and abilities that youths must possess in order to manage daily living and to establish and keep constructive personal relationships, as well as the potential roles of foster parents and of biological family members in the preparation for interdependent living and afterward.

Support of Biological Family Involvement

Some new activity may well be required of the agency initially to identify, locate, inform, and/or engage biological families. It is reasonable to consider any and all family members who might be available, starting with the family members with whom the youth has had or wants contact. These family members may be interested in strengthening connections and may be able to help identify, locate, or involve other family members.

If it appears that few or no family members are involved or available, other means of locating them can be tried. Agency case records may provide a source of information on kin; previous foster family or group homes may possess information; old correspondence, birthday cards, or scrapbooks may furnish clues to availability and interest. One overlooked way to "find" family members is to ask the foster youth where they might be. Foster children are often in contact with, or aware of, siblings or other family members about whom the agency does not know.

It is important not to dismiss ahead of time family members who may appear to lack the capacity for beneficial involvement. If family members are interested in possible connections, are geographically accessible, and/or are likely to be in contact with the emancipated youth, efforts to involve them should be made. Various ways to reconnect them and to support that connection can be considered. It might be necessary to provide transportation, day care service, or other resources to enable the family to participate. One way to approach the family is to emphasize the voluntary and positive nature of participation toward interdependent living. Agencies might consider, with the consent of the youth, sending to family members written invitations to participate in the youth's preparation for life after foster care. Such a positive action emphasizes to everyone involved a "graduation" and new goals, rather than a last-resort situation.

Visits by family members are another good point at which to inform and engage them; both social workers and foster parents can actively help here by using telephone and in-person contacts with the family to encourage participation. Where independent-living centers are available, they may well be the best environment in which to involve the family. The settings are likely to be perceived by family members as less threatening, more accessible, and more familiar environments than agency meeting rooms or foster homes.

As soon as family members have shown any interest whatever in the efforts toward interdependent living for their teenager, joint consideration by family, foster parents, youth, and agency of the possibilities for family participation is a good idea. The social worker's assistance is necessary in such a complicated activity. Once a plan, even if preliminary, has been jointly formulated, it is helpful to put that plan into writing, as part of an explicit agreement, and on a calendar for all involved parties. These concrete reminders of agreed-upon goals and tasks will support appropriate and continuing family participation and will assist foster parents in their work with the family as well.

Once some connection has been made, agencies could include the family in the services and activities they already provide to foster youths and foster parents. For example, activities described by Mauzerall [1983] for foster youths facing emancipation include group discussions, skills development, a contract on budget and responsibilities, inclusion in review staffings, and use of a resource book. Family members could successfully be involved in some way in each of these activities, particularly in group discussions and in contracting [Maluccio and Simm 1989].

Other activities, such as compiling a life history [Pasztor et al. 1986] or involvement with a youth and his or her foster parents in counseling sessions [Tiddy 1986], might appropriately include family members in some circumstances. Social workers have a central responsibility to seek appropriate possibilities for family involvement in these services and to work actively to achieve them.

Conclusion

Involvement of family members as contributing participants together with agency staff members, foster youths, and foster parents represents recognition and use of a frequently overlooked resource in preparing adolescents for life after foster care. This involvement offers foster youths the assistance of persons uniquely important in their lives. It also offers family members and foster parents a variety of positive roles in this final phase of foster care service. It provides agency staff members with both a resource and a reminder to maintain a focus on the family in work with emancipating youths. It emphasizes the importance of the family to the foster child's well-being throughout the continuum from entry to exit from foster care, and the significance of establishing kinship ties for life after foster care.

REFERENCES

Anderson, J. D., and Simonitch, B. "Reactive depression in youths experiencing emancipation." Child Welfare 60 (1981): 383–390.

Barth, R. P. "Emancipation services for adolescents in foster care." Social Work 31 (May–June 1986): 165–171.

Blumenthal, K., and Weinberg, A. (editors). Establishing Parental Involvement in Foster Care Agencies. New York: Child Welfare League of America, 1984.

Carbino, R. "Developing a parent organization: New roles for parents of children in substitute care." In Maluccio, A. N., and Sinanoglu, P. A. (editors), The Challenge of Partnership: Working with Parents of Children in Foster Care. New York: Child Welfare League of America, 1981, 165–186.

———. "Group work with natural parents in permanency planning." In Morris, S. (editor), The Use of Group Services in Permanency Planning for Children. New York: The Haworth Press, 1983, 7–30.

Edinger, H. B. "Reuniting children and parents through casework and group work." Children 17 (1970): 183–187.

Fanshel, D. On the Road to Permanency. New York: Child Welfare League of America, 1982.

Fein, E., Maluccio, A. N., Hamilton, V. J., and Ward, D. E. "After foster care: Outcomes of permanency planning for children." Child Welfare 62 (November–December 1983): 485–560.

Festinger, T. No One Ever Asked Us . . . A Postscript to Foster Care. New York: Columbia University Press, 1983.

Furrh, P. E., Jr. "Emancipation: The supervised apartment living approach." Child Welfare 62 (1983): 54–62.

Hess, P., and Proch, K. Family Visiting in Out-of-Home Care: A Guide to Practice. Washington, DC: Child Welfare League of America, 1988.

Hess, P., and Williams, L. B. "Group orientation for parents of children in foster family care." Child Welfare 61 (1982): 456–466.

Kluger, M., Maluccio, A., and Fein, E. "Preparation of adolescents for life after foster care." In Aldgate, J., Maluccio, A., and Reeves, C. (editors), Adolescents in Foster Families. London: B. T. Batsford and Chicago: Lyceum Books, 1989, 77–87.

Laird, J. "An ecological approach to child welfare: Issues of family identity and continuity." In Germain, C. B. (editor), Social Work Practice: People and Environments. New York: Columbia University Press, 1979, 174–209.

Maluccio, A. N., Fein, E., and Olmstead, K. A. Permanency Planning for Children—Concepts and Methods. London and New York: Routledge, Chapin and Hall, Inc., 1986.

Maluccio, A. N., and Simm, M. "The use of agreements with adolescents in foster family care." In Aldgate, J., Maluccio, A., and Reeves, C. (editors), Adolescents in Foster Families. London: B. T. Batsford and Chicago: Lyceum Books, 1989, 102–121.

Maluccio, A. N., and Whittaker, J. K. "Helping the biological families of children in out-of-home placement." In Nunnally, E. W., Chilman, C. S., and Cox, F. H. (editors), Troubled Relationships. Volume 3 of Families in Trouble. Beverly Hills, CA: Sage Publications, 1988, 205–217.

Mauzerall, H. A. "Emancipation from foster care: The independent living project." Child Welfare 62 (January–February 1983): 46–53.

Millham, S., Bullock, R., Hosie, K., and Haak, M. Lost in Care: The Problems of Maintaining Links between Children in Care and Their Families. Aldershot, England: Gower, 1986.

Murphy, D. A. "A program for parents of children in foster family care." Children Today 5 (1976): 37–40.

Pasztor, E. M., Clarren, J., Timberlake, E. M., and Bayless, L. "Stepping out of foster care into independent living." Children Today 15 (March–April 1986): 32–35.

Pasztor, E. M., and Associates. Preparing Youth for Interdependent Living. West Hartford, CT: Center for the Study of Child Welfare, University of Connecticut School of Social Work, and Atlanta, GA: Child Welfare Institute, 1988.

Pine, B. A., and Jacobs, M. "The training of foster parents for work with adolescents." In Aldgate, J., Maluccio, A., and Reeves, C. (editors), Adolescents in Foster Families. London: B. T. Batsford and Chicago: Lyceum Books, 1989, 151–165.

Simonitch, B., and Anderson, J. L. "On their own: An Oregon experiment." Children Today 8 (1979): 28–31.

Tiddy, S. G. "Creative cooperation: Involving biological parents in long-term foster care." Child Welfare 65 (January–February 1986): 53–62.

Timberlake, E. M., Pasztor, E., Shagren, J., Clarren, J., and Lammert, M. "Adolescent emancipation from foster care." Child and Adolescent Social Work Journal 4 (1987): 264–277.

Zimmerman, R. B. Foster Care in Retrospect. New Orleans, LA: Tulane University School of Social Work, 1982.

8

Building on the Strengths of Black Foster Families

ALMA J. CARTEN

Foster care services have long been a target for child advocates and social reformers. The deficits of this and other components of the child welfare system have been acknowledged by key players at every level and by the general public. The services and programs that have evolved have been accused of taking neither a well-articulated, integrated direction planned in consideration of families' total needs, nor a purposeful course toward the achievement of clearly defined goals emphasizing the expressed value of family life [Maas and Engler 1959; Meyer 1984; Rimer 1985].

Black families and their children, who—along with other minority groups—are disproportionately represented in the child welfare system, have been especially vulnerable to the effects of inadequate programs and services. The perspective that guided child welfare policy development in the past has emphasized self-reliance and individualism, thus failing to give sufficient consideration to the effect of environmental influences on individual and family functioning. This perspective has been reflected in foster care services that sought to rescue children from inadequate families, resulting in large numbers of black children being unnecessarily placed away from their own homes. These children were not always viewed as suitable candidates for adoption, nor did their families receive the kind of services that supported their reunification [Billingsley and Giovannoni 1972; Chestang 1978; Mech 1983; Olsen 1982]. Consequently, it is not surprising that permanent foster care became the reality for many of them and that we now see a disproportionate number of black youths who have grown up in care and who have a discharge plan of independent living.

Foster care has remained a service used primarily by poor, minority families whose problems are a result of poverty, compounded by the conditions of their social environments. Therefore, agencies need to equip their staff members with adequate knowledge about minority groups, their family lifestyles, and the relationship between family functioning and the social environment. Black foster parents can be a valuable source of such knowledge to agencies, and they are in a key position to advocate for services needed by youths approaching discharge from care in order to ensure that these services are provided in culturally sensitive ways (see Chapter 9 by Stovall and Krieger in this volume).

First, care of unrelated children and informal adoption have been enduring traditions of black families, who view children as the collective concern of the community. These attributes can serve as assets in providing care for a wide range of children and youths. Second, interdependence and mutual supports, which are also characteristic of black families, can serve as models for the foster adolescent in the transition to successful adulthood, a transition complicated by the youth's minority group and foster care status. Third, black foster parents' familiarity with negotiating the demands of two worlds, and preparing their own children for successful functioning in these worlds, has enabled them to develop parenting skills that may be transferred to the fostering experience.

This chapter outlines principles and guidelines for agency practice and foster parent training that enhance the contribution of foster parents to the preparation of black foster adolescents for competent adulthood. They derive from the experiences of a private New York City child-care agency, in its implementation of a pilot project designed to improve services to black adolescents in care.

Description of Project

The conceptual framework of the project was based on the premise that the family performs the essential function of preparing children for successful adulthood. Underlying assumptions that informed program practices acknowledged the strengths of the black family and the attributes that make it well suited to prepare the adolescent for interdependent community living. The project compared two different approaches to foster parent training and evaluated the agency's work with foster parents and youths in light of these findings.

The training programs were carried out concurrently and differed in group composition and instructional format: one was attended by the foster parents only; the other by foster parents and adolescents together. Although both programs dealt with content and process, the foster parent-only group emphasized a didactic teaching format, and the foster parent-adolescent group was more process-oriented, drawing training content from the participants' experiences in group interactions. Both programs consisted of a series of eight two-hour sessions jointly led by two social workers. Teaching approaches included role-playing, case materials, readings, small-group exercises, log assignments, and playing back selected segments of videotapes of the actual group sessions.

In general, the project emphasized partnership and collaboration between the agency and the foster parents. Innovative aspects of the project were its use of a group of experienced foster parents in developing the program and a contractual placement model. Foster parents were viewed as an extension of the agency staff, acting as mentors and role models for the youths in their care rather than as substitute parents. The contractual placement agreement among the agency, the adolescent, and the foster parent encouraged mutuality and further strengthened partnerships.

Principles and Guidelines for Program Design and Training

The project yielded principles and guidelines that are useful in program design and training of foster parents, particularly for work with black adolescents. These principles and guidelines emphasize the fact that social workers can build on the strengths of black families.

Uniqueness of the Black Foster Family

The family is central to the life of every society and is best suited to perform the essential task of preparing children for successful adulthood. Perhaps the degree to which offspring are able to function as contributing members of adult society is an indirect measure of how well the family has carried out one of its fundamental purposes. Yet families cannot be understood separately from their environments, and black families in America have historically functioned under the often dual burdens imposed by minority group and low economic status.

The ecological perspective recognizes the influences that transactions with the larger systems of society have on individuals and families. It acknowledges the coping and adaptive capabilities of the individual and identifies the purpose of the helping process as focusing on those transactions that, by enhancing opportunities for growth and change, promote an adaptive fit with the environment [Germain and Gitterman 1980].

In his seminal study of the American black family, Billingsley [1968] incorporates this ecological perspective in his formulations for understanding the structure and functioning of black families. His conceptual model stresses the network of naturally interdependent relationships within the black community and wider society, the influence of these larger social systems on black family life, and the adaptive patterns that have emerged to serve positive functions. Billingsley concludes that the black family is a sustaining, resilient, and nurturing social system, possessing characteristics that make it particularly well suited to assist black children not only to survive but to achieve in the broader, non-supportive environment. Hill [1971], in his classic study of black families, identifies five family strengths that have been keys to the survival and development of the black community: kinship bonds, work orientation, adaptability of family roles, achievement orientation, and religious orientation. In light of the attributes delineated by these two authors, among others, the black foster family is a unique system of strengths, particularly suitable for providing the educational and socialization experiences needed by the black adolescent who is in transition to interdependent living.

Carten [1986] cites many examples of these special capacities in her detailed report of the project that is the subject of this chapter. Foster parents who participated in the project modeled the development of mutual support networks. Group members talked by telephone between group sessions and shared travel arrangements. Those foster parents with automobiles transported other group members who would otherwise have had to use public transportation during unsafe hours. A number of the foster parents attended a special Family Day on strengthening the black family, sponsored by one group member's church. Participants also reached out to non-participating foster parents to share new information and resources with them. When the project terminated, the group asked that an address and telephone list be circulated to provide a means for "keeping in touch" and "helping one another out."

With the encouragement of their foster parents, this mutual support aspect of the black experience also emerged in the relationships among the youths who participated in the project. Three had known each other from previous social or school experiences but had not known of the others' foster care status. Over a period of time, attachments were formed among the youths, suggesting the potential for establishing peer relationships leading to shared apartment arrangements in community living and long-term ties of friendship with others who share the common bond of the foster care experience.

Mutual aid and support were also in evidence in the foster parent-adolescent training group, particularly in helping the youths to cope with fears about living on their own. For example, with the encouragement of the group, one young man was able to complete a homework assignment—interviewing a local bank official about banking services and the requirements for opening checking and savings accounts. With support, he was able to overcome his initial reluctance and later told the group enthusiastically, "Yeah man, the dude was calling me sir and everything."

Such an activity may seem commonplace; however, many black foster youths have had few such experiences. Because of this lack as well as fears of rejection, they often do not avail themselves of the services needed for living successfully on their own. At a practical level, this activity supported the development of another important life skill—being an effective consumer. Through group discussion of the banking experience, the youths learned that the check-cashing establishments they customarily used cost more and offered no benefits. This discovery led to additional discussions about organizations with practices that exploited poor, inner-city communities, thus making it necessary to travel outside the immediate neighborhood to obtain necessary goods and services at a lower cost and of higher quality.

Partnership and Collaboration with Foster Parents

Foster parents have always been the primary on-the-line providers in foster care agencies. In the past, however, they have held a quasi-staff-client relationship with the agency and have frequently been viewed as targets for treatment and change. Black foster parents have been especially vulnerable to this view of their role and in their relationship to the agency, since many have life-survival concerns with which they need assistance. In contrast to this view, services to adolescents in foster care must emphasize partnership and collaboration between agencies and foster parents, as discussed in Chapter 5 of this volume. Foster parents must be recognized for the wealth of knowledge derived from their previous on-the-job experience, life experience, and the racial sensitivity that they bring to the foster parenting role.

Agencies successful in putting this principle into action will stress foster parent participation in the design and delivery of training programs for staff members and for other foster parents, and for joint training of both groups. They will also provide opportunities for foster parent input into the formulation of agency policy and practice.

Foster Parents as Role Models and Mentors

The conceptualization of the role of foster parent as parent substitute, which characterizes traditional foster care, provides the young child with opportunities for bonding experiences that meet psychosocial needs for attachment to parental figures and a nurturing family. This model, however, may conflict with the psychosocial needs of the adolescent, which necessitate achievement of separation and autonomy from family and parental ties and integration into community living. Moreover, the view of foster parents as substitute parents may impede the youths' development of renewed relationships with their biological families. Because of the often troublesome nature of these relationships, foster parents serving as substitute parents may be inclined to discourage connections to the family, thus isolating and estranging the youths from potential future supports.

Instead, the foster parents' role can be shifted from substitute parent to that of mentor and role model. In this approach, placement is guided by a contractual agreement that focuses on mutuality in the adolescent-foster parent relationship and teaches competence and mastery of the skills needed for self-reliance. This approach also frees foster parents from the need to compete with biological parents, minimizes feelings of personal failure and responsibility for the adolescent's limitations, and promotes a greater objectivity in the caretaker role. Hence, the adolescent benefits from the least restrictive environment of the foster family home with its capacity to meet emotional needs, while also working to accomplish the necessary tasks of this stage of life.

At the same time, the foster parent-mentor is regarded as a collaborating member of the agency's child-care team, as one who brings special skills and intuitive insights to the fostering experience, and as a specialist in understanding the needs of the individual foster youth. Continuation of the mentor relationship should be encouraged after discharge, so that the young adult can receive continuing guidance and advice on resolving problems that emerge during the transition to this new life status. Such assistance is important, since many youths in foster care profit from relationships with their foster parents following emancipation [Kluger et al. 1989].

Use of Adult Learning Approaches

Various adult learning principles should underlie foster parent training and, in particular, the preparation of black foster parents as caregivers for adolescents. These techniques include a diversity of training styles and approaches to meet varied learning needs. Research has shown that different approaches lead to the achievement of different learning objectives. For example, in the project described earlier, the researcher found that the foster parents who experienced a more didactic teaching approach increased their identification with the teaching role in fostering more than did similar foster parents who experienced the process-oriented training program. In contrast, the latter group was better able to demonstrate improved fostering practice skills following training [Carten 1986].

Lee [1979: 132], in a project using the small-group modality for work with new foster parents, found that neither the didactic nor the experiential approach to the learning-teaching process could stand alone. Her study explored the connection between educational and social work approaches to learning through an analysis of John Dewey's experiential educational approach and those of social work educators Bertha Reynolds and William Schwartz. Lee suggests that the "method is to 'work from the experience out,' or inductively derive the concepts and content to be 'taught' from the experiences presented and shared by the learners." Carten's [1986] design followed that of Lee, in that the training curriculum for foster parents was developed around predetermined content, and the life experiences of the participants were essential to adjusting that content in process.

While the life experiences of participants are fundamental to the training process, it is equally important that training reflect planning, coherence, and integration. Each module should be directed toward the achievement of clearly articulated learning objectives that have been cooperatively established. Thus, the challenge for successful training is to balance planned structure and flexibility.

This approach was aptly demonstrated by the co-trainers of the foster parent-adolescent training group in the project. Although the topic of black family lifestyle had been scheduled for a session late in the program, at an early session the suggestion was made to use first names among group members. This suggestion initiated a discussion of the black experience, including the negative feelings many blacks have with the use of first names early in relationships, the valuing of relationships with elders that are based in the African heritage, and the expectation that children and youths refer to non-related adults by their surnames. This exchange of ideas in turn led to a discussion of the sensitivity of older adolescents to the use of names in the fostering relationship, since many maintain a continuing tie to biological families. Issues emerged about how the foster adolescent is introduced to outsiders, how differences in surnames are explained, and the discomfort that some adolescents experience when expected to refer to the adult caregiver as mother or father. Throughout the project, the trainers had to be not only flexible in the teaching of the prearranged content areas, but able to identify the subtle nuances of the black fostering experience as these emerged.

Another key principle involves the ability of the trainer to create an environment for learning by demonstrating knowledge of the subject matter, respect for the strengths and expertise of the participants, and a valuing of their cultural uniqueness. This ability is greatly aided when the trainer of black foster parents is sensitive to issues related to the black experience, since the trainer's skill at entering into the life space of the participants is central to the educational encounter. In the 1986 study, age and ethnicity were experienced by foster parents as distancing variables. Foster parents observed that the frequently young, white workers did not fully "understand the situation of our kids" or that "we [black people] have been doing this [caring for black children] for a long time" [Carten 1986: 163].

Another adult learning principle that is reflected in effective foster parent training programs is the participation of trainees in setting the training agenda. Adults learn best when they feel a need to know something. Hence, training should meet the needs foster parents have identified and should offer real-life examples of problems and the challenges they present. In the project, foster parents and adolescents were consistently involved in a collaborative search for answers to the questions: "What are the skills needed for independent living?" and "How are these skills best taught and learned?"

In the approach using foster parents and adolescents together, role-playing and small-group exercises were found to be effective. For example, one activity was the development of each individual youth's discharge plan, such as intermediate and long-range goals; potential obstacles, including the youth's own limitations and the lack of community resources; and solutions for overcoming these limitations. Each youth and his or her foster parents were to develop the plan at home, as well as to identify any tension that resulted from their work together on it. At a later group session, another foster parent reviewed with the adolescent the plan's viability. This exercise underscored the need to plan consciously and deliberately for establishing and achieving goals, as well as the need for increased opportunities for foster parents and adolescents to work objectively and cooperatively in problem-solving activities related to discharge planning.

Skills for interdependence were also emphasized when the group celebrated the birthdays of two youths. One, who had difficulties managing money, received a gift subscription to *Black Enterprise;* the lead article in the first issue dealt with money management. The other youth was struggling with developmental issues of identity, sexuality, and establishing autonomy in her relationship with her biological mother; she was given Toni Morrison's *In Search of My Moth-*

er's Gardens. Practical skills for living on one's own and for developing a positive racial identity and self-concept were explored informally by the group within the context of the black experience. In relating to the concerns of the second youth and her troublesome relationship with her mother, the trainer was able to focus on the need of black foster adolescents to achieve identity consolidation by establishing a sense of comfort with their roots and acceptance of the limitations of their biological parents. This process enables both the biological and foster parents to become resources who can be called upon after discharge.

Joint Training Sessions for Foster Parents and Youths

Additional benefits from training can result when foster parents and adolescents participate in joint training sessions. As previously noted, two approaches were tested, one involving joint training and the other involving foster parents alone. Qualitative and quantitative measurements of program outcomes clearly indicated that the presence of the adolescents increased the foster parents' sensitivity and ability to respond to the individual needs of youths in their care. The foster parents who participated in training with their foster youths verbalized new insights into the behavior and feelings of the adolescents, with such comments as "My son is surprising me" and "I never knew he felt that way before." Joint training can provide opportunities for foster parents and adolescents to demonstrate their competence to each other and to work cooperatively on problem solving related to interdependent living. Such training promotes learning and further emphasizes for both foster parents and adolescents that the process of formulating individual plans must be monitored, goal-directed, realistic, and completed within a specified time.

This training strategy also supported a greater variation in the patterns of subgroups that were formed. The adolescents became a distinct subgroup that performed support and teaching functions. The behavior modeling and feedback that came from peers were far more effective than the "lecturing" of adults. The subgroups formed around gender of the adolescents also enriched content concerning family planning, responsible sexual behaviors for both males and females, and social/interpersonal relationships, all important attributes for achieving successful adulthood.

Facing Difficult Issues Squarely

The program design and training for work with emancipating foster adolescents must take into account a number of issues. The normative needs of the adolescent to challenge adult authority and traditional values have resulted in foster adolescent placements being at high risk for disruption and breakdown [Berridge and Cleaver 1987; Fein et al. 1983]. Consequently, the older child in care often experiences multiple placements and does not have an opportunity for consistent experiences that teach adult life skills. Similarly, the adolescent's need to achieve a consolidation of identity, positive self-concept, and separation from family ties creates a further dilemma for the minority adolescent, who must continually struggle with these issues as they are complicated by foster care and minority group status.

In addition, a number of studies correlate low achievement levels of blacks to a devalued sense of self. Since there are many successful, high-achieving blacks who have positive self-concepts and a strong sense of racial identity, it might be postulated that a strong sense of racial identity and a sense of group identity are critical to the development of a positive self-concept. Barnes [1972] attributes the positive self-image of many blacks to experiences within the black family and community that serve as mediators between the individual and the larger society. These associations enable them to distinguish their own sense of worth from how they are defined by the larger society and develop a view of self that enhances both self and group. As does Billingsley [1968], Barnes emphasizes the interdependence of the black child and family with other systems in the society.

Black foster parents have cited many examples of the need to advocate for their foster children or to serve as buffers between them and negative community encounters perceived as racially motivated, particularly in relation to the public school system and employers. Some reported such experiences with the child welfare agencies with which they work. These reports suggest that foster parents do perceive, as an important part of their role, supporting the development of a positive racial identity and mitigating the negative effects of encounters in the wider community [Carten 1986].

Chestang's [1978] discussion of the character formation of blacks also possesses relevance for understanding the process of identity consolidation of black foster adolescents and their achievement of successful interpersonal functioning. He suggests that life in a racist majority culture demands that black individuals develop interpersonal skills that allow them to relate within two worlds. One adaptive response that has emerged in the individual's efforts to mediate the demands of these two environments is that of "getting over," which implies a seduction of the environment.

The child welfare system provides vast opportunities for the adolescent to manipulate the environment in ways that will permit him to "get over," since the major players in the system have differing sets of priorities. These priorities are shaped by competing policies that influence the behavior of the social workers, biological parents, and foster parents, who must relate to the foster adolescent. Often the adolescent's attempts at "getting over" have resulted in serial terminations of placement that decrease opportunities for constancy in relationships with adults with whom he or she can identify to learn the roles needed for adulthood. "Getting over" also leads to a pattern of inauthentic relationships, which can carry over to nonproductive, manipulative behaviors in adult life.

Black foster parents, because of their own experiences in negotiating the demands of two worlds and their own parenting experiences, can be sensitive to this dynamic and transfer their understanding of it to the fostering relationship. James was fortunate to have such a sensitive foster parent:

> An attractive, charming, and articulate young black man, James acknowledged that in relating to his foster mother, very little "got by her" and there were few opportunities for "getting over" [Carten 1986: 140].

Foster parents and social workers must squarely face these issues and the reality of these burdens on the foster adolescent. A common adage in the black community, and also a consistent theme of the project discussed, is that "in order to know where you are going, you have to know where you came from and know whose shoulders you were riding on to get there." Training and other group approaches should promote full and open discussions on adolescent growth and development and identify those transactions in the process that represent stressors typical of this life stage, as well as particular stressors on black youth.

"Family tree" exercises with both foster parents and their adolescents can identify common themes of the black experience as well as those unique to foster care. Also, open discussions of the progress of the placement increase a youth's chances of "making it." This process occurs first by diminishing the chances of placement disruption; second, by modeling communication and negotiation skills necessary for competent adulthood, particularly important for success in a hostile environment; and, finally, by allowing for a confrontation of less adaptive "getting over" behaviors. Such an approach to work with youths in foster care emphasizes reciprocity and partnership among the key players—the foster adolescent, foster parents, and the social worker, and, where appropriate, the biological parents (see Chapter 7 by Carbino in this volume).

Conclusion

Preparation for emancipation and interdependence is a lifelong process. Families provide for children, within a nurturing supportive environment, the experiences that further a developing and incremental competence and mastery of life skills. Within a complex social environment, the transition to adult status has become increasingly difficult for all adolescents. For black foster adolescents, this process is further complicated by their minority group as well as their foster care status. Service delivery strategies should, therefore, address those issues that create additional stresses for this group of young people.

Child welfare policies have traditionally developed with an absence of sensitivity to the special needs of minority group children. The emerging programs for independent living and the concepts that are embodied in them reflect these past practices. There is, however, the potential for developing, within the new concept of preparation for interdependence, programs that capitalize on the strengths inherent in the black foster family and community. These can serve as natural resources for ensuring the adolescent's successful transition to community living.

Black families have a long tradition of valuing children. Because children are viewed as the responsibility of the collective community, these families show a proclivity for the care of unrelated children and the informal adoption of children. In mediating the demands of the larger society, black families have also developed coping, adaptive responses that place value on extended family and kinship ties, mutual support, self-help, and interdependence. These attributes can serve as assets for promoting in the adolescent approaching discharge from foster care the development of an orientation to adult life that recognizes its interdependent nature and the need for connectedness to a vast network of relationships and institutions within the immediate and the larger community. Agencies charged with the care of black foster children must develop policies and practices designed to enhance these assets and to use them for the fullest benefit of young people and their community.

REFERENCES

Barnes, Edward J. "The black community as the source of positive self concept for black children: A theoretical perspective." In Jones, Reginald L. (editor), Black Psychology. New York: Harper and Row Publishers, 1972, 166–192.

Berridge, D., and Cleaver, H. Foster Home Breakdown. Oxford, England: Basil Blackwell, 1987.

Billingsley, A. Black Families in White America. Englewood Cliffs, NJ: Prentice Hall, 1968.

Billingsley, A., and Giovannoni, J. Children of the Storm—Black Children and American Child Welfare. New York: John Wiley & Sons, 1972.

Carten, A. J. The Independent Life Skills Preparation Project: A Model for the Development of a Specialized Foster Parent Training Program. Unpublished dissertation, Hunter College School of Social Work, The City College of New York, 1986.

Chestang, L. "The delivery of child welfare services to minority group children and their families." In Child Welfare Strategies in the Coming Years. Washington, DC: U.S. Department of Health, Education and Welfare, Office of Human Development Services, Administration for Children, Youth and Families, Children's Bureau, DHEW. Publication No. (OHDS) 78-30158, 1978.

Fein, E., Maluccio, A. N., Hamilton, V. J., and Ward, D. "After foster care: Outcomes of permanency planning for children." Child Welfare 62 (November–December 1983): 485–560.

Germain, C. B., and Gitterman, A. The Life Model of Social Work Practice. New York: Columbia University Press, 1980.

Hill, R. B. The Strengths of Black Families. New York: National Urban League, 1971.

Kluger, M., Maluccio, A., and Fein, E. "Preparation of adolescents for life after foster care." In Aldgate, J., Maluccio, A., and Reeves, C. (editors),

Adolescents in Foster Families. London: B. T. Batsford and Chicago: Lyceum Books, 1989, 77–87.

Lee, Judith B. "The foster parent workshop: A social work approach to learning for new foster parents." Social Work with Groups 2 (1979): 129–143.

Maas, H., and Engler, H. Children in Need of Parents. New York: Columbia University Press, 1959.

Mech, E. V. "Out-of-home placement rates." Social Service Review 57 (1983): 659–667.

Meyer, C. H. "Can foster care be saved." Social Work 29 (December 1984): 499.

Olsen, L. "Services for minority children in out-of-home care." Social Service Review 56 (1982): 572–585.

Rimer, S. "From foster care to life on New York City streets: Three case studies in failure." The New York Times (July 19, 1985).

PART III

Meeting the Challenge: Practice Methods and Strategies

*A*ll young people making the transition to adulthood struggle with creating a comfortable separation/dependence balance in their connections to significant figures. Relationships with parents, siblings, teachers, peers, and others are all arenas in which youths can assert their growing self-reliance while coming to terms with their needs. The presence of additional key figures intervening in the lives of foster youths can make progress toward adulthood more difficult. Foster youths typically face many sources of intervention: the agency, social workers, foster parents, biological family, cultural influences, and the court system. Conflict among interveners can create for youths a "crisis of loyalty," as they become drawn into power struggles that erode, rather than promote, healthy interdependence. Part III examines a range of intervention methods and strategies that make use of a team approach to help young people solidify a sense of self, overcome past trauma, and create realistic plans for the future.

Minority foster youths face even greater obstacles than Caucasian youths as they make their way toward adulthood, and, being less prepared, remain at greater risk of dependence on government systems throughout their lives. In Chapter 9, Stovall and Krieger demonstrate that fostering minority youths requires special skills that should be learned so that ethnic identity can become part of self-identity, and young people's needs can be met in ways that are culturally relevant. They consider a range of systemwide, consistent, and carefully implemented methods for developing ethnic competence that involve the agency, staff members, foster parents, and the community.

Helping youths to overcome the negative effects of abuse and neglect requires that foster parents and social workers deal effectively with potential obstacles to achieving developmental milestones. In Chapter 10, McFadden examines the consequences of maltreatment on adolescents in foster care and offers intervention strategies involving mental health services, health care, employment, education, and recreation and leisure.

In Chapter 11, Ryan examines approaches to disciplining young people in foster care and provides guidelines for developing individualized plans to help them to take responsibility for their own lives. Basic strategies for helping adolescents to develop self-control are explained.

In Chapter 12, Pine and Krieger discuss the importance of working with adolescents to assess independent-living skills and to plan for their attainment. A model is presented that identifies the goals, both task- and process-related, of assessment and case planning with youths in foster care. A range of instruments are reviewed in order to illustrate criteria for selection.

9

Preparing Minority Foster Adolescents for Adulthood: The Need for Ethnic Competence

BENNIE M. STOVALL AND ROBIN KRIEGER

I t is generally agreed that minority foster adolescents, who largely belong to black, Hispanic, and Asian ethnic groups, face even greater obstacles than their Caucasian counterparts as they make their way toward adulthood. "Ethnicity patterns our thinking, feeling and behavior in both obvious and subtle ways. It plays a major role in determining what we eat, how we work, how we relax, how we celebrate holidays and rituals, and how we feel about life, death and illness" [McGoldrick 1982].

The ethnic differences of minority teenagers are frequently perceived as emotional disturbances; legitimate psychological difficulties are more likely to be met with restriction or even entrance into the criminal justice system rather than treatment; educational and career goals are often scaled down; cultural values and related goals are frequently misunderstood and maligned; and the critical need of every minority adolescent to discern and cope with the effect of racism is largely overlooked. As a result, minority foster adolescents are often less prepared to lead productive lives than their Caucasian counterparts and remain at greater risk of dependence on government systems throughout their lives.

In an effort to alter this picture, child welfare practitioners have been addressing the need to become ethnically competent in the planning and provision of services for young people in foster care. This goal is a critical concern because of the large number of black, Hispanic, and Asian-American young people in placement who are being cared for by white foster parents and social workers, even though it is increasingly recognized that it is preferable to place children with foster families of the same race. While all caregivers, regardless of heritage, need to be ethnically competent in their work with children, misunderstandings related to cultural differences are most likely to take place when the ethnic backgrounds of young people differ from those of the adults caring for them. Ethnic competence can help to overcome those differences, and it has been defined as being able to "conduct one's professional life in a way that is congruent with the behavior and expectations that members of a distinctive culture recognize as appropriate among themselves" (Green 1982: 52). Yet, as they strive to develop comprehensive programs, policies, and procedures, practitioners find that they are unclear about what such practice really means. Building on the concept of ethnic competence, this chapter considers the special challenges that minority adolescents in foster care face as they prepare for adulthood and explicates ethnically relevant policy and practice implications for foster parents, agencies, and social workers.

Minority Foster Adolescents

Most foster parents and social workers would agree that competence, coupled with empathy, warmth, and genuineness, is required when caring for young people who are working to overcome the challenges of leaving the foster care system. Additional competence is needed, however, when working with minority adolescents because they bring to the client-helper relationship cultural differences that must be understood if help is to be effectively given. These differences involve perceptions of self and others, styles of interacting, personal grooming, language, history, family patterns, relationship and parenting styles, self-image, values, and tastes in food and music. Frequently minority teenagers also face difficult challenges that stem directly from discrimination against their racial group. For example, they must learn to overcome rejection not only by biological parents but by the dominant society as well. This double rejection can result in pervasive feelings of anger and despair, which greatly impede progress toward adulthood. Youths who are hostile and hurt by the compounded rejection of family and community are especially vulnerable to insidious traps that are so often waiting for them: crime, substance abuse, early and unwanted pregnancies, and dropping out of school. Each of these alone has a deleterious effect on the attainment of adult life skills; in combination, a rewarding life may always remain elusive.

Ethnicity is expressed in myriad ways throughout one's life, including the ways in which one prepares for adulthood. The nuances must be understood and respected if minority adolescents are to be readied effectively for adulthood. For example, reactions to the onset of sexual maturity are ethnically determined. It is at this time that some cultures prescribe a set of behaviors for males that differ greatly from those for females. Awareness and respect for these differences are necessary for minority adolescents to be helped to take culturally acceptable steps toward adulthood.

> A white foster father, whose love of classical music was something that he wanted to share with his Puerto Rican foster son, was terribly hurt when the boy castigated him for his "acting just like a girl." The social worker helped the foster father to recognize that his foster son was attempting to communicate something about himself and his culture and was not trying to hurt. The worker further encouraged the foster father to expand his love of music to include Latino music, which his son might be more willing to accept. The social worker also helped the foster father to see that the young man's interest in more traditional male activities reflected his ethnic reality and should not be challenged at the time. As a result, the foster father later encouraged his foster son to become a protector of his younger sister, which was a more ethnically meaningful way for him to demonstrate his acceptance and understanding of his son's values. At the same time, this action increased the young man's willingness to take on adult responsibilities.

It is also important to remember that the effect of oppression can lead young people to seek ways to feel free of others and in control of themselves.

Hector was an excellent skater and got a job at the local skating rink. The hours were long and the pay was low; however, the manager of the rink told Hector that he could skate as long as he wanted, and that he could maintain the status of a rink employee at all times. His foster family felt that Hector had the skills to command a different and higher-paying job, which would then allow him to pay for skating as often as he would like. In a lengthy conversation with Hector, his social worker recognized that the skating job was something that gave him status, and that his peers thought Hector was to be envied. Hector told her how important it was to him that he did not have to report to anyone during his work shift, but rather, that others needed to ask his permission for things. This freedom and the opportunity to be in a decision-making role outweighed the value of a higher-paying job for Hector. The social worker helped the foster parents realize that the chance to possess status and authority were empowering for Hector, who had been the target of oppression throughout his life, and that they should encourage him to find equally appropriate and satisfying sources of personal strength.

As part of their adult responsibilities, minority foster youths are ultimately responsible for passing on their culture and values to their own children. To do so, they must have the opportunity to experience their culture and be familiar with its special foods, values, language, holidays, and more. Minority foster adolescents need to know their roots because this information will be used to shape the next generation. Soon enough, shaping the next generation will become a major life task.

Betty had a black father and a white mother. Betty's mother assumed the sole parenting role until she died, when Betty was nine. Betty appeared to be Caucasian and was placed in a white foster home. The placement, though nurturing and positive for Betty in many ways, provided no opportunity or encouragement for Betty to learn about or experience the black culture.

When Betty was 16, she became pregnant and gave birth to a baby whose physical characteristics clearly conveyed Betty's black heritage. Although the foster family was accepting, caring, and loving toward Betty and her child, they were unable, as was Betty, to convey adequately to Betty's child all that it means to be black.

Betty's placement in a white home could have been an appropriate choice had it provided opportunities for Betty to experience both of her cultures. The placement would require, however, that the foster parents understand Betty's cultural needs as a biracial child, and that they become ethnically competent to assist her with the transition to adulthood.

Finally, minority adolescents typically experience less personal power and control than their white peers and indeed may feel that they *should not* be directly responsible for themselves or take charge of their lives [Dana 1981]. Efforts to ready young people for life after foster care must appreciate this perspective. It seems misguided that independent-living training programs and materials for foster youths often have autonomy, initiative, and accomplishment as their foundation, when so many, as a result of being oppressed, have learned submission and have developed values that are contrary to initiative and accomplishment. This condition requires that efforts to prepare these young people for adulthood acknowledge their limited expectations and include goals related to empowerment.

Thus, in addition to the range of needs that young people may have due to their foster care status, minority adolescents present exigencies that require caregivers to become ethnically competent to prepare these youths effectively for adulthood.

Role of Foster Parents

The issue of ethnic competence is relevant for all foster parents, but especially those whose culture is different from that of the adolescent in their care. Ethnically competent foster parents are aware of their own cultural limitations; are open to cultural differences; possess a client-oriented, systematic learning style; use the youth's cultural resources; and acknowledge the youth's cultural integrity [Green 1982].

These foster parents understand that "the remarkable is sought in the most commonplace and that one's professional obligation is to discover the cognitive and affective weight of even the most mundane objects and events" [Green 1982: 56]. This behavior requires a willingness to look to the young persons as instructors of their culture, able to teach foster parents about their own ethnically determined preferences and needs. Ethnically competent foster parents also make differences in cultural backgrounds easy to talk about. Just as preparation for life after foster care must be openly addressed, including the parental expectation that the young person will move on, so too must the foster parents address the differences in ethnic identities and values. As foster parents welcome learning more about their young person's culture and his or her personal characteristics, they can become better able to adapt their independent-living preparation efforts to fit cultural expectations. The following example emphasizes the ways in which ethnic competence is critical in preparing minority adolescents for adult life.

Fifteen-year-old Juanita, of Mexican ancestry, was placed with the Anderson family in a white middle-class suburb of Houston. Mr. and Mrs. Anderson had reared two sons, who were both in college. They had also cared for an adolescent niece for two years because she had difficulty living at home with her parents. The Andersons felt proud of their abilities to work with, and even enjoy, teenagers. They welcomed the chance to become foster parents to Juanita, hoping that they could be trusted with the same degree of confidence that their niece had given them.

From the time Juanita moved into the Anderson home, however, she seemed mistrustful, withdrawn, and resentful. The Andersons expected that she might take a while to warm up to her new foster family, but by the third week together, after they had served a special welcoming meal, taken her to an outdoor concert, bought her some new school clothes, and borrowed a cassette player for her to have in her room, they felt hurt by Juanita's continued efforts to remain distant from them. The Andersons began to consider that perhaps she, like many teenagers, wanted to break free rather than join them, so they began to talk with Juanita about how she might learn to take care of herself once she reached adulthood. Their questions about earning money and arranging for a place to live were met with vague interest, though Juanita did agree she would like to earn some spending money. She said that she would contact the fast-food restaurant near her school and let Mr. Anderson know by the weekend how her job search progressed. Three weeks went by, during which Mr. Anderson periodically asked her about her job search, and Juanita always had an excuse for not making any efforts. The Andersons became concerned about her procrastination and were at a loss as to how to proceed without making Juanita retreat even further away.

Family life reached a shaky low when, in response to being invited to join the Andersons on a family picnic, she screamed, "So you can show me off and let everyone know what a good deed you're doing." The Andersons went to the picnic alone. When they came back, they found that Juanita had been in a fight with a girl at school and had several cuts and bruises. She refused to answer their questions about the reasons for the fight. Feeling that this was the last straw, the Andersons called Juanita's social worker to discuss whether she might be better off in another setting.

They felt they had made every effort to reach out to their foster daughter and had lost interest in trying any further.

Consider how this example might be changed if the Andersons knew more about their own cultural biases and how these conflict with Mexican culture. The Andersons share the five key values that characterize the dominant culture in the United States: active self-expression; equality and informality in social relationships; achievement and accomplishment; control of oneself and one's destiny while in pursuit of a better future; and individualism and autonomy experienced in democratic, nonauthoritarian relationships with others [Stewart et al. 1969]. These values shaped the way the Andersons treated Juanita and influenced their expectations of her. If they had been aware of Juanita's cultural differences, they would have understood that, as a Chicana, she had different characteristics:

Juanita expresses her emotions, and expects to be understood, intuitively, without having to give words to her feelings. The failure of her foster parents to nurture in response to her more spiritual manner of communication left Juanita feeling isolated and unloved. She responded by becoming withdrawn and hostile.

She finds it essential to connect to others as a way of realizing and empowering herself. Juanita saw little in the Andersons' household with which to affiliate; their choice of food, music, religious expression, and communication styles were signals to Juanita that she did not, and could not, belong.

She wishes that her foster home were cleaner and was shocked that Mrs. Anderson would leave the house for her evening activities without making sure that the house was completely in order. She began to think the Andersons expected her to clean the house, as if she were a servant.

She cannot understand why Mr. Anderson wants time alone to read the paper after returning from work. She experienced this behavior as a rejection and responded by keeping her distance from him.

She is being cautioned by her Latino friends that the Andersons "are doing her a favor" and are using her to make a political statement about their liberalism rather than being motivated by their concern for Juanita.

She expects to defend physically any assaults to her dignity with "*parar en seco*," or "stopping dry," which refers to guarding oneself. A Latino schoolmate began to deride Juanita with taunts of "Your parents are gringos." She was compelled to defend their, and her own, honor.

Had the Andersons been ethnically competent to care for Juanita, they would have done the following:

They would have chosen, for their welcoming dinner, tortillas, jalapeno peppers, and refried beans and would have played Mexican music, such as mariachi. They would learn about her other food and music preferences, and enjoy them with her regularly.

They would have paid attention to subtle communication cues, such as those that are best conveyed through the eyes and body language, to discern and feed back to Juanita what they thought she might be expressing.

They would have let Juanita know that it is acceptable for them to leave dishes in the sink and laundry unfolded if it means they will make it to an appointment on time. In an effort to respect her feelings about cleanliness, they would have encouraged Juanita to keep her room in a manner in which she would be comfortable. They would have also made an effort to keep the house cleaner.

They would have told Juanita about their own need for psychological and physical space as a way to refuel themselves. They would help her to see that a choice for time alone can be a good way to take care of oneself and is not always a rejection of others. They might have helped Juanita to try this technique for herself, in addition to understanding this behavior in others. And they would also have tried to accommodate her need for closeness and availability.

They would have warned Juanita that her peers may try to make her suspicious of their reasons for becoming foster parents. They would have shared the events leading up to their own decision to care for Juanita, including their experiences with their sons and niece, and the qualities they see in her that make them care.

They would have acknowledged that assaults on one's dignity should never be tolerated and that they recognize how painful her schoolmate's words were. They would also have pointed out how violence often leads to more violence and could lead to legal jeopardy as well. They would have talked with her about other socially acceptable ways to defend oneself, offering to accompany her to school where she could explain her actions to officials, and encouraging her to invite friends home, who could then serve as a support network.

They would have engaged closely with her in a search for employment, They would have helped her to connect an interest she has, such as music, with a job, such as clerk in a record shop. They would have been ready resources throughout the initial phases of the search, perhaps helping her to fill out applications, thereby respecting her need for connection.

They would have shown interest in whether Juanita would like to attend mass, whether a Latino parish would be preferred, and what religious figures she might like to have in her room (e.g., the statue of the Virgin of Guadalupe).

They would have affirmed their commitment to helping her prepare for life after foster care, expressing their hopes that Juanita can have a happy family life of her own. They would also discuss with her the skills that are needed by all adults, regardless of their future plans, and help her plan to achieve them.

As this example demonstrates, an ethnically competent approach to fostering adolescents is essential if their preparation for adulthood is to be accomplished; if the relationship between foster parents and young people is to be satisfying; and if opportunities for a productive life are to be increased. The example also points to the following range of characteristics of ethnically competent foster parents of minority adolescents:

Recognition of both the strengths and limits of their own cultural values
Appreciation of cultural differences, recognizing that there is no single correct way of thinking or behaving
Valuing of cultural identity, with conviction about the important place that it has in shaping one's self-image
Acknowledgment that one does not have to be a member of a particular ethnic group to be ethnically competent to parent a child of that heritage
Recognition of human strengths

Role of the Agency

Agencies, like the individuals they comprise, can develop and project ethnic competence. In fact, agency support of, and attention to, the needs of minority youths send essential messages to foster parents, social workers, and young people that ethnic heritage must be upheld. Here are some ways to develop and promote an agency's ethnic competence.

Reflection of Ethnic Styles

An agency's ultimate reason for developing ethnic competence is the cultivation of minority empowerment, or "a true working partnership between minority and nonminority staff members, who cooperate to provide services that in turn empower clients to meet their needs" [Gallegos 1982]. One way for the agency to accomplish this task is to identify and work with minority consultants, who should represent the range of cultural groups in the community. Possible sources include religious and spiritual leaders, community settlement houses, and local chapters of ethnically focused organizations. Perhaps convened as an advisory group, the consultants would be responsible for ensuring that the agency is cognizant and respectful of the community's ethnic preferences, styles, strengths, and needs. To achieve this goal, the consultant can identify and help to recruit minority board members, staff members, and foster parents, all of whom are necessary for an agency to develop and carry out ethnically sensitive policies and practice. The consultants can also suggest minority mentors, who can serve as role models and community anchors for minority youths leaving care. In addition, the consultants could provide foster parents and staff members with regular in-service training sessions on issues related to that particular agency's progress toward achieving ethnic competence.

Some members of ethnic groups, such as Puerto Ricans, typically seek mental health assistance from family or friends. Agencies planning on serving such clients must establish themselves as capable of functioning as quasi-extended family. Relationships between staff members and clients should be mutual, personal yet respectful, and non-hierarchical. Clients should feel able to stop in to say hello or report on various elements of their lives; children should feel free to drop in to show off a report card; and staff members and clients might easily work together on painting the agency's community room or coaching a baseball team. In addition, rather than focusing on the future-oriented, structured time frame that is characteristic of many institutions, agencies serving more present-time-oriented cultures would start sessions around rather than at specific times, avoid the use of waiting lists, and be able to respond immediately to crises. Moreover, they would emphasize home visits and staff involvement in community activities that would allow interactions to take place in natural settings [McGowan 1988].

Systemwide, consistent, and carefully implemented information sharing is certain to produce the kind of useful change and growth that agencies seek. The process of developing ethnic competence is slow and serious. Efforts to trivialize it, through such inadequate means as offering intermittent workshops or recruiting token minority board members or staff members, must be avoided.

Training Considerations

Training for ethnic competence should be required of all service providers, regardless of race or ethnicity, thus underscoring that all foster parents and social workers alike can increase their ethnic competence. It should also be provided for board members, administrators, and others affiliated with the agency so that the process of becoming ethnically competent can permeate the agency.

It is recommended that training be offered by integrated teams made up of foster parents, staff members, board members, minority consultants, and youths and that it emphasize the importance of the following considerations:

Understanding human behavior from different cultural points of view
Clarifying values in light of dominant and minority perspectives
Debunking myths and biases about minorities
Identifying barriers to effective engagement of clients and competent service delivery, including the effect of interpersonal and institutional racism
Eliminating the fallacy that minority helpers do not need training, or that nondirect-contact staff members, board members, administrators, and others do not need to become ethnically competent
Stressing self-awareness, and the influence of one's personal beliefs, values, and biases on one's behavior
Disseminating information about various ethnic groups to highlight history, ethnic realities, cultural expressions, language, food, music, religion, perceptions about the dominant group, role of and relationships with government, norms, family views, values, and the strengths of ethnic individuals and families
Pointing up the influence of ethnic realities on the daily lives of minorities, and other survival issues
Modifying traditional practice to include consideration of ethnic factors such as responses to persons of power, eye contact, and the meaning of self-determination

Outcome Assessment

Agencies can discern whether minority youths are being prepared for adulthood in an ethnically competent way by monitoring their independent-living plans. Administrators, perhaps aided by minority consultants, must be sure that minority adolescents are being encouraged to identify and work toward goals that are consistent with their cultural values and interests.

> Damon is sixteen years old. His mother is Vietnamese and his father a black American. His physical features reflect his Asian ancestry, yet all agency records identify him solely as a black child. Damon has been in and out of foster homes for the last ten years; throughout the long case record on Damon, there were no references to any efforts to make him aware of his Asian background or to acquaint him with Asians in the community.
>
> Damon's social worker, Mr. Allen, made use of Damon's having just seen "Platoon," a film about the Vietnam War, to talk with him about his own Vietnamese background and to begin to find answers to many of Damon's questions that were stirred by the film. Damon was particularly interested in the identity of his mother. Through work with a local refugee-serving organization, Mr. Allen was able to locate a church whose congregation was largely Vietnamese, and to identify a family that was interested in having Damon join them in church activities, including a family picnic and several trips to the beach. Through continued record searches, Damon eventually learned that his mother had been killed in the war, but that she had two sisters who had immigrated to the United States. As Mr. Allen helps Damon mourn the loss of a mother he never knew, plans are under way to locate and connect Damon with his aunts. Well aware, however, of the historic tensions between many Vietnamese people and the children of black American soldiers, Mr. Allen sought counsel from members of both groups to find ways to smooth Damon's entry into his family.

We know that as adolescents prepare to move on, they must be able to look back on as complete a picture as possible in order that their identities be solid enough to carry them through the stresses of becoming a young adult. Agency leadership in recognizing the importance of filling in the details related to a young person's unknown heritage, unidentified family members, and untapped ethnic resources in the community is essential if minority foster adolescents are to be prepared for adulthood.

Role of the Social Worker

Competent social workers are always attuned to the quality of the fit between foster parents and young people. The process of learning to live together can be difficult for foster families, and social workers are often called upon to help. These negotiations become more complex when foster parents and youths come from different racial and ethnic backgrounds. It is the responsibility of the social worker to be ethnically competent; that is, sensitive to the importance of ethnicity generally, and aware of the values and preferences of their minority clients, specifically. This approach translates into the practice of empowerment, as social workers share power with the adolescents in their care. That result can be achieved by conducting with each youth a needs assessment that identifies culturally relevant strengths, needs, and goals (see Chapter 12 by Pine and Krieger in this volume). Linking adolescents to ethnic mentors in the community is another step toward empowerment, as is being attuned to culturally relevant rites of passage to adulthood.

Social workers should be cautioned that with empowerment comes an adolescent's greatest expectations, which can ease depression but create anxiety, as youths overestimate their abilities to meet expanded challenges. Furthermore, social workers must recognize the need to help young people manage their anxiety by practicing new behaviors in attainable steps and by affirming each success; the key here is setting the adolescents up to succeed and helping them to resist the temptation to set overly limited goals as a way of preventing anxiety. The latter step may be particularly difficult if the young person's previous case plans have been influenced by racist tendencies to misunderstand or underestimate the abilities of minorities. Ethnically competent social workers have a mandate to help minority youths to reach as far as they can. When necessary, therefore, case plans should make use of a repertoire of treatment approaches offered by the best providers available; education and career goals should be defined in accordance with a youths' potential and interests, without being scaled down; and efforts to have youths visit with kin should be made to reflect the full range of individuals who might be considered family within a given culture. It is also the responsibility of the social worker to help foster parents understand that care is not, as many might believe, "color-blind," and that fostering minority adolescents requires special skills that can be learned. Social workers can encourage foster parents to see the adolescents in their care as teachers, pointing out the esteem-enhancing aspects as well as the educational values of casting young people in this role. They can join foster parents at culturally oriented training sessions and follow these by identifying ways in which foster parents might reach youths in ethnically meaningful ways. Ethnicity, however, is an experience that, in its most complete form, is reserved for members of that ethnic group. It is unrealistic to expect that social workers and foster parents can become sufficiently competent in a culture other than their own to absorb its richness completely; consequently, while social workers can learn about and appreciate a new culture and share their awareness with foster parents, they must make every effort to link young people with adults and peers of the community who share the adolescent's background. Thus, when foster adolescents are placed with families from different cultures, social workers must appreciate that the youths need a "dual placement," that is, one that requires the social worker to use the agency's ethnic mentors to augment the work of foster parents in order to ensure that the young person is properly exposed to cultural influences. This intervention is likely to be consistent with the youth's expectation, in that it makes use of extended "family" and relies on mutual help. It also eases the otherwise unfair burden on the foster parent of being the sole communicator of ethnic identity.

Conclusion

Foster parents, social workers, and agencies can and must become ethnically competent in order to help minority foster adolescents as they make their way to adulthood. Interdependent-living preparation that does not include respect for and attention to the special needs of ethnic minorities will leave a substantial portion of emancipating young people unequipped to handle even the usual stresses of adulthood and even less so the additional demands posed when minority adolescents face the effect of racism. Ethnically competent preparation for interdependent living requires a systemwide, consistent, and carefully implemented effort to change attitudes and practices of all those responsible for providing services to this population of adolescents: foster parents, social workers, agency administrators, and board members. Pride in one's ethnic heritage is a tremendous source of joy and identity for many people. Ethnically competent caretakers and service providers can help ensure that minority foster youths experience this necessary and very human connection to themselves, their past, and their future.

REFERENCES

Dana, Richard H. (editor). Human Services for Cultural Minorities. Baltimore, MD: University Park Press, 1981.

Gallegos, J. S. "Planning and administering services for minority groups." In Austin, M. J., and Hershey, W. E., Handbook on Mental Health Administration. San Francisco, CA: Jossey-Bass, 1982, 87–105.

Green, James W. Cultural Awareness in Human Services. Englewood Cliffs, NJ: Prentice-Hall, 1982.

McGoldrick, M. "Ethnicity and family therapy." In McGoldrick, M., Pearce, J. K., and Giordano, J., Ethnicity and Family Therapy. New York: The Guilford Press, 1982, 3–30.

McGowan, Brenda G. "Helping Puerto Rican families at risk." In Jacobs, C., and Bowles, D. (editors), Ethnicity and Race—Critical Concepts in Social Work. Silver Spring, MD: National Association of Social Workers, 1988, 48–64.

Stewart, E.C., Danielian, J., and Festes, R. J. Stimulating Intercultural Communication Through Role Play. Alexandria, VA: Human Resources Research Organization, 1969.

10

Maltreatment: Obstacles to Successful Emancipation

EMILY JEAN McFADDEN

Physical, sexual, and emotional abuse and physical and emotional neglect create negative effects that may hinder an adolescent's strivings for emancipation. For the youth without a history of maltreatment, adolescence is a time of profound change and development cognitively [Elkind 1968], emotionally [Erikson 1950], physically and sexually [Silber 1980], morally [Eisenman 1968], and socially [Havighurst 1972]. Growth in these areas is likely to occur much less evenly in maltreated youths, who may remain fixed at earlier developmental levels. Consequently, they may have different experiences in interacting with the normal institutions of adolescent life (for example, the family—biological and foster, school, work, and the peer group) than will their peers without a history of abuse or neglect. Helping a youth in foster care to overcome the negative effects of maltreatment requires that caregivers understand and deal effectively with potential obstacles to achieving developmental milestones.

Following a brief overview of the effect of maltreatment on development, this chapter examines the consequences of specific types of abuse and neglect on adolescents in foster care. Then, with a focus on the partnership of foster parent and worker, various interventions are considered for meeting foster adolescents' needs for health care, educational and vocational, or recreation services, as they are helped to overcome the effects of earlier abuse and to prepare for interdependent living.

Effects of Maltreatment

Konopka asserts that "the period of adolescence is as significant a period in life for the development of the total personality as are the first years in childhood" [Konopka 1982: 93], and that there are six key experiences to be worked through that she calls "firsts." She delineates these as experiencing physical/sexual maturity, experiencing withdrawal of and from adult benevolent protection, consciousness of self in interaction, reevaluation of values, becoming an active participant in society, and a life force or extraordinary physical capacity.

The adolescent in foster care who has been seriously abused or neglected experiences these challenges, so necessary to the transition to adulthood, problematically. For example, sexually abused youths may have a very negative reaction to the onset of sexual maturity. They may be terrified of normal body changes and believe them to be the result of early sexual injury. Sexually abused youths may hate their bodies or regard them as a thing to be used, much as their perpetrators did.

The withdrawal of benevolent adult protection can be profoundly alarming to youths who have been maltreated. Some youths exiting foster care may never have experienced benevolent adult relationships, while others may have finally landed, emotionally wrung out, in a caring foster home. After a possibly wrenching struggle to develop trust in nurturing caregivers, these youths are unlikely to see foster parents' efforts to support emancipation as benevolent. Instead, they are more likely to feel rejected or pushed out of the nest.

For maltreated youths in foster care, experiencing consciousness of self in interaction may be confusing and overwhelming. If the consciousness of self evolves from reflected images of others, then the multiplicity of caregivers and the host of conflicting messages given to the youths over the years will yield, at best, a series of warped and distorted images, reflecting back with the nightmarish quality of distorted mirrors in a carnival fun house.

The reevaluation of values will also create difficult challenges for maltreated youths in care. They will have learned, early in life, a number of powerful lessons such as "Might makes right" and "Big people hurt and use smaller, weaker people." Moral development depends to a significant degree on the presence of empathy and an awareness of the rules. Youths who have not been treated with kindness will have difficulty with empathy; those who have lived in a series of environments with conflicting and confusing rules will not have internalized a consistent sense of fair play. Moreover, maltreated youths may have little or no reason to trust in adults, let alone absorb their values.

Becoming an active participant in society may also be a difficult challenge for maltreated youths. Maltreatment creates passive victims, not autonomous actors. Compliance ensures survival but may seriously undermine a youth's sense of competence and self-esteem, which are necessary to achieving normal social growth and responsible citizenship.

Finally, the life force, that exuberant physical energy that carries many adolescents forward into adulthood, may be stunted or at least minimized by earlier maltreatment. Many physically abused youths have lived so long with chronic pain that they do not know what it is like to feel good. Years of emotional neglect may have left them depleted and exhausted, unable to bounce back from even the minor woes of adolescent life and impending adulthood.

These effects of maltreatment on development and consequently on a youth's ability to master the skills needed for interdependence will, of course, be influenced by the youth's individual experiences. Specifically, the age of onset, severity of maltreatment, and relationship with the abusing adult will be vital factors in determining the effect of abuse or neglect. Equally important in mediating its effect are the availability of support and nurturance from other adults and the child's own constitutional or genetic qualities that may serve as a defense. Moreover, in addition to the overall effect of maltreatment, other consequences may result from specific types; that is, physical abuse, sexual abuse, and emotional neglect.

Consequences of Physical Abuse

Adolescents who have been physically abused may experience a variety of developmental blocks and difficulties, exhibited in a wide range of behaviors, any of which may impede a smooth transition to adult roles. Some abused youths may set up situations in which they will be scapegoated and punished, others develop patterns of being the aggressor rather than the victim [Bender 1976]. Overt, aggressive behavior often reflects the foster child's effort to escape from painful feelings, as well as an identification with the aggressor. Some abused children have serious emotional problems with respect to self-concept, relationships with peers and adults, attachment, and the capacity to trust others [Timberlake 1979; Kinard 1980; Burch 1980].

Anger and Fear

The abused child is both angry and fearful. If the youth who was abused as a child has not had the opportunity to resolve the anger and fear, these feelings may perpetuate a cycle of acting-out behavior that may provoke further retaliation by foster parents and others and present serious impediments to the achievement of life styles (see Chapter 4 by Levine in this volume). Tyrell's case is an example.

> Tyrell had been severely abused at age thirteen. He had many difficulties in obeying limits set by foster parents, leading to placement disruption, a runaway episode, and, in his last foster home, an abuse episode when his foster father beat him with a belt. Tyrell was both angry with parental figures and fearful of them. He would do "sneaky" things to anger his new foster parents and then appear to be "asking for it."
>
> This pattern carried over to his work relationships. In his first job at a fast-food restaurant, Tyrell blew up at the manager when asked to do things he didn't want to do. First he would comply with the request, but not do the job well. Then, when reprimanded, his explosive anger would surface and overcome his fear of reprisal. When Tyrell was fired, he took money from the cash register. The foster parents recognized that Tyrell had difficulties both at home and at work and insisted on therapy for him. They also helped him to see how expressing anger in this way made keeping a job impossible and encouraged him to talk it out with them when he was feeling this way.

Adolescents with a history of physical abuse face a constant struggle with anger and aggression. Much of their energy is spent in trying to keep the anger under control because of the earlier learned fear of the anger of others. If anger is extremely controlled, however, it is turned inward, resulting in depression or, worse, potential suicide [Sharlin and Shenlar 1987]. Erupting outward, the anger may take the form of aggression toward peers, adult authority, or younger youths. It may carry over to adult behavior in future intimate relationships or parenting roles.

Distorted Body Image

The youth who has been physically abused may have a distorted body image. The whole sense of self is built on the way one feels *in* one's body, and the way one feels *about* one's body. The ego is first and foremost a body ego. Physical maltreatment, therefore, causes emotional damage as well as physical damage.

Diminished Self-Esteem

Physically abused children have more difficulty with self-concept than nonabused children, see themselves as different from others, and are more likely to perceive themselves as unpopular [Kinard 1980]. If these problems are not dealt with, the adolescent's difficulty with self-esteem may lead to other problems. For example, there may be a relationship between adolescent pregnancy and the effects of physical abuse and neglect—specifically, low self-esteem. And, while the rates of teenage pregnancy have risen primarily because more adolescents are sexually active, a combination of factors may render a young woman leaving foster care more vulnerable to premature parenthood. Deprivation of body pleasure, fear of rejection, feelings of isolation, and low tolerance for frustration are all associated with the low self-esteem that often results from abuse [Haynie 1980; Crawford and Furstenberg 1985].

Trisha's case illustrates how low self-esteem can cause serious problems for a youth in foster care and how foster parents can intervene to help a youth make important decisions in preparing for her life after foster care.

Trisha had been through a series of foster home placements. She felt that she must be unlovable because her mother had not tried to get her back nor had she wanted to see Trisha for the past few years. Trisha was overweight, did not date, and was not popular. She told her foster parents that she wanted to have a baby to love and wished she had a boyfriend. She often reverted to babyish ways of seeking attention and affection from her foster mother, yet in many ways she seemed afraid of physical closeness.

The foster parents were surprised when Trisha had a miscarriage; they had not known she was sexually active. They were concerned that she might have been exploited, and that if she had a child she would not be able to cope. In talking to the worker, they realized that more was at stake than just preventing a pregnancy. Trisha became involved in counseling to improve her self-esteem, and the worker helped her enroll in a teen charm school. The foster mother began going to Weight Watchers with Trisha and both lost unwanted pounds. Trisha began to make a few friends and joined the youth group for adolescents facing emancipation. She decided that she did not want a child until later, when she would be more prepared for adulthood.

Impervious to Pain

Some youths who have experienced serious physical trauma have developed the emotional defense of appearing impervious to pain. As children, they learned to disconnect from body sensation. Having lived with chronic pain, they have difficulty in identifying what bothers them or in realizing that they hurt. They may ignore physical signals of pain or illness and fail to get needed medical attention. Some abused youths may dig or pick at their bodies without any apparent expression of pain. Foster parents are rightfully appalled at such evidence of self-mutilation and need help in dealing with the behavior. Moreover, an adolescent who has not received adequate health care services may still experience physical problems related to the earlier abuse. One youth had lived with chronic shoulder pain for years because his shoulder had been dislocated and wrenched when he was thrown by a parent against the wall. He did not complain of the pain, but an alert foster parent noted that he did not appear to have free and normal use of his left arm. The foster parent sought medical services for him, which included an extended course of physical therapy.

Poor Coordination

A similar aftermath of earlier physical abuse is difficulty with motor coordination. An adolescent who has not learned body boundaries may be constantly banging into doorways, falling over furniture, or generally displaying the stiff, rigid, or awkward movements indicative of poor coordination. For some, poor coordination may have a physical basis in minimal brain damage received from earlier battering or shaking. For others, it may have been a maladaptive response to an unsafe environment. Tonya's case provides a good illustration of problematic motor coordination and how she was helped to overcome this potential obstacle to getting and keeping a job—essential skills of adulthood.

> Tonya got her first job at a local fast-food chain, working behind the counter. Her supervisor was concerned because she was clumsy: dropping money, spilling the customer's drinks, and bumping into other counter persons. She had earlier gone near the grill and burned her arm. She had not complained, and the foster parents didn't notice the burn, which was covered by her long sleeves. Several days later, her manager noted the burn and insisted that she get medical treatment. Tonya became angry, said the burn didn't bother her, and refused to go to the doctor. The manager was concerned that she was accident-prone and called the foster parents about Tonya's injury and "attitude."
>
> Tonya's foster parents found that the situation was more complicated than simply persuading Tonya to get medical attention for the burn. They requested an evaluation, which revealed minor neurological damage. The foster parents and worker helped Tonya to locate different employment where her poor coordination would not be a deterrent to success, and her body image could be improved.

Indicators of Physical Abuse

In sum, there are many negative consequences of physical abuse. In their efforts to help adolescents overcome these and prepare for interdependent living, workers and foster parents should be alert for the following signs:

Low self-esteem
Poor body image
Problems in coordination
Absence of normal reactions to pain
Chronic minor physical problems
Alternating cycle of anger and fear
Aggression
Emotional neediness
Difficulty in forming relationships

Consequences of Sexual Abuse

Awareness that sexual abuse of children is widespread is growing. Current estimates are that one in four girls is sexually abused. Although the corresponding figure on male victims is lower, there is agreement that sexual abuse of boys is seriously unrecognized and underreported [Brown 1979; Nasjleti 1980; Zaphiris 1986].

The author believes that far more than half of the adolescents in care have been sexually abused. Many are unidentified by the agencies responsible for them. They may have come into care for reasons of dependency, delinquency, or abuse. They may have returned to care as the result of a broken adoption. Some may even have been sexually abused by earlier foster parents (McFadden and Ryan 1986). Few of these youths are able to trust a social worker, therapist, or foster parent enough to reveal painful secrets. Male youths especially are fearful of making such revelations for fear of losing a shaky sense of masculinity. These youths are obviously at risk for further problems if they have not faced and laid to rest the trauma of earlier sexual abuse.

Paradoxically, youths who are in care because they were sexually abused may have also been placed at risk by the interventions of various helping systems. Some youths feel it is better not to tell than to face police investigations, further reprisals on their families, or painful and frightening court appearances in which one is forced to testify against a parent or other significant person. Seeing one's family break up, or facing a brutal cross-examination, can create ineradicable painful feelings that may seriously inhibit a youth's ability to ask for help in the future.

For both males and females, sexual abuse may have been devastating or minor depending on a number of factors: age of onset, relationship with the abuser, severity of the abuse, whether force was used, reactions by significant people to the disclosure, whether treatment was obtained, and whether professional intervention caused further trauma.

Even though adolescents in foster care may have received earlier treatment for sexual abuse, many of its consequences persist. Unresolved issues may reappear each time the youth reaches a new developmental stage. Since therapeutic intervention can help children to express feelings and understand a situation only at their current cognitive level, it may be necessary for a youth, male or female, to return to counseling at each new stage. Clearly, the process of emancipation from foster care, with its inherent loss of security and movement toward the world of adult sexuality, may be a critical time for youths who have been sexually abused. Such was the case with Lisa:

When Lisa reached puberty she had alarmed her adoptive parents by leaving her soiled sanitary pads lying around in public view. She had also refused to bathe and developed an offensive body odor. After her adoption broke down and she was placed in residential treatment, she dealt with sexual abuse issues that had resurfaced. She had believed that menstruation was a sign that her body had really been damaged by sexual abuse. The presence of menstrual blood seemed irrefutable evidence. She had hoped to keep people away from her by neglecting hygiene. Treatment had helped her to understand and come to terms with her changing body. Her later adolescence, spent in foster care, was uneventful until she began to prepare for emancipation. During her senior year in high school she broke up with her boyfriend, stopped eating, refused to go to school, and began having nightmares.

The worker and foster parents were puzzled and Lisa could give no explanation except that she had been upset by something that had happened with her boyfriend. Counseling helped Lisa to understand that when she had intercourse with her boyfriend, it had triggered old feelings from the childhood sexual abuse. She had felt frightened and out of control, just as she had at age eight. The only place she felt safe and protected was in her foster home. She had had a panic attack at school after her health and hygiene class. With counseling and the support of her foster parents, Lisa was able to return to school. She was also encouraged to assert herself with her boyfriend and take more control of her sexuality.

Adolescents who have been sexually abused may respond to the maltreatment in a variety of ways. Some will receive therapy and begin to move toward recovery. Others will repeat past patterns of victimization and continue to be sexually exploited or become sexually promiscuous. Still others will defend against their fears of victimization by identifying with the perpetrator [Brandt and Tisza 1979]. They reduce their anxiety about the past trauma by victimizing instead of being the victim:

Kimberly had been babysitting for a neighbor as a way of earning money for incidentals. The neighbor's four-year-old son began crying whenever Kim came to the house, and begged his mother not to leave. Finally he complained to his mother, "Don't make me stay with Kim. She kisses my peepee and puts her finger up my butt." Kimberly was fired immediately.

As they are helped to prepare for adult roles, foster youths who have been sexually abused may need to learn that there is a difference between sexual feelings and sexual behavior. This was Hank's struggle:

Hank had gotten a summer job with a recreation department as a counselor in training at its day camp. One day after roughhousing with the younger boys in his team, he walked off the job and quit. He refused to give an explanation to his supervisor, worker, or foster parents. Only much later did he confide to his foster father that he had quit his job to protect himself, because he had been aware of feeling sexually aroused by the younger boys while they "rassled." He said "I didn't want to hurt them like I'd been hurt, but I was all turned on and scared I would get out of control. I'm afraid I'll never be able to work with kids."

Some youths who were sexually abused feel they need strong limits to help control their behavior. They also need therapy to help them understand their feelings. It is not unusual for adolescents in care to have sexual feelings about a foster parent. Workers should discuss this matter openly with foster parents and help foster parents to set boundaries around sexualized behavior. Many youths in care have over the years developed eroticized or seductive behaviors as a response to earlier emotional neglect and sexual abuse. Significant adults in their earlier lives may have reinforced inappropriate behavior such as touching by giving them attention only when they touched in this manner. Unfortunately, some foster parents and other adults misinterpret the youth's behavior as being seductive, when in reality the youth is simply using a repertoire of earlier developed survival behaviors, asking for attention or affection, not sex.

Sexually exploited youths struggle with a number of other consequences of the earlier sexual abuse. Some remain mistrustful of adults and are suspicious of any one who may reach out to them. This attitude presents a real challenge for a youth such as Darryl who, in preparing for interdependence, needs to be able to make essential social connections to others in the community:

Darryl was working with a paint crew, painting houses in the neighborhood. The boss of the crew took an interest in him and invited him out for dinner. Darryl refused, just as he had refused an opportunity to go to a ball game with an older neighbor.

Although sexually abused youths may have experienced too much sex at too early an age, it should not be assumed that they are sexually sophisticated. Most sexually abused children are emotionally neglected and brought up in an atmosphere of secrecy, sexual ignorance, and a denial of sexuality. Thus they may know even less about sexuality than peers who received a normal sex education. Many adolescents who were sexually abused still retain childish fantasies about sexuality and are as uninformed as Ronald was:

> When Ronald was seven, he had been repeatedly orally penetrated by his stepfather, who ejaculated in his mouth. Ronald never told anyone. He remembered that his mother told him, "Babies grow in your tummy when you swallow a seed." For many years, Ronald had worried that somehow a baby would grow inside of him from the semen he had swallowed. As he grew older, he knew that males didn't have babies, but he continued to worry about the semen that had gone into his stomach.
>
> In early adolescence, Ronald engaged in oral sex with a stranger for money, and his fears resurfaced. This time he was afraid his stomach was rotting. He began gagging and even vomiting when he had certain types of food. By age sixteen he had an ulcer. His foster mother gently inquired why bland foods such as milk and ice cream seemed to upset his stomach. After Ronald blurted out that it reminded him of semen and told them of his worries, his foster parent and worker saw that he received both treatment and appropriate sex education. Ronald's health improved.

Boys who have been sexually abused may have great concern about their gender identity and sexual orientation, which is confounded by homophobia. They may not be aware that for the majority of adolescents homosexual experiences constitute a discrete period of developmental curiosity, which is discarded as heterosexual interests predominate [Cates 1987]. These youths need reassurance that the abusive incidents do not necessarily determine sexual orientation.

The emergence of sexuality in adolescence and the need to achieve sexual maturity in preparation for adult roles are particular challenges for the adolescent who has been sexually exploited or abused. To help youths in foster care overcome any of the problems resulting from past abuse, foster parents and workers need, as a first step, to recognize behaviors that might give clues to such a history. In summary, these include:

> Problems with digestion such as gagging and vomiting, spastic colon, and fecal impaction
>
> Inappropriate sexual behaviors such as excessive masturbation, inappropriate touching, fear and revulsion or preoccupation in relation to sex, sexual promiscuity, and sexual aggression with younger children or animals

Fear and anger expressed as fear of being alone with other people, nightmares, and overly aggressive behavior
Low self-esteem, particularly a damaged body image as expressed in
poor hygiene or a deliberate attempt to appear unattractive

Moreover, even though youths may have been appropriately identified, diagnosed, and treated for sexual abuse at an earlier stage of
their development, it is critical that caregivers understand the potential need for further help. Otherwise, developmental blocks may impede the emancipation process, or the youths may leave care only
to be revictimized.

Consequences of Emotional Neglect

Physical abuse and sexual abuse are almost always accompanied
by emotional abuse or neglect. Even when a child has not been physically abused, emotional neglect may be devastating. Indeed, some
research suggests that emotional neglect is potentially more damaging
to development than abuse [Augoustinos 1987]. The damage to development may be caused, in great part, by the inconsistent and negative
parental attention that was part of the actual abuse. For example,
children who are sexually abused are also emotionally neglected by
parents who have failed to protect them and provide the nurture
and attention all children need, made the child responsible for the
adult's happiness, created an atmosphere of secrecy that denied reality,
and valued the child only for sexual activity. Parents who physically
abuse a child frequently diminish a child's self-esteem with verbal
abuse, create an atmosphere of fearful unpredictability, expect more
than the child can ever accomplish, set up a role reversal in which
the child is supposed to nurture the adult, and punish the child for
normal expression of feelings. Thus, the feelings of loss associated
with abuse may be even more difficult to deal with than the bereave-
ment following the death of a parent [Kinard 1980].
Emotional neglect may not be solely the result of earlier abuse
or rejection by biological parents. It may also represent the culmina-
tion of many traumatic moves within the child welfare system [Garba-
rino 1980]. The child who has been rejected by foster and/or adoptive
parents finds in adolescence that the earlier sense of loss from biological parents is intensified; thus the youth's self-blame and self-hatred
may be reinforced. Institutional abuse by an ineffective foster care

system may have included a shortage of appropriate placements [Hoek-stra 1984], lack of treatment or misdiagnosis [Shaughnessy 1984], or actual physical or sexual abuse by foster parents or other caregivers [McFadden and Ryan 1986; Vera Institute 1982]. The system is often guilty of physical or medical neglect in its failure to provide adequate health care services for youths in care [Hochstadt et al. 1987]. Emancipating youths have often had a long succession of workers and have learned that even caring workers are busy and do not stay long at their jobs. Hence, the child welfare system is viewed by some adolescents in foster care as an abusive, authoritarian, or indifferent parent. Such was Mary's view:

> After telling of abuse in an institution and her difficulties in adjusting to a foster home, seventeen-year-old Mary was asked in an interview what she thought of the child welfare system's care of her. Her face contorted in a scowl. "Bullshit," she said. "Disgusting."

Alienated youths are at particular risk of depression and suicide [Loppnow 1985].

Because of their experiences with abusive parents and perhaps an equally abusive system, some adolescents may be wary and mistrustful of their foster parents. They may use negative behavior to test the relationship. If foster parents can look beyond the acting-out of an abused youth and focus on the unmet emotional needs of the young child within, some of the mistrust and emotional neglect can be alleviated. Alicia was fortunate in her placement with foster parents who understood this.

> Alicia was a sixteen-year-old who had been physically and sexually abused at age seven. She had been removed from her mother's custody, returned, removed again, returned again, and removed again before parental rights were terminated. Several foster placements and an adoptive placement had broken down because of Alicia's inappropriate and sexualized behaviors.
>
> Her foster parents worked closely with the therapist on building Alicia's self-esteem and trying to provide enough nurturing attention that she would not have to behave in an overly flirtatious manner or touch others inappropriately to be noticed. While setting limits with Alicia, the foster parents focused on her emotional needs. They spent a great deal of time with her doing skill-building activities, playing games, reading, and nourishing their relationship. They realized that Alicia's emotional

development had lagged around age seven and that she had not yet caught up. Although Alicia lived in a physically mature adolescent body, she had the needs to be nurtured of a seven-year-old.

As Alicia came to trust the foster parents and to feel that they valued her for her own sake, not her sexualized touching, she stopped trying to relate to them in inappropriate ways. She could ask for attention and communicate her needs directly.

Indicators of Emotional Neglect

As with other types of abuse, recognition of a history of emotional abuse or neglect is an essential first step in helping a foster youth to prepare for interdependent living. Behaviors that might indicate such a history include:

Suicidal ideation
Lack of controls and impulsivity
Poor self-esteem and little sense of self
Withdrawal, running from closeness, or escaping through fantasy
Difficulty in relationships
Hostile-dependent behaviors and relationships
Poor school performance
Chronic depression, sometimes masked by anxiety
Little hope for a positive future
Difficulties in handling separations
Testing for rejection

Intervention Strategies

The problems and behaviors resulting from maltreatment of all types influence an adolescent's efforts to face the major challenges of the transition to adulthood. Foster parents and workers are particularly essential in helping these youths deal effectively with and overcome the physical, social, and psychological scars of the past, while mastering the developmental tasks of their approaching adulthood. Working together and involving the foster youth, the three—worker, foster parent, and adolescent in care—constitute a team. The team engages others from various sectors as the youth's needs for services are determined, including mental health services, health care, education, vocational services, and recreation. Hence, the youth benefits directly from the service received as well as learning from trusted adults essential consumer skills in obtaining needed services. This dual approach is critical since the skills—tangible and intangible (as discussed in Chapter 1 in this volume)—that the maltreated adolescent must acquire in the process of becoming a competent adult depend largely on a healthy sense of self and successful interactions with peers, helpers, and caregivers, family members, co-workers, school personnel, and others in the community.

Mental Health Services

As suggested by the earlier discussion, youths with a history of maltreatment are likely to need a variety of mental health-related services. For example, the risks and challenges of moving ahead can exacerbate old feelings of fear or low self-esteem. Also, leaving home again may activate old losses (see Chapter 4 by Levine in this volume).

Foster parents and workers may need to provide informal counseling and support on these issues. It may be necessary to involve a mental health professional in working with the youth on developmental blocks that can hinder growth and the development of competence. Mental health services should be sought when an adolescent has any of the following problems: *(1)* the effects of earlier maltreatment have interfered with the youth's self-esteem to the point of blocking his or her ability to plan the emancipation process—for example, the youth feels unable to consider growing up; *(2)* these effects are interfering with the youth's bodily functioning as evidenced in problems with eating, sleeping, or elimination; *(3)* the youth is depressed or talks about suicide; *(4)* the youth shows sexualized behavior that makes him or her vulnerable to further victimization or exploitation, as was the case with Alicia, whose situation was described earlier; *(5)* excessive anxiety prohibits the youth from accepting the challenges of emancipation—for example, the youth is afraid to get a job or is unduly afraid of strangers; and *(6)* the youth is exhibiting asocial or dangerous behavior in response to the emancipation process—for example, molesting younger children, stealing, or hurting others.

In the team approach, the worker and foster parent together make the decision to pursue help, while clarifying to the youth how counseling can help. It is critical that the foster parent appreciate the importance of therapeutic support to surmount the developmental obstacle and reinforce this support by word and attitude. Equally critical is the worker's role in clarifying, for the mental health professional, the central role of the foster parent as a team member in this endeavor. Some clinicians may not want to spend the necessary time to involve foster parents or may feel that the confidentiality of their relationship with the youth precludes a working relationship with the caregiver.

The involvement of a mental health professional will be more effective in helping the maltreated youth if a number of guidelines are followed. First, foster parents should provide focused and specific information to the therapist about the developmental blocks they have noted, the youth's level of functioning, indicators of maltreatment, maladaptive behaviors, and other important observations. Second, foster parents should be informed as to the goals of the treatment, the approaches to be used, and the general prognosis for the intervention. Third, foster parents will need clarification on their roles in the intervention, for example, transporting the youth to sessions, keeping the therapist informed of developments, attending a training group with other foster parents, trying new approaches with the youth, monitoring certain behaviors, and other responsibilities. Fourth, foster parents, worker, and therapist should meet regularly to exchange information and assess the youth's progress. Finally, the foster parents will need anticipatory guidance from the therapist when sensitive areas are to be addressed in the course of treatment, and when the youth will require extra support and monitoring due to resurgence of deep depression, suicidal ideation, or an acting-out of sexual issues.

Generally, with a youth planning for emancipation, the focus of a therapeutic intervention should be supportive rather than uncovering. The challenges and demands of this period create too much insecurity for the vulnerable youth to relinquish defenses and allow old pain to surface. The youth is much more likely to move forward if the intervention builds on the youth's competence and helps him or her to understand and evaluate why progress is blocked. Moreover, if too much uncovering work is done at this sensitive time, the youth's energy may be mobilized to face old pain, rather than to meet new challenges. There are, of course, exceptions, usually when the blockage is so extensive that the youth has been completely immobilized, or when the youth is in a secure setting and the timetable for emancipation has been delayed. Whatever the approach, for many adolescents with a history of maltreatment, it is useful to think of the treatment process as a series of supportive interventions across the life cycle rather than as one intensive, time-limited intervention.

Health Services

Difficulties stemming from earlier physical or sexual abuse can be eased through the intervention of health care professionals. In Tonya's case, the worker-foster parent team was able to help her avert a poor start in the job market by obtaining an accurate medical diagnosis of her clumsiness and by helping her to find employment more suitable to her physical capabilities.

Trisha, the foster adolescent who had a miscarriage, may need medical advice on contraception and sexuality to make informed decisions about her future. All adolescents in foster care should have access to education and advice and clinical services on matters of sexuality and its related consequences as part of preparing to meet this basic challenge of impending adulthood. With respect to responsible sex, the importance of preparation for parenting should not be overlooked. Youths who have been maltreated may have grave concerns about their own ability to parent, yet, as mentioned earlier, may be drawn to premature parenthood. In addition to ensuring the youth's access to information and health care, the worker-foster parent team may want to help the youth plan activities aimed at learning about the realities of parenthood. Group activities involving young parents willing to talk about their experiences are one approach. School- or community-based programs that offer hands-on experience with young children provide a "dose of reality" as well as reassurance to the youth that maltreated children can become loving, competent parents. A visit to a parent education class or crisis drop-in center may also provide reassurance as well as information about community resources for future use.

Because a maltreated youth's health needs may have been attended to only minimally during the earlier years in care, preparation for emancipation is a critical time for health care intervention. Before leaving care, every youth should have a complete physical examination and psychological evaluation, as well as any other services available through the system to which he or she is entitled. The youth will have learned from the foster parents, we hope, how to be an intelligent consumer of health-related services and will have developed relationships with practitioners willing to continue service following emancipation. Foster parents and workers may need to advocate with providers to ensure continuity of service after the youth has left the system. As young adults, all former foster youths should know sources of affordable medical advice and care so that their health and mental health needs can be met.

Employment

Whatever services the worker may have marshaled to increase a maltreated youth's employability, foster parents remain critical partners in the team. Their support in the discussion of values about work, offering practical advice, helping the youth to dress appropriately, sometimes providing transportation, and countless other ways of keeping the youth connected with the world of work are all essential to a positive outcome. Moreover, the work of foster parents with adolescents on the performance of household chores and on accepting limits is also a critical part of preparation for employment.

Earlier experiences with adults who were capricious, abusive, punitive, or exploitative create a precarious position for youths entering the job market. Foster parents must often listen to many incidents of relationship difficulties with employers and supervisors and help a youth to sort out the reality of the current situation. The foster parents' steady concern and unflagging attention to the youth's work stories will reinforce progress and protect the youth from the possibility of failure or of being exploited in the job market. If the youth's past experiences seem to be played out in maladaptive patterns in the workplace, it may signal the need for therapeutic intervention.

Education

Physical or sexual abuse and emotional neglect can create problems that adversely affect cognitive development and school performance [Martin 1976; Mayhall and Norgard 1983; McFadden 1987]. Youths in care may experience difficulties ranging from neurological damage to emotional problems that deflect energy needed for learning and that inhibit concentration.

Youths would benefit from a teaching team that includes foster parents, workers, school personnel, and other interested helping persons. The team would examine formal academic education and vocational training, as well as informal independent-living skills groups and self-learning opportunities that contribute to the youths' educational options. Because many youths have had a history of negative experiences in schools and have damaged self-esteem, they need help in seeing that learning not only takes place in a formal classroom, but in many ways and places. Ramon's case is a good example of this variety of learning opportunities:

> Ramon hated school and threatened to drop out at age sixteen. Not only were his grades poor, but he had also received many negative comments from teachers on classroom behaviors such as talking out of turn or not paying attention. He had been suspended from school several times for cutting classes. When his foster mother realized he was serious about wanting to quit school, she met with the worker and Ramon and then had a series of meetings with Ramon's school counselor. Ramon took several aptitude and vocational tests, which showed an interest in working out of doors. The educational team listened carefully to Ramon's thoughts on school and realized that his current school program was not meeting his needs and was reinforcing his negative self-image.
>
> Ramon confided that he had never done well in school, and that as a younger child he had been mocked by other children who called him "Sped" (special-ed) and "Dummy." He was afraid whenever his teacher called on him, feeling that he might be ridiculed by the class. He worried about school a lot and felt like a "loser." He could see no connection between the remedial courses he was taking and the needs of his life. He wanted to be able to take care of himself, because he felt that no one else would be there to take care of him.
>
> In planning for Ramon's education, the team helped him to enroll in a vocational program that provided practical skill training and a co-op program that helped him build employability skills. Ramon also joined a Youth G.O.A.L.S.[1] group, and began working with his foster parents on the employability module of his G.O.A.L.S. curriculum. He became interested in landscaping and even checked several books out of the public library. His attendance, reading ability, and motivation improved as he made the transition to a program that met his needs. Ramon's foster parents, worker, and vocational instructor were pleased when he announced a new goal—graduation from the vocational school and going to work for a landscaping company.

Youths in care are at risk of being negatively labeled or falling between the cracks in the public education system unless they have a committed advocate who knows how to work with the system.

---

[1]Youth G.O.A.L.S. is a program using small groups of adolescents in foster care to augment training that their foster parents are receiving on preparation for interdependence [Ryan et al. 1988].

Determined intervention by the foster parent-worker team can ensure that youths in foster care obtain needed services. Some agencies are employing a teacher or other educational specialist as liaison between the agency and the school, as well as a resource person to educational programs and policymakers. Most educational systems have a wide range of services available: vocational testing; psychological evaluation; remedial reading; academic and vocational counseling; cooperative education and job placement; special education planning, placement, and classes; G.E.D. certification and high school completion classes; community education classes for life enrichment; and alternative schools. Working as a team with the school special-services personnel enables foster parents and workers to help youths gain entrance to a variety of services that may prove useful and interesting.

Training foster parents to take an active role in supporting emancipation prepares them to become primary educators of youths in their care. The Independent Living Project of Eastern Michigan University trains foster parents to take leadership roles working with youths on tangible skills (laundry and cooking) and supportive roles on intangible skills (decision making and emotional preparation for leaving home). Foster parents learn how to help youths to master their own Youth G.O.A.L.S. curriculum, in which youths assess their ability and determine where they wish to begin [Ryan et al. 1988]. Several important messages about education are modeled in this approach: learning is a lifelong process; important real-life learning takes place outside the classroom; education seems important when it gains you what you want; and it is all right to ask for help from a supportive adult mentor.

Working together, foster parents and workers will be able to maximize the educational opportunities for youths preparing to leave care. For youths who are academically talented, financial aid and planning for college will be the focus. For others, the team will need to ensure the youth's access to a more immediate educational goal. Every youth, in becoming an active participant in society, will, we hope, be helped to learn that education is a lifelong process and that there are many resources to meet these needs as life goes on.

Recreation and Leisure

As the team works together on a plan that will answer a youth's particular needs, recreation and leisure are important aspects of preparation for interdependent living. For example, physically and sexually abused youths have experienced damage to their body images. Therefore, physical activities involving the mastery of the body or acquisition of new skills may be highly therapeutic. Martial arts and self-defense courses can inspire greater confidence and security. Dance or swimming might improve motor skills in a youth with poor coordination. Sauna, jacuzzi, or massage might help a youth reconnect to body sensations. Weight Watchers or exercise class might be useful to the overweight youth who feels damaged, fat, and unlovely. Similarly, anorectic youths may need special attention. A modeling course or charm school can give new poise and confidence to one who feels awkward and unattractive.

Maltreatment often results in "lost childhood." Some youths with a history of maltreatment may have missed the fun of being a child by having had prematurely to assume adult roles and responsibilities, for example, serving as caregiver for younger siblings. As young adults on their own, these youths may be at risk of becoming involved in exploitative, addictive relationships in which they are expected to give a great deal and get little or nothing in return.

In short, an important part of preparing for appropriate adult roles and relationships is learning how to enjoy leisure time: how to have fun alone; how to pass an evening alone; how to entertain oneself when one is lonely; and how to relate to peers without the crutches of drugs, irresponsible sex, and other artificial highs.

Many foster parents of adolescents urge each youth in their care to be involved with one outside sport or activity in the community. For one youth, that might mean being on a bowling team; for another, it might be attending a church group. Others may volunteer at hospitals or nursing homes. Among the many benefits, involvement in these activities helps the emancipating adolescent to develop reference groups and to practice the skills needed for active participation in society.

Small groups have been found to be an effective intervention with adolescents in care [Rice and McFadden 1988]. Bringing adolescents together in groups to prepare for independent living enables them to develop a range of important social skills as well as to explore common interests and concerns. Groups can deal with self-help skills, choices and consequences, jobs, and leaving home again. In a group context, adolescents in foster care can learn that they are not alone in their feelings about growing up. They can share ideas on music, sports, television, and other leisure activities. They may take field trips together. They can try simulations of real-life experiences: choosing an apartment, disagreeing with a friend, or interviewing for a job [McFadden in press; Ryan et al. 1988].

Conclusion

Maltreated youths have issues that may surface and resurface throughout the life cycle as they reach new stages of development. The emotional effects of maltreatment, such as poor self-image or inability to trust, may impair the youth's later adult relationships and impinge on the achievement of life tasks.

Social workers and foster parents must be prepared to continue their teamwork, advocating continually to develop resources that meet the lifelong developmental needs of these former maltreated children. Perhaps the greatest single resource will be the committed foster parent who will remain emotionally available as the newly launched adult takes on the challenges of the life cycle. Realistically, although effective teamwork can heal many wounds, there are no guarantees. Workers and foster parents must become able to support each other with the hope that the preparation youths received in foster care was sufficient to carry them forward into a future that is, for all youths, unpredictable at best.

REFERENCES

Augoustinos, Martha. "Developmental effects of child abuse: Recent findings." Child Abuse and Neglect International Journal 2 (1987): 15–27.

Bender, Barbara. "Self-chosen victims: Scapegoating behavior sequential to battering." Child Welfare 55 (1976): 417–422.

Brandt, Renee, and Tisza, Veronica. "The sexually misused child." American Journal of Orthopsychiatry 47 (1979): 80–90.

Brown, Selma. "Clinical illustrations of the sexual misuse of girls." Child Welfare 58 (1979): 435–442.

Burch, Charles. "Puppet play in a thirteen year old boy: Remembering, repeating and working through." Clinical Social Work Journal 8 (1980): 79–89.

Cates, Jim. "Adolescent sexuality: Gay and lesbian issues." Child Welfare 66 (1987): 353–364.

Crawford, Albert, and Furstenberg, Frank. "Teenage sexuality, pregnancy and childbearing." In Laird, J., and Hartman, A. (editors), A Handbook of Child Welfare—Context, Knowledge, and Practice. New York: Free Press, 1985, 532–559.

Elkind, David. "Cognitive development in adolescence." In Elkind, David (editor), Understanding Adolescence. Boston: Allyn and Bacon, 1968, 128–158.

Eisenman, Russell. "Values and attitudes in adolescence," In Elkind, David (editor), Understanding Adolescence. Boston: Allyn and Bacon, 1968, 183–197.

Erikson, Erik. Childhood and Society. New York: Norton, 1950.

Garbarino, James. "Meeting the needs of mistreated youths." Social Work 25 (1980): 122–126.

Havighurst, Robert J. Developmental Tasks and Education, 3rd Edition. New York: David McKay, 1972.

Haynie, Roena. "Deprivation of body pleasure: Origin of violent behavior? A survey of the literature." Child Welfare 59 (1980): 287–297.

Hochstadt, Neil, Joudes, Paula, Zimo, Deborah, and Schocter, Jayne. "The medical and psychosocial needs of children entering foster care." International Journal of Child Abuse and Neglect 2 (1987): 53–62.

Hoekstra, Kathleen. "Ecologically defining mistreatment of adolescents." Children and Youth Services Review 6 (1984): 285–298.

Kinard, E. Milling. "Mental health needs of abused children." Child Welfare 59 (1980): 451–462.

Konopka, Gisele. "Stresses and strains in adolescents and young adults." In Ziefert, Marjorie (editor), Adolescent Abuse and Neglect. Ypsilanti, MI: Easter Michigan University, 1982, 93–105.

Loppnow, Donald. "Adolescents on their own." In Laird, Joan, and Hartman, Ann (editors), A Handbook of Child Welfare—Context, Knowledge, and Practice. New York: Free Press, 1985, 514–531.

McFadden, Emily Jean, and Ryan, Patricia. "Characteristics of the Vulnerable Child." Paper presented at 6th International Child Abuse Congress in Sydney, Australia (August 1986).

McFadden, Emily Jean. Counseling Abused Children. Ann Arbor, MI: ERIC, University of Michigan, 1987.

———. Youth Leaders Guide, PUSH for Youth G.O.A.L.S. Ypsilanti, MI: Eastern Michigan University, in press.

Martin, Harold. The Abused Child. Cambridge, MA: Ballinger, 1976.

Mayhall, Pamela, and Norgard, Katherine E. Child Abuse and Neglect. New York: John Wiley and Sons, 1983.

Nasjleti, M. "Suffering in silence: The male incest victim." Child Welfare 59 (1980): 269–275.

Rice, Dale, and McFadden, Emily Jean. "A forum for foster children." Child Welfare 67 (May–June 1988): 231–243.

Ryan, Patricia, McFadden, Emily Jean, Rice, Dale, and Warren, Bruce. P.U.S.H. for Youth G.O.A.L.S. Independent Living Curriculum. Ypsilanti, MI: Eastern Michigan University, 1988.

Sharlin, Shlomo, and Shenlar, Aliza. On Adolescent Suicide and Poetry. King George, VA: American Foster Care Resources, 1987.

Shaughnessy, Michael. "Institutional child abuse." Children and Youth Services Review 6 (1984): 311–318.

Silber, Tomas. "Adolescent sexuality." In Advocating for Children in the Courts, 2nd Edition. Washington, DC: National Legal Resource Center for Child Advocacy and Protection, American Bar Association, 1980, 339–551.

Timberlake, Elizabeth. "Aggression and depression among foster children." Children and Youth Services Review 1 (1979): 279–291.

Vera Institute of Justice. Foster Home Child Protection. New York: City of New York Human Resources Administration, 1982.

Zaphiris, Alex. "The sexually abused boy." Preventing Sexual Abuse, Newsletter of National Family Life Education Network, Santa Cruz, CA, 1 (Spring 1986): 1–4.

11

Disciplining Adolescents in Foster Family Care

PATRICIA RYAN

How to discipline and the appropriate amount of discipline are major concerns of today's parents. Child development researchers, family therapists, and the mass media debate the merits of various approaches. Arguments about deleterious effects of harsh and rigid punishment are countered with the accusation that overly permissive parenting styles are responsible for most current social problems involving youths and young adults. These controversies are exacerbated when attention is turned to disciplining adolescents.

Finding the correct approach to discipline is even more critical for young people in foster family care, because they may have suffered severe neglect, emotional, physical, or sexual abuse and thus have an even greater need for appropriate discipline [Ryan 1984; Bayless 1986]. Social workers and foster parents dedicated to providing a nurturing and healing environment must confront and handle behaviors that are difficult and sometimes antisocial. Their personal beliefs as to how to handle children are frequently at odds with agency or state policies, limiting the forms of discipline that can be used with children in out-of-home placement.

This chapter reviews various approaches to the use of discipline, especially with adolescents. It then explores the implications for discipline with adolescents in foster family care, with emphasis on helping foster parents to enhance their knowledge and skills in use of discipline and on developing individualized plans for disciplining a particular youth. The chapter also considers guidelines for helping adolescents assess the consequences of their behavior in preparation for independent living after foster care.

Approaches to Discipline

Research on Discipline

Much research has focused on the short-term consequences of various forms of discipline and the extent to which corporal punishment and other harsh forms of discipline may be related to later adult aggression and child abuse. Elder [1963] reports that emphasis on verbal forms of discipline is most likely to result in youngsters modeling parent behavior and believing in the legitimacy of parental power. He postulates that use of explanations leads to the desire to model, compliance, and eventual autonomy. Kuczynski [1983] finds that children perform better when other-oriented reasoning is used, as compared to simple rules or self-oriented reasoning. Kelly and Goodwin [1983] conclude that children react more positively to parental power when democratic rather than authoritarian parenting techniques are used.

Herzberger and Tennen [1985] argue that sensitization techniques, including yelling and corporal punishment, encourage children to think primarily of the consequences of misbehavior for themselves. There is general consensus that the use of corporal punishment or physical discipline leads to aggression at the punishing person and/or others in the environment [Bandura 1973; Gordon 1970; Waters 1983].

Approaches to Discipline

In conjunction with selected theories of child development, research findings have led to a variety of popular approaches to parenting in general, and discipline in particular. The most prevalent approach underscores the need for parents to be reflective and to take the point of view of the child [Driekhurs and Grey 1970; Gordon 1970; Ginott 1970]. The emphasis is on the healthy development of autonomous personality, maintenance of family harmony, allowing children to learn from the natural consequences of their behavior, and use of clear or structured communication styles [Ginott 1970]. When rules are necessary, they should be spelled out ahead of time. Children are to be encouraged to make decisions after being clearly informed of the consequences, and the parents then make sure that the consequences follow.

Another approach focuses on parental manipulation of responses to children in order to affect their subsequent behavior [Bijon and Baier 1966; Patterson 1975]. In general, the message for parents is that discipline is not punishment, but teaching that leads to the development of responsibility. Overreliance on reward and punishment is regarded as generally ineffective. When rules are necessary, they should be accompanied by explanations. An important mechanism for providing the arena for explanations and practicing democratic procedures is the family meeting. Here the parents have the opportunity to explore the reasons for inappropriate behavior, establish rules, explain the rationale for the rules, determine consequences, model appropriate behaviors, and create a learning environment for the children.

Disciplining Adolescents

Advice on parenting younger children carries over to adolescents, though with some modifications; there is more emphasis on the reflective approach to parenting [Tavormina 1980]. Adolescence is generally recognized as a difficult stage developmentally and as a time of emotional ambivalence, as youths alternate between wanting the independence of adulthood and the security of childhood [Fisher and Fisher 1976]. This ambivalence is often accompanied by a high level of disorganized energy [Josselyn 1972].

Therefore this stage is also difficult for the family, and the family changes as members adjust their demands and responses to their new conceptions of the child and his or her idiosyncratic reactions to adolescence [Steinberg 1980; Savin-Williams and Small 1986]. Parents find themselves obliged to give up some authority, as competing social systems make demands on their adolescents, and to adjust to their emerging sexuality [Winch and Gordon 1974]. For parents, the central problem becomes how to facilitate autonomy and independence while maintaining restraints and limitations [McHenry et al. 1981].

In this regard, Steinberg [1980: 12] advises parents to "maintain their emotional involvement in the form of concern and caring while gradually moving toward a relationship characterized by greater behavior autonomy." Adolescents, however, still need some parental guidance and limits. Vogelsong and Guerney (1980) point out that this stage is a critical time for identity formation and that lack of communication with adults leads to emotional disturbance. Harsh criticism, rejection, and inconsistent parental behavior, on the one hand, and disinterested permissiveness, on the other, are both likely to cause problems for adolescents [Waters 1983]. Gould [1977] suggests that teenagers be given broad areas for making choices in such matter as use of their time, selection of courses and extracurricular activities, and their personal appearance.

Adolescents in Foster Family Care

Like other adolescents, those in foster family care are caught in the ambivalence and conflicts prevalent for that age group in our society. Although the research on the effect of the foster care experience on the child is inconsistent [Maluccio and Fein 1985], there is at least some evidence that a significant minority suffer [Rest and Watson 1984; Rice and McFadden 1988]. Youngsters in long-term foster care may have experienced many moves due, at least in part, to their own behaviors or may have been made to feel as if their behaviors were responsible for the moves [Proch and Taber 1985].

As a result, adolescents in foster care may be even more likely than other youths to harbor unresolved conflicts that may emerge with adolescence [Ziefert 1984]. They may have experienced poor or inconsistent role models in the past. They may be developmentally behind their peers [Ziefert 1984; Ryan 1988]. In addition, they generally suffer from low self-esteem and unresolved grief [Levine, Chapter 4 in this volume; McFadden et al. 1987].

Foster Parenting and Discipline

In working with adolescents, foster parents encounter the same problems as other parents. They approach their tasks from a variety of backgrounds and with a variety of parenting skills and styles. In addition, they are often restricted by agency policy at the very time they are most pressured to control rebellious behavior, and so they often feel frustrated and helpless. Many parents of adolescents are overwhelmed by parenting, in part because of their high expectations for themselves [Gould 1977]. This feeling may be even more true for foster parents, who are often held up by the agency and community as exemplars. Foster parents, moreover, are faced with the challenges inherent in disciplining someone else's son or daughter, such as needing to set limits, often without the benefit of an established relationship to offset what appears to the youth as control or punishment; being unaware of a youth's cognitive and emotional capacities for developing self-control; and lacking familiarity with a youth's history in regard to discipline specifically and relationships in general.

To be successful with adolescents, foster parents may have to change their approach to discipline just as other parents must adjust their parenting style as their children reach adolescence. It is most helpful if foster parents begin by recognizing that much adolescent behavior is learned behavior that was at some point adaptive for the youngster. For example, the only attention some children have ever received has been the result of negative behaviors; these children therefore view punishment as better than being ignored. For others, inappropriate approaches to adults are the only ways that they know to survive emotionally.

Understanding the reasons underlying adolescent behavior should help the foster parent to approach the young person more calmly. Recognition of the general conflicts of adolescence helps foster parents to develop a style of discipline that resembles that of counselor more closely than that of parents.

For younger teenagers, especially those who are developmentally delayed, the foster family may have to provide a great deal of structure. For older teenagers, the demands and skills needed for young adulthood and emancipation from foster care will demand greater freedom. Maier's [1987: 29–30] advice for child-care workers in group residential settings is also appropriate for foster parents: "Much of a caregiver's energies need to be invested in rehearsing with adolescents a variety of life experiences that are apt to be encountered away from" the residential center.

In short, foster parents are faced with a major challenge as they seek to use discipline as a means of helping to prepare adolescents for life after foster care. Social workers can participate in meeting this challenge by helping foster parents to enhance their knowledge and skills in the use of discipline and to develop individualized plans for discipline with a particular youth.

Enhancing Foster Parents' Knowledge and Skills

Definition of Discipline

A survey of standard dictionaries shows that the first meaning of discipline is generally "teaching or training." Other meanings include "the behavior resulting from such training;" "a set of rules or orders;" "punishment;" and "a branch of knowledge or learning." Also, the author has found that parent educators, when asked to give a formal definition, equate discipline with teaching. When asked to report on the way in which they were disciplined as children, however, they usually speak of punishment. This response demonstrates the prevalence of the confusion of discipline as punishment.

As with others, foster parents therefore need help to distinguish between discipline as punishment and discipline as teaching. Toward this end, the author has found it useful in foster parent training programs to define discipline as follows: Teaching children those things they need to know in order to be responsible adults, while maintaining limits and rules necessary for their safety and the comfort of others until they have the experience, knowledge, and ability to establish and maintain their own behavioral rules.

Strategies in Using Discipline

Building on this definition of discipline, four basic strategies that foster parents can use in helping adolescents learn self-control and grow into competent and responsible adults follow.

Explanation and Verbal Instructions: Parents and other caregivers vary in the amount of explanation they use in discipline, often expecting children to do what they are told without asking the reasons why. Foster parents must recognize that the typical adolescent has developed the cognitive structure to appreciate the reasoning underlying rules and to demand explanations [Kuczynski 1983].

Modeling: The importance of modeling is widely documented and provides the basis for general socialization theory and explanations of individual behavior patterns [Bandura 1973]. Children of all ages model their behaviors on those of significant others. With adolescents, the importance of parental models is often obscured because of the youths' negative behavior and seeming lack of attention. Even the most rebellious youths, however, will be quick to point out any inconsistencies between what adults say and what they do.

Positive and Negative Reinforcement: Virtually all human beings will avoid behavior that is followed by unpleasant consequences and repeat behavior that leads to pleasant consequences, unless there are other overriding reasons for repeating or avoiding the initial behavior. In accordance with this principle, foster parents can help adolescents in their care to reinterpret discipline as negative consequences for inappropriate behavior. Foster parents can also learn to appreciate the importance of rewarding or providing positive consequences for appropriate behavior. They should also learn that ignoring behavior is often an effective extinguisher of the adolescent's negative actions.

Experimentation: Learning also occurs through experimentation; that is, trying various forms of behavior and discovering what happens. Wise parents provide their children with safe opportunities to explore the physical and social environment and learn from the natural consequences of behavior. Adolescents are usually more concerned with exploring their social world and discovering their place in it. Much of their behavior can be regarded as testing limits, as they develop their identity through the reactions of others.

The following example illustrates the use of these strategies in preparing an adolescent for interdependent living.

Danny, aged seventeen, wanted $90 to take his girlfriend to her prom. His foster parents were pleased that he had carefully figured out how much he would need for the event. Since he had only two weeks to earn the money, and their basement badly needed painting, they agreed that they would pay him $90 to paint the basement. They bought the paint with the agreement that he would start the job on Saturday and work on it every afternoon when he got home from school.

Saturday morning Danny slept late and then said he had to go to visit a friend. When reminded of his commitment to paint the basement, he said he would be back within an hour. He did not return until mid-afternoon. His foster parents were extremely irritated. Mr. K said he was going to do the job himself. He felt especially annoyed that Danny had broken his promise. As they waited for Danny to return, they discussed the reasons why he might be avoiding the painting job. Mrs. K wondered if they were taking too much for granted: Did Danny know how to paint a basement? Was he afraid to start the job?

When Danny finally came in, Mr. K asked if he was ready to start on the job. When Danny hesitated, Mr. K said, "I know you want to get started so you will be able to finish this week and get your money. Let me help you get set up."

In the basement, Mr. K then explained the importance of preparing the walls properly, the way to mix the paint, and how to get started. He and Danny worked together for a half hour; then he left Danny to work by himself. The K's were very pleased with the progress Danny had made by supper time.

When Danny returned home, the K's could have used a number of strategies. Perhaps the most common response in this situation is to nag at a youth or to keep repeating the negative consequences of not carrying through (i.e., no money for the prom). Some foster parents would want to punish the youth for breaking his promise. The K's chose to use this as an opportunity to teach.

Working Directly with Adolescents

In their direct work with adolescents, it is crucial that foster parents—and social workers—show that they value and respect them. If the adults appear to be condescending or omniscient, the youths will react negatively. It is essential to praise youths for the things they can do and to point out that many young people are unable to do them, not just those who are in foster care. Youths need adults who will listen carefully to their opinions and respect them even when disagreeing. They need adults who will share their own values and explain why they feel these are important, but not insist that the youths accept the values.

As they are guided by these principles, foster parents may find the following points useful in their efforts to use discipline to teach adolescents in their care and thus promote their growth.

No matter how limited youths may be, they can learn some things.

We cannot work on everything at once; it is important to set priorities.

It is important to concentrate on specific behaviors and not allow inappropriate behavior and responses to lead us to allow the youths to feel that we do not value them.

We will probably get further in our efforts to teach youngsters if we concentrate on rewarding what is learned rather than punishing when something is not learned.

We will not get very far with most youths if we try to control their behavior or to argue about who is right and who is wrong.

We will be most successful if we establish a few rules for safety and convenience and then concentrate on helping youths to learn. For older youths, the emphasis should be on determining what they want to learn and how they might accomplish it. We will probably be most effective with this age group if we concentrate on helping them to meet their own standards and get the job done to their satisfaction.

We will be most successful if we concentrate on increasing the youth's self-esteem. We can do so by stressing the following:

I value you and think you are important.

I want you to learn these things so you will be able to take care of yourself and live the kind of life you want to live.

Most of the time, when we do something new, we find the task difficult at first. As we do it more often, it becomes easier.

I am confident you will be able to do these things eventually.

I will work with you until you can do it on your own.

The following example shows the application of some of these principles with adolescents in foster family care.

Mary Lou seemed very young for her sixteen years. Although she wanted to learn independent-living skills and appeared willing to help her foster mother with a number of household tasks, she seemed incapable of starting and finishing even the simplest chores on her own. When she did try to help, she would soon get angry and storm off, leaving the job undone.

Finally her foster mother, Mrs. S, began to realize how little Mary Lou knew about running a household. She could not prepare the simplest of foods without careful instructions. After several discussions with the caseworker, Mrs. S understood that a good deal of Mary Lou's anger was triggered by frustration at her own limitations, and that the more often she failed, the more upset she became at having to try again.

Mrs. S was able to lower her expectations for Mary Lou. She started assigning small and relatively simple jobs. She was careful to make sure that Mary Lou knew how to accomplish every step. She used a lot of encouragement and praise. Mary Lou responded well and over time learned to do more on her own.

Developing Individualized Plans for Discipline

Sooner or later most foster families working with adolescents will face a behavioral crisis requiring the use of discipline. The most serious crises frequently arise from behaviors that the family feels are inappropriate or even intolerable. They may range from minor issues to serious offenses such as substance abuse, vandalism, truancy, or other dangerous behaviors. Foster families often also face a youth's failure to behave appropriately: not doing homework, not completing chores, or not following other house rules.

Social workers can help foster parents to cope with behavioral crises by developing an individualized plan to handle specific behavioral problems. The following sequence of six steps, which is illustrated in Figure 1, provides a framework for developing such a plan for a particular youth [Ryan 1984]. Learning the sequence of steps is a useful part of every foster parent's general preparation. The framework is worded for extinguishing undesirable behaviors, but it can easily be modified for encouraging desirable behaviors.

FIGURE I. SEQUENCE OF STEPS FOR DEVELOPING
INDIVIDUALIZED PLANS
FOR DISCIPLINE.

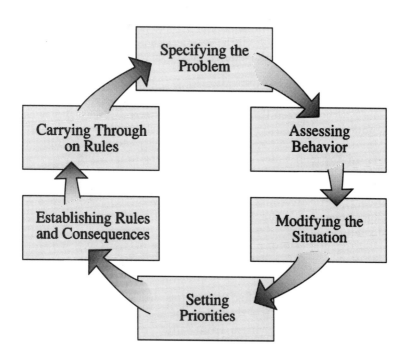

Specifying the Problem.

The first step is clear specification of the problem. This is necessary in order that both the worker and the foster parent agree as to the behavior they are discussing and, if appropriate, formulate a definite rule. For instance, stealing can refer to a number of behaviors, ranging from taking pennies off the dresser and borrowing others' clothes to taking $50 from someone's wallet or selling the family stereo. An example of a problem is "arriving late to school at least twice a week or more."

Assessing Behavior

It is important to determine the reasons underlying a youth's behavior or failure to behave as desired, if one is to change that behavior. Although some behavior may seem random or unmotivated, most foster parents can appreciate that there is always a reason for it. Many youths find that misbehavior is an effective way of gaining attention. In addition, adolescents in foster care have had certain experiences in their lives that may lead to exaggerated behaviors, such as excessive need for attention, fear of excessive consequences, lack of socialization to appropriate behaviors, and developmental lags or delays.

As considered by McFadden (Chapter 10 in this volume), previous life experiences of foster adolescents have frequently included abuse and neglect that may have seriously affected their development. In addition, these youths have usually experienced many unresolved losses. Their emotional and cognitive energy has been concentrated on grieving and on trying to make sense of their situation, leaving little energy for normal development (see Chapter 4 by Levine in this volume). Understanding a youth's stage of development, rather than chronological age, may therefore provide a clue to greater understanding of his or her behavior.

An additional step in behavioral assessment is determining the situations or circumstances leading to the behavior. Although it may seem that some youths are always in trouble, careful analysis will usually show that it is most frequent at certain times of day, or before or after certain events. Such analysis again provides a clue to understanding the purpose of the behavior and how it might be handled most effectively. For instance, reasons for a youth's late arrival at school might include, among others:

Anxiety about performance either in the academic setting or with peers

Getting up late
Taking too much time for other things in the morning
Loitering with friends outside of school

Modifying the Situation

Once a foster parent has determined the situation or events leading to undesired behavior, it may be relatively easy to extinguish or decrease the frequency of the behavior through minor changes in the situation. Some foster parents will not be enthusiastic about making changes in their schedule, and most have family and other constraints; however, minor schedule changes and adaptations may result in fewer confrontations and greater family comfort. For example, a youth might be better able to get to school on time if he or she fixes lunch, gets clothes ready, and makes other preparations the night before rather than waiting until morning.

Setting Priorities

Attempting to change all of a youth's undesirable behaviors and habits will seldom be successful. Foster parents who attempt too much will feel frustrated, and their unsuccessful attempts are likely to make the youth feel a failure and further undermine self-esteem. Setting up a long list of rules leads either to a constant battle and strain or to the youth's learning that adults will not abide by what they have said. Establishing priorities and working on a few behaviors at a time allow both the foster parents and the youth to experience success.

Each family will have to determine its own priorities, but behaviors that are dangerous for the youth or for others, destructive of property, or illegal must receive top priority. Other behaviors may also be given high priority, especially those that undermine the youth's confidence or those that the family finds intolerable. If a family cannot control these behaviors, they need more help, and the agency must assist them in finding this help.

Establishing Rules and Consequences

Once the family has determined those behaviors that will receive top priority, it is appropriate to establish rules and determine the consequences for adherence to or failure to adhere to each rule. Adults working with adolescents will find that including them in determining the rules and consequences will lead to the greatest degree of success.

Not only does their involvement make it more likely they will comply, but it also provides an opportunity for them to learn how to state their side of an argument, how to assess other persons' points of view, and how to develop skills in negotiating compromises—all of which are needed for competent adulthood. It is important that the rules be agreed upon whenever possible. The foster parent, however, within limits set by agency guidelines, has ultimate responsibility for these decisions.

Discussing expectations with youths and encouraging them to express their perspective provide foster parents with an opportunity to learn more about the youths' values and open the way for reinforcement of positive attitudes. Involving youths in determining consequences, both positive and negative, provides additional understanding of the youths and increases their motivation for compliance. Also useful is the development of a written contract outlining the rules and the positive and negative consequences [Ziefert 1984]. An example is that of the tardy youth, who agreed to perform an hour of household chores for every hour he arrived late to school. Each week that he arrived at school on time every day, his Saturday night curfew was extended by an hour.

Carrying Through on Rules

The final step is reviewing the plan to establish that family members can persevere with it. If they are unable to do so, the plan will not be effective. Two of the reasons that make it difficult to implement a plan are unrealistic rules and extreme consequences. The foster parents, worker, and youth should evaluate the rules to make sure that the desired behavior is under the control of the youth and that he or she has the self-control to do what is required or to refrain from doing what is prohibited. Whenever possible, prohibitions should include acceptable alternative behaviors. The rules should also include a plan for the foster parent to monitor the behavior.

The consequences, both positive and negative, should also be realistic. Those that are too large or exaggerated will be difficult to implement. It is usually wiser to have relatively small consequences that can be applied frequently. For instance, grounding a youth for an extensive period because of curfew violation often leads to a feeling of resentment on the part of the youth or guilt on the part of the foster parents. In addition, a youth who is late may stay out even later, if it will be the last time for a while. Grounding for one night for each half-hour late may be easier to implement and stimulates motivation for the youth to get home as soon as possible.

Helping Adolescents Assess the Consequences of Their Behavior

The foregoing discussion has concentrated on the foster parent as the locus of control and on the use of logical consequences. This method is consistent with the need of adolescents for firm limits. The major focus of discipline, however, and especially discipline for older adolescents, should be the teaching of responsibility [Dinkmeyer and McKay 1982; Ryan 1984, 1988]. Once young people are emancipated from foster care, the consequences of their behavior will no longer be mitigated and modified by foster parents or child welfare agency staff members. Thus, youths need help in developing a paradigm for assessing and evaluating the consequences of their own behavior. It may be helpful to divide potential consequences into different areas. Workers and foster parents should be alert to ways that will help young people practice how to determine the potential consequences, both negative and positive, in each of the areas considered below.

Natural Consequences

These consequences include behaviors that are the results of the natural order rather than patterns or regulations established by other human beings. Eating usually makes one more comfortable unless one eats too much. Staying up late leads to feeling tired in the morning. Driving while drunk may well lead to an accident.

Social Consequences

These consequences are the reactions of other people to our behavior. Their reactions are often difficult to ignore and can be critical if we care about a person or if that person has power over us. Being consistently late for appointments may put a strain on a relationship, while doing someone a favor most often supports the relationship. Calling the boss a name may result in losing a job.

Legal and Economic Consequences

These consequences are based on the laws of our society. They determine how we go about getting what we need and what happens if we disobey the formal rules. For example, most objects and services cost money that has to be earned. Even welfare and other forms of support depend upon meeting legal criteria of eligibility. If we are caught driving over the speed limit, a fine usually ensues. If we do not pay the electric bill, we will have no electricity. If we are caught shoplifting, we will probably be arrested and may be given a jail sentence.

Emotional Consequences

These consequences involve our own reactions to a situation. Doing something well usually leads to pride. When we are unsure of how people will react to our behavior, we may be anxious. When we fail to live up to our own standards, we feel shame.

Merely teaching youths a set of rules and making sure they obey them leaves the youngsters in a vacuum once the rules no longer apply or there is no one available to enforce them [Ryan 1988]. In contrast, adolescents can be empowered to take charge of their behavior by learning to use this framework; to evaluate the positive and negative consequences; and to make the best possible, or least negative, decisions in their lives.

Conclusion

Developing an appropriate style of discipline for use with adolescents is a difficult task; the characteristics and life experiences of youths in foster care can complicate this process for foster parents. The challenge of helping to promote self-control in youths who often have not benefited from positive role models and harbor unresolved conflict and grief is great. This challenge can, however, be met by foster parents as they learn to counsel and teach youths with respect, imbue them with a sense of responsibility over their own lives, and develop plans that reflect the individual needs of each young person.

REFERENCES

Bandura, A. Aggression: A Social Learning Analysis. New York: Prentice Hall, 1973.

Bayless, Linda. "Discipline: The case against corporal punishment." Foster Care Journal 9 (1986): 5–6.

Bijon, Sidney W., and Baer, Donald M. "Operant methods in child behavior and development." In Honig, Werner K. (editor), Operant Behavior: Areas of Research and Application. New York: Appleton-Century-Crofts, 1966, 718–789.

Dinkmeyer, Don, and McKay, Gary D. Step/Teen: The Parents' Guide— Systematic Training for Effective Parenting. Circle Pines, MN: American Guidance Service, 1982.

Driekurs, Rudolph, and Grey, Loren. A Parents' Guide to Child Discipline. New York: Hawthorne Books, 1970.

Elder, Glen H. "Parental power legitimation and its effect on the adolescent." Sociometry 26 (1963): 50–65.

Fisher, Seymour, and Fisher, Rhoda L. What We Really Know About Child Rearing. New York: Basic Books, 1976.

Ginott, Haime G. Between Parent and Teen. New York: Signet, 1970.

Gordon, Thomas. Parent Effectiveness Training. New York: New American Library, 1970.

Gould, Shirley. Teenagers: The Continuity and the Challenge. New York: Hawthorne Books, 1977.

Herzberger, Sharon D., and Tennen, Howard. "The effect of self-relevance on judgments of moderate and severe disciplinary encounters." Journal of Marriage and Family 47 (May 1985): 311–318.

Josselyn, Irene M. The Adolescent and His World. New York: Family Service Association of America, 1972.

Kelly, C., and Goodwin, Gail C. "Adolescents' perception of three styles of parental control." Adolescence 71 (Fall 1983): 567–571.

Kuczynski, Leon. "Reasoning, prohibitions and motivations for compliance." Developmental Psychology 19 (1983): 126–134.

Maier, Henry W. "Developmental group care of children and youth: Concepts and practice." Child and Youth Services 9 (1987): 1–225 (entire issue).

Maluccio, Anthony N., and Fein, Edith. "Growing up in foster care." Children and Youth Services Review 7 (1985): 123–134.

McFadden, Emily Jean, Rice, Dale, Ryan, Patricia, and Warren, Bruce L. "Leaving Home Again: Emancipation From Family Foster Care." Paper presented at First North American Conference on Treatment Foster Care. Minneapolis, MN: August 1987.

McHenry, Patrick C., Price-Bonham, Sharon, and O'Bryant, Shirley. "Adolescent discipline: Different family members' perception." Journal of Youth and Adolescence 10 (1981): 327–337.

Patterson, Gerald R. Families: Applications of Social Learning to Family Life. Champaign, IL: Research Press, 1975.

Proch, Kathleen, and Taber, Merlin A. "Placement disruptions: A review of research." Children and Youth Services Review 7 (1985): 309–320.

Rest, Ellen Ryan, and Watson, Kenneth W. "Growing up in foster care." Child Welfare 63 (July–August 1984): 291–306.

Rice, Dale L., and McFadden, Emily Jean. "A forum for foster children." Child Welfare 67 (May–June 1988): 231–243.

Ryan, Patricia. Fostering Discipline. Ypsilanti, MI: Eastern Michigan University, 1984.

———. Choices and Consequences. Ypsilanti, MI: Eastern Michigan University, 1988.

Savin-Williams, Rich C., and Small, Stephen R. "The timing of puberty and its relationship to adolescent and parent perceptions of family interactions." Developmental Psychology 22 (1986): 342–347.

Steinberg, Lawrence D. Understanding Families with Young Adolescents. Chapel Hill, NC: University of North Carolina, 1980.

Tavormina, Joseph B. "Evaluation and comparative studies of parent education." In Abidin, Richard R. (editor), Parent Education and Intervention Handbook. Springfield, IL: Charles C. Thomas, Publisher, 1980, 130–155.

Vogelsong, Edward L., and Guerney, Bernard G., Jr. "Working with parents of disturbed adolescents." In Abidin, Richard R. (editor), Parent Education and Intervention Handbook. Springfield, IL: Charles C. Thomas, Publisher, 1980, 297–321.

Waters, Virginia. "The rational-emotive point of view of discipline." In Dor, Darwin, Zax, Melvin, and Bonner, Jack W., III (editors), The Psychology of Discipline. New York: International Universities Press, Inc., 1983: 65–98.

Winch, Robert F., and Gordon, Margaret T. Family Structure and Function as Influence. Toronto, Ontario: Lexington Books, 1974.

Ziefert, Marjorie, with McFadden, Emily Jean. "Adolescent abuse and neglect: Placement considerations." In McFadden, Emily Jean (editor), Preventing Abuse in Foster Care. Ypsilanti, MI: Eastern Michigan University, 1984, 89–106.

12

Assessing Skills for Interdependent Living

BARBARA A. PINE AND ROBIN KRIEGER

The adolescent's search for identity is so common a human experience that the question "Who am I?" has become a cliche used to sum up the teenage years. The search for answers to this question can result in the storminess that often characterizes adolescence, as teenagers attempt to sort out the components of their own identities. It is a poignant time in life that calls upon young people to master a range of tasks in six key areas of development: cognitive, physical, social, emotional, moral, and sexual. Assessment and case planning with adolescents in foster care must focus on the extent of their mastery of milestones in these areas as indicative of readiness to assume the roles and responsibilities of life after foster care.

All adolescents are forced to examine their self-images in light of their ideal images. Perception of differences in these two sets of images can result in painful feelings that, if appropriately channeled, can produce tremendous growth and change. Without such direction, usually provided by parents, self-assessments may erode a self-concept that, for an adolescent in foster care, may already be damaged by the experiences of family separation and placement. Thus, foster parents and social workers can mitigate the pain of such examinations, as well as guide the formation of plans to prepare for adulthood, by working with teenagers in their care to identify developmental strengths and limitations. This chapter discusses the importance of assessing independent-living skills, describes selected approaches available to foster parents and workers, and identifies the principles for engaging in an assessment with an adolescent in foster care.

Definition of Assessment

The most effective work with foster adolescents, as in any social work intervention, is based on a careful process in which all of the pertinent aspects of the situation are considered, the critical factors are identified, consideration is given to all of the possible alternatives for intervention, and a decision is made as to the approach that will be taken [Bartlett 1970].

This view of assessment is further developed in Maluccio's reformulation of assessment [1981] as competence clarification. This concept refers to the person-environment transaction. Understanding a client's competence in dealing with the environment requires clarification of both client characteristics such as skills, attitudes, and motivations, and those of the impinging environment that serve as resources or obstacles. In addition, competence clarification emphasizes the extent of the goodness of fit between these two sets of characteristics and identifies this fit as the focus of asessment and case planning.

The application of these perspectives to work with adolescents preparing to leave foster care must deal with at least three dimensions of the situation: the youths' individual development emotionally, physically, socially, morally, cognitively, and sexually; those features of the youths' foster care experience as these have influenced the course of that development; and, finally, the requisite skills of adulthood—the minimum expectations for all adolescents as they mature to adulthood.

Individual Development

All adolescents must accomplish a set of developmental tasks as they move toward adulthood. Tasks or changes in the physical domain include the maturation of the body, including size, shape, and reproductive organs. Intellectual tasks include gaining the ability to think more abstractly and creatively and to reason and make decisions. Social and emotional tasks include being able to establish and maintain same- and opposite-sex friendships, developing an individual identity, and becoming increasingly self-reliant. Moral tasks involve the development of a value system and the ability to distinguish and make choices between right and wrong. Sexual tasks include coming to terms with one's sexual identity, taking care not to contract or spread sexually transmitted diseases, and preventing unplanned pregnancies.

Foster Care Experience

The experience of separation from family and placement in out-of-home care, as well as the events that precipitated the placement, can have a profound effect on the achievement of tasks in any or all of these developmental areas. The achievement of a sense of self can, for example, be negatively influenced by internalized parental identities or self-blame for the placement itself [see Chapter 3 by Land in this volume]. A history of abuse, physical or sexual, may cause an adolescent to be terrified of normal body changes. The abuse may leave scars, result in poor coordination, or otherwise impede healthy physical development [see Chapter 10 by McFadden in this volume]. The reality of abrupt emancipation and lack of preparedness may cause an adolescent in foster care to avoid opportunities for autonomy and independence [see Chapter 3 by Land in this volume]. Moreover, maltreatment often creates passivity, a survival mechanism, which is the antithesis of the drive for independence so necessary for achieving developmental tasks. Other effects of maltreatment, such as aggressive behavior or setting oneself up as a scapegoat, preclude the development of satisfying, mutual friendships that are the requisite of social development [see Chapter 10 by McFadden in this volume].

Multiple placements and other aspects of the foster care experience may result in abridged educational experiences, affecting cognitive development [see Chapter 3 by Land in this volume]. Ironically, achievement of the cognitive task of abstract thinking stimulates a youth's reexamination of the reasons for being in care, a process that may cause pain and a diminished sense of self-worth that impede emotional development [see Chapter 4 by Levine in this volume]. Moral development may be complicated by a multitude of moves and exposures to many different, and perhaps conflicting, sets of family values. Finally, a well-defined sexual identity requires a sense of separateness and individuality and a healing of past trauma, any of which may be compromised by inadequate and inconsistent care [see Chapter 6 by Wedeven and Mauzerall in this volume].

Requisite Skills of Adulthood

As described in Chapter 1, there are two interrelated types of skills—tangible and intangible—that adolescents must master in preparing for competent adulthood. The key components of competency were delineated there as follows:

Satisfying and mutually gratifying relationships with friends and kin
Responsibility for one's sexuality
The ability to nurture one's own children
A positive sense of self
Contributing to and participating in the community
The ability to make essential connections

Maluccio notes that a "person's autonomy and competence evolve in response to the dynamic transaction between person and environment" [Maluccio 1983]. Thus, assessment of adolescents in foster care must attend not only to the three dimensions described above but to their interaction with one another.

Rationale for Assessment

Interdependent-living skill assessment for foster youths is a powerful intervention strategy that brings together a caring adult, usually a foster parent or a social worker or both, and a young person in foster care to evaluate his or her readiness for adulthood and develop plans for life after foster care. Some type of inventory or data-gathering format usually guides the assessment process.

The power behind the use of a particular assessment tool or approach is two-pronged, including both tasks and process. Its benefits include the tangible product—information needed for the tasks involved in case planning, which is now required by law for agencies providing child welfare services to adolescents in foster care, and the intangible benefits of the assessment process itself. Chief among these are the use of a naturally occurring self-assessment process to reduce the negative effects of the experiences related to foster care placement; the opportunity for caregivers to model important adult skills such as setting goals, decision making, and teamwork; a chance for individual attention and a deepened relationship with caregivers; and an opportunity to explore previously untapped biological family resources.

Policy Requisites

Evaluation and case planning are required by federal law since the passage of the "Adoption Assistance and Child Welfare Act of 1980" (Public Law 96-272). This law amended the Social Security Act, creating a new foster care program under Title IV-E, requiring, among other provisions, a written case plan for every child in foster care for whom federal funds are to be claimed [Allen and Knitzer 1983; Maluccio et al. 1986; Pine 1986]. In 1985, the Title IV-E program was amended with the addition of the Independent Living Initiative, providing $45 million to state child welfare agencies for a range of services and programs for adolescents in care. Among other desired outcomes of the use of these funds is a written transitional independent-living plan, based on each youth's needs, that would be incorporated into the overall written case plan. Currently, over two-thirds of the state agencies conduct individualized assessments and develop case plans for adolescents in their care [Allen et al. 1988].

Despite these policy reforms, there continue to be obstacles to careful assessment. Cook [1988] notes that while state agencies support the concept of individually assessing each adolescent's strengths and needs, too few are systematically incorporating such assessments into practice. Too often, available resources and existing programs determine intervention strategies with adolescents in foster care, rather than the individual needs of youths, thus encouraging premature foreclosure of the assessment and case-planning process. For example, a foster care agency might receive funding for an employment program and, since employment skills are generally considered essential for independent living, refer all of its seventeen-year-olds to the program. In fact, some of these adolescents in care may have other, more pressing needs that impede, and may even preclude, the development of employment skills. Moreover, when intervention strategies are driven by policies and programs rather than carefully assessed individual needs, premature action can lead to failure and frustration for the young person and wasted resources for the community. In contrast, individualized assessment to identify basic skills and social and emotional strengths and weaknesses enhances each youth's commitment to participating in the services provided [Cook 1988]. Other benefits derived from conducting assessments are discussed below.

Benefits

A Natural Occurrence
Self-assessment is a naturally occurring event that takes place in the life of every adolescent. Most adults can recall how important it was to be popular, or to excel in sports, or to be considered smart. Feelings of exquisite joy or despair rested on one's reputation in matters such as these. An adolescent caught up in this kind of self-reflection is at a critical juncture. On the one hand, successes breed more courage to test oneself in new areas, and opportunities for growth present themselves again and again. Conversely, mirror images that show failure can produce tremendous frustration and hopelessness that inevitably thwart future progress.

Unfortunately for adolescents in foster care, whose diminished self-esteem often leaves them with little hope for a brighter future, the process of self-evaluation can produce more anguish and suffering. "My family was no good—and I'm no good either" was how one adolescent described himself. Teenagers who see only shortcomings and weaknesses are doomed to enter adulthood poorly prepared to meet its demands unless their caregivers intervene to help them gain a more positive sense of self-worth.

Situations of this sort can present major challenges for foster parents and workers, who must assume dual roles in preparing adolescents to emancipate from foster care. As caregivers, they must be reactive, stimulating resolution of lingering conflicts as well as helping adolescents link the past to the present. At the same time, they must be proactive, helping adolescents to improve day-to-day functioning and confront the tasks of maturation and emancipation [Timberlake and Verdieck 1987].

The critical ingredient for deriving benefits from this naturally occurring self-assessment is active and thoughtful attention from foster parents and social workers. For adolescents in foster care, many of whom have suffered from too little or intermittent attention, and who have been controlled by a variety of systems, engaging in skill assessment may represent the first opportunity to focus on oneself in a positive light, to speak up about choices and preferences, and to address future goals concretely.

Learning Adult Skills

The process of assessment provides opportunities for an adolescent to learn important adult skills such as planning, setting goals, decision making, and collaboration. Adult caregivers can model and thus teach adolescents these skills, particularly if the assessment brings together in mutuality and partnership those who are most likely to have pertinent information and to carry out activities—the foster care worker, the foster parents, the teenager, and, in some cases, biological family members. Moreover, assessment provides a context in which to focus carefully on skills and their relationship to goals. Adolescents are given a chance to label as skills a range of behaviors not previously framed as such and to recognize their relationship to future plans.

Tom, sixteen, was known among his peers as a video game whiz. He spent many afternoons and evenings at the arcade, winning one free game after another because of his considerable knowledge of and flair for the games. Rather than deriding Tom for wasting his time, his foster mother, Mrs. Coti, used the assessment to help Tom see the many attributes that resulted in his developing a video whiz reputation: perseverance, patience, keen eye-hand coordination, and ambition. Tom had not considered how important these skills were in becoming a video game expert, but he had to admit, happily, that they were essential. Furthermore, Mrs. Coti encouraged him to apply for a job in one of the many computer stores downtown. Soon after, Tom was offered a sales position at a store near school and was thoroughly enjoying the chance to demonstrate his skills *and* get paid for it.

Building Relationships

Positive changes in relationships can occur between caregivers and adolescents as they work together on an assessment. Consider the effect on a despairing young person of an attentive adult who takes the time to say, "I'd like to get to know you better . . . to learn what you'd like to do . . . and to learn what you would like to have happen for yourself." Nurturance sincerely offered can deepen many such relationships.

One foster mother, during a support group for foster parents, talked animatedly about her success in using an assessment as part of the process of welcoming a teenager to her home. She was impressed with how the assessment quickly aided them in feeling comfortable with each other and helped them to identify her foster son's likes and dislikes. Particularly notable was her discovery that he very much wanted to stop smoking cigarettes. It was a goal that the foster mother shared, so together they enrolled in a Smokenders program, with the result that neither had smoked in three months. In addition to the obvious health benefits, the assessment helped this foster mother and son to achieve empathy with each other and engage as a successful team toward a common goal.

Other foster parents have reported the benefits of using assessment as a way to begin talking with teenagers about their eventual transition to independent living. At a training session for social workers and foster parents, one foster father talked frankly about his reluctance to broach the subject of his foster son's need to plan for living on his own.

Mr. Green had fathered Michael for nine years, and did not want to hurt Mike's feelings by suggesting that he would, at some point, need to think about living on his own. He also had to admit to his own difficulty in letting Mike go. The assessment gave him a positive way to mark Michael's coming of age, to congratulate him on reaching an important milestone, and to talk of Mike's hopes and worries about the future. Mr. Green said that without the assessment as a guide during this anxiety-provoking stage, he might never have gotten around to talking about Mike's approaching adulthood. Instead, using the assessment gave him and Mike a chance to look at all they had accomplished and to prepare confidently for the next important step.

Exploration of Biological Family Resources

A final but critical reason for conducting a careful and thoughtful assessment with each adolescent in care is the opportunity for helping him or her to identify and be able to use a range of potential family resources. This exploration is important even with the most impoverished of families. Carbino [Chapter 7 in this volume] has noted the importance to foster adolescents of renewed contact with biological family members even when past contact may not have been regular or positive. Parents and other relatives, who earlier were unable to serve as a placement resource, may be able to contribute in other ways to an adolescent's move toward interdependent living.

In exploring potential contributions from family members, it is important to consider the breadth of kinship ties, including those to parents, siblings, grandparents, aunts and uncles, and godparents. The wide variety of resources these relatives may provide includes information on group membership, a sense of belonging and a place to be, and other tangible aid.

Information from family members could include medical or genetic history as well as facts about the family and the adolescent's earlier years before foster placement. This kind of information can aid in the teenager's search for identity and in the development of a sense of belonging to a family group. Family membership is further enhanced by family records, photographs, and other memorabilia that relatives may be able to provide. Moreover, for the adolescent in foster care whose lineage is uncertain but may be Native American, the discovery of tribal membership would be an essential family resource to help that young person to realize.

Family members who were unable to provide a permanent home for a child may now be able to provide a young adult with a place to visit or spend holidays or perhaps an interim living situation between foster care and independence. Even job opportunities may be available through kinship ties. With the help of her worker, one young woman in foster care made contact with her aunt, who lived in another part of the state. The aunt had been unable to take custody of her niece when she was originally placed because of the long hours she worked as the owner of a small beauty salon. She was delighted to renew the relationship and, after a period of regular visiting, offered the young woman a job in the salon as well as an invitation to share her apartment.

Finally, information obtained from relatives could lead to other tangible resources for the adolescent. These include the right to receive veterans and Social Security benefits earned by parents who may have died, as well as the inheritance of property, funds, or other valuables. In sum, the opportunity to explore and tap the widest range of resources from the broadest network of kin is another key reason for engaging the adolescent in foster care in a comprehensive assessment and case-planning process.

Approaches to Guide Assessment

The final section of this chapter further encourages systematic assessment and case planning with adolescents in foster care by presenting several instruments that can be used. Then, to guide in their selection and use, a number of principles are outlined. Finally, case examples illustrating the use of selected approaches are described.

Description of Selected Instruments

The following descriptions are of six assessment methods developed for use with foster adolescents. Several are drawn from two national foster parent training curricula [Ryan et al. 1988; Pasztor et al. 1988], while others have been developed in conjunction with recent efforts to strengthen agency foster care programs [Jacobs and Gilrane 1988]. The assessments selected for inclusion here are windows on the strengths and needs of adolescents preparing to leave foster care. Each provides a different view: some are comprehensive; others focus attention on a particular aspect of an adolescent's profile.

1. ASSESSING ESSENTIAL CONNECTIONS
    Source: Eileen Mayers Pasztor et al. *Preparing Youth for Interdependent Living.* West Hartford, CT: Center for the Study of Child Welfare, The University of Connecticut School of Social Work, and Atlanta, GA: Child Welfare Institute, 1988, III—4–19.
    Available from: Child Welfare Institute
                          Center for Foster and Residential Care
                          1430 West Peachtree St., Suite 510
                          Atlanta, Georgia 30309
    Description: Hansell [1976] identified seven categories of attachment to the environment, representing a human being's transactions with the environment that are necessary for survival. Using this categorization, Polowy and others [1986] devised a means of ascertaining a foster adolescent's connectedness or disconnectedness in the seven key areas. Pasztor et al., in the curriculum cited above, further refined this approach, identifying a set of nine connections essential for achieving interdependence:

Information and knowledge
A significant person
A group
A meaningful role
A means of support
A system of values
A source of joy
History
A place

The material, organized in a chart format, includes indicators of disconnection for a youth in foster care in each of the nine areas, as well as guidelines for assessing connectedness, including sample questions and strategies that can be worked into a case plan for building those connections that are needed.

2. STRENGTHS/NEEDS ASSESSMENT
Source: Eileen Mayers Pasztor et al.: III—5 handouts (3, 4) *(see above)*.
Available from: Child Welfare Institute
(see above)

Description: This method engages a caregiver and an adolescent in a discussion of the young person's strengths and needs in relation to six major interdependent-living categories: special interests and activities; school and work; religion and values; physical and emotional health; family and friends; and social services. The adult is instructed to present the assessment to the adolescent as a way of seeing what the young person looks like in terms of future planning. This "picture in words" is made possible by the adult asking a range of non-threatening questions that enable key strengths and needs to emerge, such as "What do you like to do?" "How do you spend your time?" "What would you like to be proud of accomplishing?" "What would you like to feel good or better about?" An action plan follows the assessment, which provides directions so that the adult and the young person can jointly decide to work on the need that is most pressing for the adolescent in preparing for adult life. A 20-minute audiotape of an assessment, which was done between an adult and a youth, and a completed assessment, based on the tape, are included.

3. ECO-MAPS
Source: Emily Jean McFadden. *P.U.S.H. for Youth G.O.A.L.S.: Leaving Home Again.* Ypsilanti, MI: Eastern Michigan University, 1988, 7–10.
Available from: The Institute for the Study of Children and Families
Eastern Michigan University
Ypsilanti, Michigan 48197

Description: The eco-map is one of a number of interactive techniques that have been used by social workers to explore families' relationships with various systems in their environment. Completed, eco-maps provide a visual representation of the significant components of the family's environment, as well as the stresses and supports the family derives from each [Hartman and Laird 1983].

In this foster parent training curriculum, the eco-map approach has been modified for use with adolescents in foster care. Although the eco-map exercise is for adolescents to complete on their own, it can be easily adapted as an interactive approach involving the adolescent, the foster parents, and the worker. The instructions call for the completion of two eco-maps. The first shows the foster teenager's current connections to important parts of his or her life, such as work, school, friends, and family; the second represents the connections needed when he or she is emancipated.

The first eco-map appears as follows: The adolescent draws connections from self to significant components in his or her environment. The type of line characterizes the connection, as in this example:

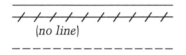

————————————	A strong, supportive connection
—/—/—/—/—/—/—/—/—/—	A stressful connection
(*no line*)	No connection
— — — — — — — — — — — — — —	A weak connection

In the second eco-map, the adolescent is asked to think about future goals for independence and to diagram them as follows: the adolescent selects the goals, fills in the circles, and draws the lines showing the type of connection to each goal. By comparing the two eco-maps, the adolescent can observe how they differ and can identify what will be needed to achieve the goals shown in the second eco-map, including new connections that will need to be made. Thus, both assessment and case planning are facilitated.

4. Your Plan for Adult Living

Source: Marc Jacobs and Lenore Gilrane. *The Planning Index and Life Skills Profile Handbook.* Boston, MA: Judge Baker Children's Center, 1988.

Available from: National Resource Center for Youth Services
The University of Oklahoma
131 North Greenwood Avenue
Tulsa, OK 74120

Description: These approaches have been designed to offer caregivers and young people a non-threatening framework for organizing strengths and needs and determining action steps toward preparation for adulthood. The Planning Index emphasizes discussion and relationship support in the following areas: school—job training—work; money and shopping; the people in your life; family history and relationships; health and medical care; where am I going to live when I am out of care; and leaving home. Questions are designed to explore hopes and values and to identify activities and people to promote preparation for the future. For example, questions related to school include: What subject do (did) you enjoy the most? What subject do (did) you feel you've learned a lot in? What subject do (did) you find the hardest? Who at school do you feel supports your efforts? Who at school would you like to be more involved with you?

Following completion of the index, young people are asked to review their answers and to identify one item they would like to accomplish, one area they wish to improve, and one thing about themselves they would like to change. For each of these, they are asked to determine the steps to be taken, those who can help, and a time schedule for reaching the goal. As each goal is reached, they are invited to add a new one. With the signatures of the youth and the caregiver, the plan may serve as a contract and as part of the adolescent's overall service plan.

As a companion to the *Planning Index*, the *Life Skills Profile Handbook* takes initial assessment, planning, setting goals and taking action to the next stage by viewing the living-skill competencies related to preparation for adulthood. For example, after answering the questions mentioned above concerning school, the young person is instructed to turn to the school, career, and work section of the handbook. Here the youths are asked about ability, willingness, readiness, or need for more training in relation to knowing how to solve problems at school; planning for additional education; finding vocational training; choosing work or career goals; learning about various occupations; and deciding whether they might like or hate a particular job. Following completion of the handbook, young people are asked to list all areas in which further training or support will be needed and then to order their importance by rank. They are next asked to identify actions to learn the skill, who will help, and a time schedule.

5. Understanding Developmental Tasks for Youth in Care
    Source: Eileen Mayers Pasztor et al. III—2 (19–22) and handout 3 (1–4) *(see above).*
    Available from: Child Welfare Institute
        (see above)
    Description: The developmental tasks of adolescence are usually more difficult for young people in foster care than for their peers. This assessment method identifies the developmental needs and tasks of teenagers, common behaviors associated with each task, and the ways in which placement negatively affects the ability of youths to manage these demands and prepare for interdependent living. Also, strategies for partnership efforts in helping

youths manage this stage of development are presented in two case examples. Assessing young persons' behaviors and ability to prepare for adulthood by considering developmental demands can be very illuminating for them and for caregivers; the approach can increase empathy and give rise to intervention strategies that might otherwise not emerge.

6. Strategies for Helping Youth in Care Make Connections among Past Experiences, Present Needs and Future Plans
    Source: Eileen Mayers Pasztor et al. III—3 handout 5 (1–6) *(see above).*
    Available from: Child Welfare Institute
        (see above)
Description: The authors of this foster parent training curriculum emphasize the effect of past losses on efforts to help adolescents in foster care master interdependent-living skills—for example, unresolved grief. It is important, therefore, to understand the grieving process and to recognize typical behaviors that adolescents in a particular stage of the process may exhibit. The material on grieving is organized as a chart presenting the stages of grieving, listing typical behaviors that may be observed, and suggesting ways to help adolescents manage the grieving process and become better able, willing, and ready to master necessary skills.

Principles for Selection and Use

To gain maximum benefit from the assessment, a number of guidelines should be followed when engaging foster adolescents in this activity.

Identification of Positive Attributes
Bearing in mind the shaky self-esteem of most foster teenagers, it is essential that assessments begin with a concentrated focus on existing skills: what the adolescents like to do, any accomplishments, and their admirable qualities. Since it is essential that some assets be noted, an expanded view of the concept of skills may be needed. For example, a seventeen-year-old foster daughter, whose withdrawn behavior, slow speech, and slovenly appearance matched her depressed emotional state, began to make lengthy eye contact with her foster mother when the woman commented on how long her foster daughter's hair was, and how much she herself had always wanted long hair. When engaging a young person in an assessment, foster parents and social workers *must* find a door through which some self-appreciation can be felt.

Linkage of Results with Action Plan

Assessments must do more than identify a strengths-needs profile; they must accompany the profile with a plan to capitalize on strengths and turn needs into accomplishments. Otherwise, young people, foster parents, and social workers can become overwhelmed with information and stymied in their efforts to improve the image that the assessment presents. Robert, age fourteen, became visibly anxious as he looked over the long list of needs that emerged from having done an assessment with his social worker. She, however, was able to reassure Robert that, through hard work and careful planning, together they would be able to help him become the adult he wanted to be. They began by focusing on the need that Robert felt to be most pressing, and then devised a set of steps that each would take for Robert to turn his need into an asset. It is this kind of focused attention, coupled with diligent planning and unwavering support, that allows the full benefits of the assessment process to be realized.

Identity Formation Is Comprehensively Addressed

It is essential that the assessment look beyond evaluating only the presence of tangible skills. Skills related to all six key developmental areas—cognitive, physical, social, emotional, moral, and sexual—must be considered. It is important to remember that adolescents are preparing to lead adult lives that will demand a complex range of coping skills, as the following example illustrates:

> Ms. Cobb, Gail's foster mother for the past five years, at first resisted the urgings of their social worker to conduct an assessment. She was convinced of Gail's readiness to live on her own and pointed with pride to all the evidence: Gail's employment, her many household abilities, and her well-managed checking account. Finally Ms. Cobb, out of curiosity, did complete an assessment with Gail. They both realized that while Gail was accomplished in the hard skills that her foster mother had taught her, she was reluctant to make decisions on her own, since her opinions and feelings were unknown to her. Together they realized that Gail was quite capable of following directions, but, without a defined sense of self, she was unable to direct her own activities. The assessment led them to find ways for Gail to make choices and engage in new activities without her foster mother's direction. The social worker cautioned Ms. Cobb about the possibility that encouraging Gail's self-expression might result in as yet unexpressed rebellious behavior; she was thus helped to see any acting

out as her daughter's positive steps toward autonomy [see Chapter 4 by Levine in this volume].

Partnership among Youths, Foster Parents, Biological Family,
and Social Workers Is Strengthened

As noted earlier, conducting an assessment can be a potent means of strengthening the connection between a young person and a caring adult. In fact, it can represent an ideal opportunity for significant adults to join with youths to supply information and feedback. For this process to occur, though, the assessment must be interactive in design, permitting adults to express their interest in the adolescent's profile, as well as affording opportunity for discussion. Simple checklists of skills that do not allow for spontaneous conversation cannot provide the same opportunities for intimacy as approaches that encourage mutual exploration of an adolescent's self-perception.

One social worker used the assessment process as an occasion to engage the young person, his foster parents, his biological father, and his older cousin in considering the youth's readiness for adulthood and to prepare an action plan. The social worker competently prepared all of these "team members" for their roles in discussing the boy's strengths and needs. Later, each adult talked about the pleasure they had derived from being part of such an important time in the teenager's life, and he was flattered by the expression of so much support and concern.

Case Illustrations

The following case illustrations demonstrate the use of four assessment methods. The Spaulding family used *essential connections* with their foster adoptive son; Mrs. Muhamed used the *eco-map* approach with her foster daughter; Mrs. Nicholson, a foster mother, and Ms. Thomas, a social worker, worked with fifteen-year-old Beth to assess her achievement in various developmental areas and to gain insights about problems she was having; and Mr. Mendez, with the help of his foster son's social worker, developed strategies to help his foster son deal with the loss and disappointment he feels about his biological family.

The Spaulding Case

Tim was placed with the Spauldings at age thirteen after a series of placements that had begun when he was nine. The Spauldings had raised a number of children and were committed to assessing Tim's status as an adolescent whom they would be preparing for adulthood. After Tim had lived with them for several months, the Spauldings decided to use the *essential connections* approach to engage Tim in talking about his past, particularly his more recent placement history, and to begin planning with him for the future. Because Tim had a communication problem—he had difficulty articulating thoughts and feelings because of earlier brain damage—they found it helped to diagram the nine essential connections and his relationship to each.

In exploring Tim's connection to information, specifically his understanding of why he had been placed in foster care, the Spauldings learned that he lacked connection with vital information about his placement history. Indeed, they felt that he had become stuck in the grieving process, mourning past losses without even an understanding of what they were. By piecing together information from Tim and that provided by the placing worker, the Spauldings found that he had been in one foster home from infancy to nine years of age. When he was nine, his foster mother had had to be hospitalized and had died quite suddenly in the hospital. Tim was immediately removed from the foster home with no preparation for leaving, no opportunity to participate in any aspect of the family's mourning rituals, and without a chance to say goodbye to any of his foster relatives.

The Spauldings located the foster family and planned a reunion visit. The event also included a visit to place flowers at the former foster mother's grave. As it turned out, the foster family, especially the grown siblings, were delighted to see Tim again and remembered the added grief they had felt when he was abruptly removed while they were mourning the loss of their mother.

Thus, Tim was helped to build essential connections to information and to people who had been significant in his life. These connections were captured in a photo album, which included baby pictures, that he had assembled with his former foster family, who had taken them.

The Muhamed Case

Mrs. Muhamed used the *eco-map* approach to help her adolescent foster daughter to identify and work toward a goal.

As Mrs. Muhamed worked with Natasha on her second, future-oriented eco-map, Natasha identified a particular job that she hoped to have by age twenty-one; she wanted to be a management trainee in a large, high-fashion department store in a nearby city.

At seventeen, Natasha had been working part-time for several years in a variety of jobs. Currently she was working in a fast-food restaurant while completing her last year of high school. She wasn't planning to go on to college; in fact, she was unsure of her plans following graduation.

Placement of the job symbol on her eco-map provided an opportunity for Natasha and her foster mother to talk generally about the future and especially about her career plans. Together, they made a list of what Natasha would need to do to find out more about the management trainee job. As a first step, they traveled into the city, where Natasha had an informal interview with a member of the store's personnel department. She was able to learn what they looked for in applicants to their trainee program. She decided to apply for a full-time position in a local clothing store after graduation and also to explore evening courses in marketing at a nearby community college. She and her foster mother agreed that she would continue to live at the foster home to save money for the eventual move to the city and an apartment of her own.

The Nicholson Case

Mrs. Nicholson was concerned because her fifteen-year-old foster daughter Beth was interested only in lounging around the house and resisted all attempts to interest her in any activities. She even shied away from joining the family in learning to play badminton and found every excuse to avoid lending a hand in preparing food for a family picnic.

Mrs. Nicholson discussed the problem with Beth's social worker, Ms. Thomas, who was aware of Beth's past history of neglect and felt that this might be influencing her present behavior. She suggested that they assess, with Beth, her developmental achievements and see if there might be a connection between her seeming laziness and developmental demands.

They used *understanding developmental tasks for youth in care* to talk with Beth about the ways that her earlier experiences might influence how she was feeling as a teenager in the foster home. As they talked about her feelings about herself, and her self-image, it soon became clear that her search for an individual identity was actually feeding her poor self-concept, leaving her very uncertain about her ability to learn anything new. At the same time, once her difficulties were linked to her efforts to develop a sense of self, roads to helping her emerged. Both women met regularly with Beth to talk about their concern for her and to lend emotional support. Mrs. Nicholson paid special attention to opportunities for providing encouragement, reinforcement, and praise. She also began to wonder why Beth's self-image was so poor and looked for times to listen to Beth about her childhood memories.

These talks led to Beth's revealing a history of sexual abuse that had not been known before. Ms. Thomas responded to this information by encouraging Beth to join a support group for survivors of incest and also explored her willingness to seek counseling. In time, Beth began to express interest in going along on family outings and particularly looked forward to a planned camping weekend that her church youth group was sponsoring. Mrs. Nicholson, while acknowledging that Beth had a long way to go toward developing the kind of confidence that she would eventually need, was thrilled to see how much Beth's general mood and energy level had improved.

The Mendez Case

Through foster parent training sessions he had recently attended, Mr. Mendez was familiar with the assessment called *strategies for helping youth in care make connections among past experiences, present needs, and future plans.* This knowledge helped him to understand the grief process and his foster son's behavior. Together, they worked on several strategies to help the teenager deal more effectively with his feelings of loss.

Rafael was thirteen years old when he was placed with Mr. Mendez, a single father whose own two children were on their own. Rafael had been in foster care since the age of eight, and, for the two years before his placement with Mr. Mendez, he had lived in a residential facility.

His foster father described him as an "angel" at home, but his behavior at school was causing problems. He swore at and threatened some of his schoolmates and, occasionally, his teachers. He was quick to settle disputes by physical fighting.

Mr. Mendez believed the causes of this behavior to be unresolved anger and began to notice that these negative incidents seemed to occur following either of two events: a visit with Rafael's biological parents or siblings or a Mendez family gathering. He told Rafael's therapist about his observations, and the therapist agreed and suggested that Mr. Mendez try to help Rafael to deal with his feelings.

Mr. Mendez helped Rafael talk about his disappointment with his own family and their failure to meet even his most rudimentary needs as a child—a challenge, because Rafael was unaccustomed to expressing feelings. At the same time, Mr. Mendez understood that his own close and loving family made Rafael's family appear even more a failure in Rafael's inevitable comparison of the two. Mr. Mendez and Rafael's therapist worked together, reinforcing each other's efforts to help Rafael learn new ways of expressing feelings and managing his behavior.

Conclusion

Assessment and case planning with adolescents to help them prepare for leaving foster care and achieving interdependence as adults involves a process that must be based on an understanding of the developmental tasks of all adolescents, the unique aspects of the experiences related to foster care placement that frequently impede the successful accomplishment to those tasks, and the full range of skills needed for a satisfying adulthood. The use of the assessment approaches described in this chapter can facilitate and enhance this process. The application of these approaches requires that the process begin early in the placement and reflect a partnership between the worker and the foster parents, as well as mutuality with the youth in care, to make the best possible use of family and community resources.

REFERENCES

Allen, M., Bonner, K. and Greenan, L. "Federal legislative support for independent living." In Mech, E. V. (editor), Child Welfare (Special Issue on Independent Living Services for At-Risk Adolescents) 67 (November–December 1988): 515–527.

Allen, M., and Knitzer, J. "Child welfare: Examining the policy framework." In McGowan, Brenda G., and Meezan, William (editors), Child Welfare—Current Dilemmas Future Directions. Itasca, IL: F. E. Peacock, 1983.

Bartlett, H. M. The Common Base of Social Work Practice. Washington, DC: National Association of Social Workers, 1970.

Cook, R. "Trends and needs in programming for independent living." In Mech, E. V. (editor), Child Welfare (Special Issue on Independent-Living Services for At-Risk Adolescents) 67 (November–December 1988): 497– 514.

Hansell, Norris. The Person-in-Distress: On the Biosocial Dynamics of Adaptation. New York: Human Services Press, 1976.

Hartman, A., and Laird, J. Family-Centered Social Work Practice. New York: The Free Press, 1983.

Jacobs, M., and Gilrane, L. Your Plan for Adult Living. Boston, MA: The Judge Baker Children's Center, and Tulsa, OK: National Resource Center for Youth Services, 1988.

Maluccio, A. N. (editor). Promoting Competence in Clients—A New/Old Approach to Social Work Practice. New York: The Free Press, 1981, 13.

———. "Planned use of life experiences." In Rosenblatt, A., and Waldfogel, D. (editors), Handbook of Clinical Social Work. San Francisco, CA: Jossey-Bass, 1983, 134–153.

Maluccio, A. N., Fein, E., and Olmstead, K. A. Permanency Planning for Children—Concepts and Methods. London and New York: Routledge, Chapman and Hall Inc., 1986.

McFadden, E. J. P.U.S.H. for Youth G.O.A.L.S.: Leaving Home Again. Ypsilanti, MI: Institute for the Study of Children and Families, Eastern Michigan University, 1988.

Pasztor, E. M., et al. Preparing Youth for Interdependent Living. West Hartford, CT: Center for the Study of Child Welfare, University of Connecticut School of Social Work, and Atlanta, GA: Child Welfare Institute, 1988.

Pine, B. A. "Child welfare reform and the political process." Social Service Review 60 (September 1986): 339–359.

Polowy, M., Wasson, D., and Wolf, M. Fosterparentscope. Buffalo, NY: New York State Child Welfare Training Institute, 1986.

Ryan, P., McFadden, E. J., Rice, D., and Warren, B. P.U.S.H. for Youth G.O.A.L.S.: Providing Understanding, Support and Help for Youth Going Out and Living Successfully. Ypsilanti, MI: Institute for the Study of Children and Families, Eastern Michigan University, 1988.

Timberlake, E. M., and Verdieck, M. J. "Psychosocial functioning of adolescents in foster care." Social Casework 68 (April 1987): 214–222.